At the core of rock climbing sports

OREGON
ROCK & BOULDER

THIRD EDITION

OREGON ROCK & BOULDER

A selection of unique rock climbing crags in NW Oregon and SW Washington, including a comprehensive guide to this regions diverse bouldering opportunities

Oregon Rock & Boulder™
Copyright © 2022 East Wind Design

All rights reserved. No part of this publication may be reproduced, stored in or introduced into a retrieval system, or transmitted, in any form, or by any means (electronic, mechanical, photocopying, recording, etc). Requests for permission must be made in writing to the publisher.

Book Design: East Wind Design
Technical Maps and Illustrations: East Wind Design

Cover Photograph: *Karl climbing at MCS*
Frontispiece images: *MC Slab, and Empire Boulders*

ISBN-EAN: 978-0-9997233-9-5

Oregon Rock & Boulder (ORB3) v3.0

Printed in the USA

OREGON ROCK & BOULDER

Table of Contents

Disclaimer vii
Preface viii
Acknowledgments ix

Introduction 1
- NW Oregon Climate 3
- Geology Of NW Oregon 4
- Climbing Route Ratings 9
- Equipment And Specialized Gear 10
- GPS Geodetic Datum 11
- About This Guide book 11

Rock Climbing 13
- French's Dome 13
- Enola (The Swine) 21
- Pete's Pile 31
- Bulo Point 46
- Area 51 53
- Rat Cave 65
- Rock Creek Crag 69
- Monte Cristo Slab 75
- OH8 101
- Horsethief Butte 107
- Mosquito Butte Crag 121
- Hunchback Wall 124
- Salmon River Slab 134
- Wankers Columns 135

Bouldering Intro 139
- Larch Mtn Boulders 143
- Alpenglow Boulders 159
- Bridge of the Gods Boulders 165
  - Powerline Area 165
  - Upper Area 171
- Empire Boulders 175

Disclaimer

Rock climbing and bouldering contains certain inherent risks that may be dangerous to your health. The sole purpose of this book is to inform rock climbers of the many unique crag climbing opportunities available in and around our corner of Northwest Oregon. Before attempting any bouldering described in these pages you should first be proficient in the use of modern rock climbing and bouldering equipment.

This guidebook is not a substitute for personal insight, time-learned skills, or lessons taught by climbing instructors. There are no warranties, neither express nor implied, that this book contains accurate or reliable information. As the user of this or any guidebook, you assume full responsibility for your own safety. Because the sport is constantly evolving, the author cannot guarantee the accuracy of any of the information in this book, including the V-grades, location of routes, route names, route descriptions, or approach trails.

No one can offer you any assurance against natural hazards such as lightning or other weather phenomena, loose or poor quality rock, or the risk of equipment failure. Consider with suspicion all fixed protection (such as bolts). Weathering, metal quality, and impact stress loading are some of the variants that can cause fixed gear to fail.

You know the scope and the upper limit of your rock climbing abilities. Assess your prospective climb shrewdly, and make prudent decisions based on your strengths and weaknesses. If you have any doubt concerning your ability to safely ascend a climbing route today, then stop and consider a climb that is less difficult or dangerous.

This is not a how-to guide but rather a where-to book. This book explains where to rock climb, but you must honestly determine whether you have mastered the most important aspects of the sport before embarking on any rock climbing adventure.

Consult other climbers about the adventure you are planning to embark upon. A skilled climber who knows the site can give quality advice and insight as to common etiquette as well as impart ideas about climbing technique and balance that will surely be beneficial to you.

Wisely seek assistance, and attain good instruction from others, such as a diligent climbing instructor who will teach you how to become a safe, intuitive climber.

Exercise good judgment as to where the climbing route ascends the boulder, and learn to quickly perceive subtle variants you will likely encounter in route difficulty. Know your own strengths and weaknesses; develop a competent understanding of your route-finding abilities and safety skills, for these and the right equipment are your best protection against the hazards of climbing. Confidence and ability gained through many hours of physical and mental preparation are perhaps the most valuable skills you and your climbing partner will need when managing the degree of risk you both are willing to accept.

Preface

This edition of *Oregon Rock & Boulder* is the creative expression of several individuals who have brought considerable momentum to the sport of rock climbing and bouldering in this portion of the state. Key portions of this guidebook came from a core group of individuals, some of which began decades ago when various persons opted to collect their climbing and bouldering activity information in a format from which we could glean a concise storyline to build upon. Bringing their ideas and history forward into this guidebook gives it an essential unmatched value ideal for today's boulderer.

During your quest to tap into outdoor recreational sports, remember that our rock climbing and bouldering actions today impact and influence the future decisions of property owners and land managers alike. We are responsible for keeping ours a friendly, self-managed sport and for acting in full cooperation with land managers so that we will continue to be welcomed for generations to come.

By developing a perceptive, respectful awareness of the environment around us, from the peregrine falcon to *Sedum integrifolium*, we ultimately discover that we are entrusted with the keys to provide a legacy for tomorrow. Hopefully you will find the information bound within these pages both rewarding and fulfilling.

Acknowledgments

The culmination of beta in this book exists primarily because of the shared knowledge and assistance of many friends and individuals. Thank you all for sharing your expertise about the exhilarating edge of this sport.

This guidebook is the end formulation of insight from all those rock climbers and boulderers who relish this sport and choose to maintain valued historical notes on the sport. Numerous tidbits of data exist in various small articles, but a major portion of the information is through close contact with friends and acquintances who have collected a rather impressive amount of climbing information and data, each focused toward their relative prospective view of the sport.

Over many years various individuals provided expandable authoritative information, or climbing energy, or valued insight into various crags and boulder sites. A brief list of several individuals: Greg L., Hugh B., Claude M., Dave S., Jim T. (The Swinery), John R. & Tymun A (French's), Paul C. (OH8 & Area51). Many other persons not referenced here have collectively added to the wealth of knowledge of local climbing and bouldering in this region as well. Considerable photograph credit appreciation goes to several individuals: Mr Abbott, Mr Cousar, Mr Fields, Mr Jones, Mr Reynolds, etc.

A number of individuals were highly instrumental in sharing various crucial aspects of knowledge, ideas and energy that have helped to strengthen the quality and vibrant nature of this book. Those individuals are a virtual walking encyclopedia of superb detailed knowledge on multiple tangents of the sport in this region. Their wealth of local bouldering history, in-depth bouldering beta, extensive photography collection, as well as an express determination to continously explore unknown places to find the next hotspot crag or boulder site were instrumental in this project. Considerable portions of this book are reflective of that energetic personality and invaluable expertise. That information knowledge base yielded data that could be compiled accurately into a quality product that would satisfy the interest of all climbers in this region.

Together these people bring a life-time of broad-ranging highly valued climbing skills, in-depth local climbing politics knowledge, and a profound interest in the various facets of rock climbing adventures in all its wild flavors. Within the various degrees of climbing, from rock climbing, bouldering to mountain climbing, their shared optimism to explore new crags and find new boulder sites is a unique creative energy that keeps this sport moving forward by promoting an increased wealth of publically accessible rock climbing areas, each person tackling unique ways to continually expand the sport in this region.

An Introduction To NW Oregon Rock Climbing and Bouldering

INTRODUCTION

A detailed analysis of the best select rock climbing and bouldering opportunities in NW Oregon and SW Washington

This guidebook brings together a selection from the best of the best of NW Oregon's favorite rural rock climbing crags, as well as an brief study of this regions diverse bouldering sites (a brief selection in & near the Columbia Gorge). We have specifically united a selection of enjoyable rock climbing opportunities with a brief base of bouldering information, articulately combining it all into a highly detailed and effective regional guidebook. The resulting value of encompassing two broad dimensions of the sport gives you greater latitude to experience this sport by paralleling certain popular rock climbing sites with the latest rage bouldering games, all in one book. This thesis is certain to spark your interest in the entire multi-dimensional spectrum of the sport.

The dual sporting activities of rock climbing and bouldering, are two technically diverse recreation activities that can be blended together by you to provide you with a greater range of endurance training activity. The sites described herein include a fascinating array of popular outlaying rock climbing crags from Cascade Locks to The Dalles to Government Camp and beyond. The bouldering section is a brief spectrum analogy that places particular emphasis on proximity to Portland, Oregon.

The first primary section of this book details a selection of various non-urban rock climbing sites (Area51, Bulo Point, Pete's Pile, MC Slab, Enola (aka the Swinery), French's Dome, etc), thus providing the focused sport and trad climbing enthusiast with the quick answer to popular climbing options. The second section covers both major and minor bouldering sites, capturing thorough information on an increasingly popular bouldering game. This section directs your time-based efforts toward the plethora of site options, while focusing your energy choices exclusively to the bouldering goals that satisfy your outdoor sporting needs.

The bouldering section is a minor thesis in its own right, a virtual 'first' of its kind for the region, as it brings the right information together in the right way, and in the right place. A string of quality bouldering sites that incorporate a proverbial power packed enervating punch that will keep the casual boulderer heavily entertained for many years ahead. This well-designed book is written by life-long locals, originating from a thorough database built by locals, and marketed specifically for the Northwest Oregon outdoor sports enthusiast.

The original concept for this guidebook grew out from a combination of timely events. The first was a need to offer sharply focused yet specifically select information on the most popular outlaying rock climbing crags. The second reason was the importance of completing an extensive 20+ year archive by setting the entirety of the informational wealth into this quality guidebook for all rock climbers and boulderers to enjoy.

Chris at *Enola*

Both sections (rock and boulder) in this book are a detailed analysis capturing a brief moment in the history of these recreational activities. That historic curve is crossed at one brief dated moment in time, and is set herein for your reading and climbing enjoyment. This compilation of long-gathered notes relates a story-line woven around specific individuals who relish all aspects of the sport of rock climbing and the little game of bouldering.

These instrumental players have been immersed in all the sports varies aspects, tapping quality and unique little treasured crag and boulder sites well appreciated by locals. Most of these crags and boulder sites thoroughly entertain just the locals in the recreational sporting activity, but in time a few (like LLB) may eventually yield region-wide sports interest drawing traveling boulderers to Oregon, that is, if mere andesitic bouldering has enough quality to beckon. For we live in a strange time warped region [Oregon] locked between two realms of granite [Washington & California] where mere geologic fate has combined to yield a considerable quantity of outcrops composed of andesite and basalt.

Quality climbing crags and boulder sites are crucial tourism based attractions, and it is only through various climbing teams that a fair number of these sites have been successfully explored, tapped and publicly promoted. This increased treasure trove of sites enhances the overall value of this regions outdoor sports industry by giving all participants a greater freedom of choice. The quantitative increase in sites bring inherent long-term vitality and value to the strength of this regions sports, while combining it with good stewardship ideals promotes a role model legacy for many decades to come.

With determination countless outdoor enthusiasts in our region seek out and enjoy many aspects of outdoor sports, from ascending the highest peaks (such as Mt Hood) in the state, to climbing upon the lowliest boulders. The entire outdoor sports spectrum is a year-round activity (weather providing), while the specific activities of rock climbing and bouldering continue to increase in popularity.

Many cities now have indoor climbing/bouldering sports gyms that offer benefits nearly greater than the outdoor aspects, because these facilities provide participants with an avenue to maintain year-round fitness continuity goals, a crisply ideal concept well-suited for our seasonally very rainy Northwest U.S. climate.

Guidebooks (like this one) built on a stewardship framework, while at the same time effectively covering the subject of rock climbing and bouldering, also provide you with an authoritative knowledge base that heightens your skill set, and helps bring choices to your planning, so you can effectively channel your goals into the desired direction to fit your balanced strengths and needs.

Stewardship goals are one of the prime tools that will strengthen this sport. Stewardship protocols involve, not just recognition-based old bolt replacement projects, but are really giant steps beyond. Stewarding involves leadership training programs, refining site accessibility needs, and broadening effective resource use values of our local crags and boulder sites. It also involves communication interaction with various public agencies and entities, private businesses (clubs, guide services, retail stores), while encouraging climbing community advocacy involvement at our cragging sites via stewarding events (trail stabilization management projects, etc), risk minimization management efforts, various ethos statements, and leadership training, all of which are designed to help each visiting climber or boulderer to grasp a greater sense of legitimacy and purpose when delving into the sport.

So take your sport-bound experience to a tantalizing new level and allow us to bring you closer into the detailed aspects of the sport of rock climbing with our guidebook.

Tymun on Psyco Billy Cadillac

NW OREGON CLIMATE

The Northwest U.S. has a temperate climate that receives an abundance of precipitation mainly because a warm subtropical air mass and a cold polar front jet stream air mass intermix producing variant seasonal changes in the climate. The Oregon climate west of the Cascade Range is predominantly wet for most of the year. Pacific marine air weather systems bring an abundance of rainfall that saturates the region, especially from late-October through May. Most rock climbers in Northwest Oregon generally seek the local crags during the warm season (May through October). During this portion of the year mild marine air often mixes with inland Great Basin hot weather to bring a climber-friendly cycle that keeps the region quite comfortable.

During the summer months, temperatures will average in the seventies to mid eighties (Fahrenheit) with occasional short peaks of hot, sunny days in July and August reaching the nineties. Temperatures above 100°F are infrequent.

By late October, the Pacific marine air storm tracks become more active, usually bringing a consistent series of rain showers. The typical winter storm systems generate frequent cold, rainy days with average temperatures in the 35–50°F range. Infrequently, a severe storm track from the inland polar region may produce short periods of intense cold in the upper twenties to mid thirties east of the Cascade Range, but these brisk temperatures seldom penetrate into the valleys of western Oregon. Average annual precipitation in the Willamette Valley near Portland is about 40 inches; at times the winter weather is prohibitively wet. During these periods, many climbers seek the refuge of a local rock gym or sports gym for fitness continuity.

Lower elevation (3,000' to 4,000') rock climbing sites west or east of the Cascade mountain range such as French's Dome or Pete's Pile are usually accessible as early as mid-May through October. Expect heavy snow pack to hinder easy access to high-altitude (5,000' to 6,000') until mid-July.

How does this data break down for quick use by a rock climber? If it is not raining, go climbing. Is the forecast on the west side of the Cascades predicting gray skies and showery conditions in May and June? Then consider driving to an east side destination where you can often find sunnier skies and certainly less rain than the west side climbing sites.

Unique places such as Pete's Pile or Bulo Point crag make great drier climbing destinations because of the effect of the rain shadow created by the Cascade mountain range. In essence, your visit to east side climbing destinations for rock climbing opportunities is sure to be a success, although during summer thunderstorm activity can develop rapidly along the eastern slope of the High Cascades on a hot summer afternoon.

GEOLOGY OF NW OREGON

A formative discussion on the physical geology and natural processes of rock structures is beneficial to all climbers by providing a better understanding of the cliffs and mountains we climb on. This analysis is a brief summary of Plate Tectonics and continental volcanism designed to enhance your understanding of localized geologic characteristics of rock stratum and lava formation.

Plate Tectonics

The geological landscape of Oregon, like a thin fabric has been stretched and reshaped by continental and oceanic movements described systematically as Plate Tectonics. This diverse region of volcanic activity is structurally composed of igneous, sedimentary, and metamorphic rock formations creating an interwoven and complex matrix. Though our lowlands and valleys of northwestern Oregon (including the northern Coast Range) are commonly formed of sedimentary rock, much of the Cascade Mountain Range is built on multiple layers of basalt (~50% silica), andesite (~60% silica), some dacite, and infrequent formations of welded tuff rhyolite (~70%+ silica) stratum such as Steins Pillar.

The lithosphere between the upper plates and the earth's mantle moves in relation to deep ocean volcanism, while the oceanic and continental plates ride piggyback on top. Plate tectonics gradually shift and build all rock formations into similarly understandable patterns and concepts. The thicker continental plate is composed of very old granitic stock surrounded by younger uplifted sediment, and when it collides with the offshore oceanic crustal plate the heavier (denser) plate is subducted beneath the former. Some of the compositionally lighter weight sedimentary rocks (oceanic & continental) that are subducted back down into the earths mantle will melt and remix with the magma pool or core, then rise as infrequent magma intrusions through fissures or fault lines in the continental crust. Most oceanic seafloor sediment accumulates from organic marine animals and plants, as well as from terrigenous (land) or submarine volcanic sources. If the magma congeals underground it is referred to as intrusive igneous rock in the form of dikes, sills or batholiths, but when the magma erupts volcanically through breaks or fissures in the earths surface it is known as extrusive igneous volcanism.

When the magma breaks the continental crust they are observable as volcanic vent openings which can develop into mountains that expel material composed of lava flows, flood basalts, lava domes, explosive pumice, ash or tuff clouds, and debris formations. This offshore fault line subduction zone folds and warps the sedimentary perimeter continental

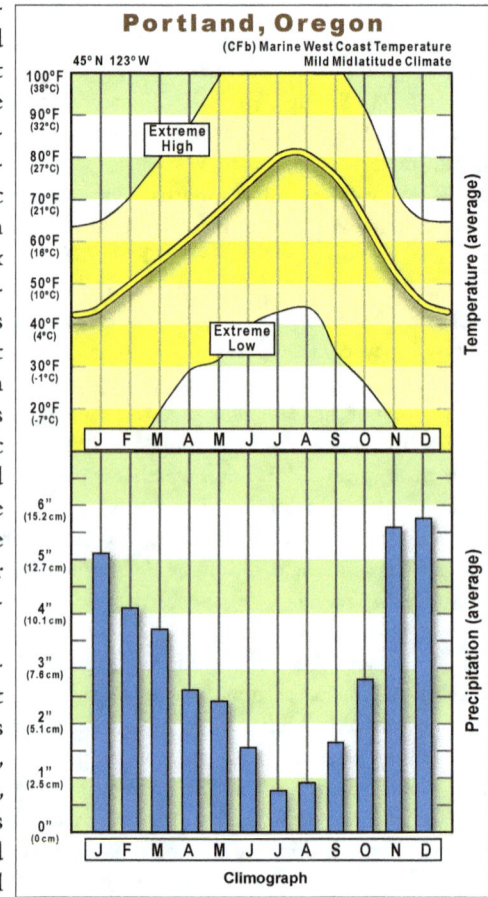

landscape creating our coastal range. These coastal foothills of sedimentary rock are folded and uplifted by the oceanic plate to form the low profile Coast Mountain range.

Certain mountain ranges such as the Olympics in Washington state are created less by volcanism and more by the ongoing tectonic folding and faulting process. The northern Cascade Mountain range of Oregon has a series of major strato-volcanoes (i.e. Mt. Hood, Mt. Jefferson) but also shield volcanoes (Newberry Crater in central Oregon) and numerous smaller cinder cones such as Olallie Butte.

Geological parameters of bedrock structures

A considerable percentage of climbing and bouldering sites in the av Oregon region are composed of andesitic or basaltic igneous rock characteristics. From a geological perspective, this is readily apparent, simply because many of the Pacific Rim volcanoes produced magmas composed of basaltic origins from deep within the Oceanic plate. From Japan to the Alaskan Aleutian archipelago, from western North America to the Andes (the origins of its "andes-ite" name) mountain range of South America, volcanoes actively expelled (in recent history and to this date) voluminous quantities of igneous lavas. Andesite rock, in essence, is water, gas content, bits of sediment, and a healthy dose of silica. This whole events begin when the Oceanic tectonic plate is subducted conveyor belt fashion beneath the Continental plate. These two plates rub and drag Oceanic basaltic (and some minor sediments) material downward into the mantle of the Earth.

During this tectonic process, sedimentary elements that form sandstone and mudstone are light weight, and like whipcream on the top of frappacino, were scraped up into hills, like our Oregon and Washington Coast Range.

During the subducting process, increased pressure upon the basalt plate increases the temperature of the rock mass (850°C-1200°C), but the tremendous pressure limits liquefaction. Once a weakness is found in the Continental plate, the basaltic rock mass travels by force up this narrow confine and liquifies as a massive molten structure or "pool" a few miles below the Earths' surface. This subsurface magma chamber displaces the surrounding sedimentary rocks, mixing it into the magma pool, altering its characteristics. Molten basaltic magmas have a much higher melting point, than light-colored rhyolitic and dacitic magmas. Molten magmas that are mixed with silica-rich sandstone and mudstone make andesitic magmas. Water tends to seep into the magma, in the chamber, and as it nears the surface, altering its final chemical balance, and effecting a drop in pressure (nearer the surface). The changing crystallization processes of the minerals in the magma chamber releases gas, thus charging the material into an explosive combination, seeking an outlet at the surface. This liquid magma then follows a weakness or crack in the Continental plates crust. Being liquid and heated, it presses upward through the surrounding older congealed rock structure, rising to the surface and venting explosively as volcanic mountain peaks. If the magma is loaded with too much silica, it may congeal right there, cooling slowly to create intrusive plutonic granite stock. If the magma pool is chemically altered by incorporating enough water into the mix, it continues upward and explodes as surface lavas, or as gaseous ash clouds (e.g. Lassen Peak, Mt St. Helens), or even extremely violently, as in the case of Crater Lake.

The results of this conjunctive igneous mix may produce 'pure' basalt (like the Columbia

Gorge Flood Basalt Group), or, as in the case of most of the entire Pacific Rim volcanic string, it may be medium-to-light colored silica-rich lava rock type (breccias, tuffs, andesites, dacites, and rhyolites) of volcanoclastics. The resultant explosive eruptive event may be a viscous dry event (obsidian), lacking sufficient water content. Water that is gathered from nearby rocks around the magma pool result in highly explosive, highly silicic steam ash (tuff and pumice) explosive events. These pyroclastic events eject gaseous clouds of fragments that solidify (whole or part) before landing on the ground. Magma that reaches the surface is an extrusive molten volcanic lava flow. Dacitic and andesitic lavas may result if the matrix has less silica content. Eventually the lava cools and solidifies.

Even after long periods of erosional and chemical weathering processes, the resultant forested landscape still reveals exposed clusters of large basaltic-andesitic boulders (or short vertical escarpments), in surprisingly extensive quantities that are readily found throughout the northern Oregon Cascade Mountain range.

If you were to take a close look at a rock specimen from one of our local bouldering sites, the apparent structure is definable. It will usually be composed of a dark to medium gray groundmass, incorporating either aphanitic (no visible crystals), or porphyritic (visible crystals). Basalts are generally black or dark gray (and generally lack visible crystals, olivine excepted). Andesites show various degrees of (small-to-large) crystals. Dacites may be light gray to brown, and rhyolites may show non- to minimally-visible crystals in a light gray to yellow (or reddish) colored matrix groundmass. The early up-building phases of numerous High Cascades Oregon volcanoes were broadly mafic (basaltic) in composition, while latter periods of explosive activity generally produced silicic magmas of basaltic-andesitic, and dacitic origins.

Considerable portions of the broad High Cascades Volcanic Arc experienced leveling by Ice Age glaciation (during the Quaternary period), including all of the Cascades of Washington state, and in the high country of Oregon a longitudinal 8-10+ mile wide swath reaching south to Mt McLoughlin. This leveling of terrain has left fingerprints on the landscape in the form of flattened knolls, and subtle morainal forms along the outskirts of the glaciation zones. Geologically landscaped examples can be observed around Olallie Lake, near Santiam Pass (Square Lake knoll), and the morainal ridge forms immediately north and south of Suttle Lake.

Andesites can be found along the entire Oregon Cascade Range, but rhyolites are more common south of the Klamath Mtn, Three Sisters, to Ochoco Mtn lineament boundary.

Geologic Episodes of the Western Cascades and High Cascades

The old Western Cascades are the compositional remnants of older volcanic activity. This older range is a mostly forested region of steeply cut foothills (up to 4,000' tall) west of a generalized north-south line from (roughly) the upper Clackamas River, to areas southwest of Detroit Lake. Heavily altered by weathering, these old peaks no longer resemble volcanoes, its magma vent sources are subdued, and the hills are a well blended mix of various deteriorated forms of dacite, basalt and andesite, where quality large boulderable sized boulders or cliffs are a rarity.

This entire broad area of the Cascade Range was developed, with a secondary, and third phase of vulcanism during the early- mid- and late-Miocene epoch. Each subsequent event period set up a row of volcanoes slightly further east of the old Western Cascade volcanoes, thus gradually burying, or subordinating those under the newer stock.

Finally, the broad uplift of the newer High Cascades Arc or range, composed of both basalt and andesite flows, formed the extensive talus and short flat top bluffs around Olallie Lake were likely laid down earlier enough to experience some grooming by glaciation. Olallie Butte, and a number of other minor cinder cones, erupted after the last Ice Age, and have retained much of their original form. Most stratovolcanoes like (the second phase of) Mt. Hood, Mt. Jefferson, and Three Sisters are relatively young High Cascades events, while the broad regional landscape upon which they are built are considerably older.

Geologic Nature Of Various Climbing & Bouldering Sites

Beacon Rock monolith is the remnant core neck of an old volcano. Mount Beacon [?] likely built a fair sized volcano in ancient history, securing the region with considerable Andesitic flows, but eventually, as the deep molten magma chamber lost sufficient pressure it congealed and cooled. Topographical extremes revised the landscape of the Columbia Gorge, river erosion being an obvious factor (and glaciation?) that has effectively removed its broad sloped tapestry, leaving the mere 900' tall core. Some subtle patterns exist that hint of this past history. The Cascade Boulders are large, fairly intact slightly roughly shaped tumbled remnants of a nearby Andesite bluff. The Andesite boulder fields that compose Hamilton Boulders are likely remnants of this ancient peak. This ancient peak likely deposited andesite flows several miles northward, but at some point peripheral subsidiary volcanic vent activity seem to have been feeding its own separate flows, differentiated from the same deep seated parent magma chamber. The volcanic event phase that formed Beacon Rock, may be directly related to parallel events that created other extensive boulder fields and lava flows extending along a broad ridge crest extending for 9 miles north to Three Corner Rock summit. This entire region is uniquely covered with an extensive variety of andesitic rock clusters.

This intertwining of volcanic events may help to explain some of the depositional Andesite flow characteristics found emanating near Three Corner Rock. The Spring Boulders cluster forms the eastern edge of a flat topped lava flow, while just south of the summit Communication Towers is a rock bluff. This relatively flat topped bluff gradually descends eastward with a brief yet abrupt northeastern scarp.

On Mt Hood various forested lower elevation ridges reveal incidences of lava flows and talus slopes from its first ancient and primary mountain building phase. These lava flows and boulders are remnants from this moderately silica-rich up-building phase. This first phase produced a broad quantitative mix of Andesitic flow activity such as found at Barrett Spur. The old central vent core of this volcano is thought to be just north of the present summit of Hood, near the site of Cathedral Spire on the north slope. Events shifted from flowing lava eruptions to pyroclastic gaseous clouds of fragmental material that built the remainder of the peak. When completed, Hood stood 12,000' high, with a base spread factor covering 90+ square miles. When the vulcanism ceased, glaciation and erosion cut deeply into the softer materials.

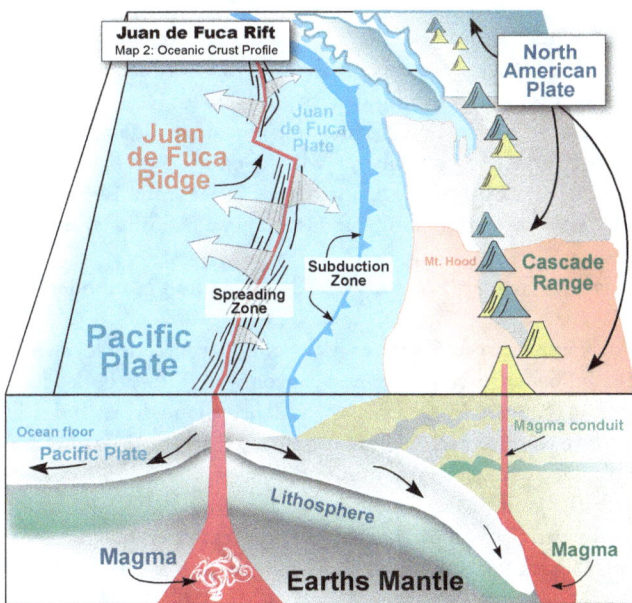

Another phase of volcanic activity ensued, with lava vents opening on the north/northeast flanks of the peak, creating extensive flows that traveled 15 miles into Hood River valley. Satellite vents occurred at Pinnacle Point, and near Cloud Cap. Barrett Spur and Cooper Spur have both survived the Fraser (Ice Age) Glaciation period, indicative of just how solid these andesitic bases have resisted erosion.

The boulder talus remnants of these vulcanism phases can be found at numerous sites around Hood, on certain alpine and forested ridge crest zones (Cooper Spur, Barrett Spur, Pinnacle Point, and the lesser yet extensive andesite talus zones west of Lawrence Lake).

About 2000 years ago, a second phase of vulcanism began. This series of renewed volcanic events produced primarily violently explosive pyroclastic events of pumice ash cloud ejecta and mud flows that are prominently displayed scattered across the southern slopes of Hood down past Timberline Lodge. The plug dome called Crater Rock was formed at this time. This series of events were similar in characteristics to the Mt. St. Helens event, and involved considerable violent gaseous cloud events, depositing zones of softer rhyolitic and dacitic material.

The Silver Star Mtn pluton comprises a unique band of granodiorite stock. This batholithic plutonic stock is a massive, slow cooled, erosion exposed system, with various peripheral bodies of dioritic contact metamorphism that provide ore-bearing veins. The full breadth of the zone effected by this granitic pluton consists of a swath beginning near the tip of Larch Mtn and rolling east across three miles of undulated forested hills. Its western lineament boundary follows nearly direct to Silver Star Mtn., continuing northeastward near the Starway ridge. Its eastern extension parallels the stream next to Skamania Mine, and includes the peripheral spires of Chimney Rocks, which are composed of aplite mantled diorite. Silver Star Mtn is an old eroded volcano, with five distinct "star-like" ridges, well eroded down to reveal various andesitic and granodiorite outcrops. The surrounding hills have long been subject to some mineral mining (such as gold, zinc, copper, quartz, and calcite). Much of this pluton barely crests the surface, but its effects are much more pronounced in the peripheral rocks (e.g. Chimney Rocks, Larch Mtn, etc).

Marys Peak sill is a remnant of a broad Gabbro sill that once covered the region from Stott Mtn in the north, south to Roman Nose west of Eugene. Much of the sill has been reduced to soil, but a few sites exist where boulderers can sample this quality product.

French's Dome is a fine example of a late stage 'plug' dome neck core of an old volcano that was likely a 'satellite' vent of the larger very old Sandy Glacier Volcano on the west flank of Mt. Hood. The ancient flows of this volcano exist below the Sandy River Glacier at the 1,650 meter elevation as a narrow profile dike or core composed of olivine andesite lava. Additional satellite vents are the Pinnacle and Cloud Cap.

The andesite lava at the Enola (aka Swinery) crag east of Rhododendron is a moderately porphyritic (58.7% SiO_2) formation.

The Pete's Pile bluff is a widely joint-spaced 60-meter high columnar andesite formation that is a moderately porphyritic lava flow exposed on the east canyon wall of East Fork Hood River near Polallie Creek. The bluff was exposed by the effects of avalanche flood debris and river cutting forces from Mt. Hood eruptive volcanic cycles. Compositionally the Pete's Pile bluff has an abundance of 2-3mm blocky plagioclase phenocrysts of silicate mineral (5-10%) with traces of olivine and amphibole in a dense medium-gray colored groundmass.

At Bulo Point chemically active water solutions increased the process of granular decomposition of the superficial structures. Rock formations in the 15-mile creek watershed are porphyritic silicic andesite (62.6% SiO2) in a blocky plagioclase phenocryst matrix of light and dark-colored minerals. The Bulo Point formation is likely an extrusive lava flow refined by erosional processes that removed the less resilient layers. A steady weathering process from water, heat and other factors gradually rounded the overall cliff features. Bulo Point has a course-grained surface texture akin to a particularly rough grade of sandpaper, great for friction so long as you are careful with how you jam your fingers or fists into rough-edged cracks.

CLIMBING ROUTE RATINGS

This guide uses the well-known Yosemite Decimal System (YDS) as the standard method for rating rock climbs. This system, first developed at Tahquitz in the 1950s, is a two-system concept connecting a Difficulty Grade and a Free Climbing Class.

Difficulty Grades

A Difficulty Grade (Roman numerals I through VI) indicates how long it will take to climb a route and is determined by the difficulty, the involvement, and the length of a route. For example:

- Grade I   Can be climbed in a few hours.
- Grade II   Can be climbed in a half day or less.
- Grade III   Can be done in less than a day.
- Grade IV   One long, hard day. Hardest pitch is no less than 5.7 in free climbing difficulty.
- Grade V   In one long day if the climbers are experienced and fast, otherwise 1½ days plus should be expected while the hardest pitch is usually at least a 5.8 difficulty.
- Grade VI   Requires multiple days to ascend and often includes extreme mixed free climbing and/or difficult nailing.

The Yosemite Decimal System concept, though designed to assist, is highly subjective and will vary from area to area. Some climbers may be able to climb very efficiently on two Grade IV routes while others may barely manage a Grade II without bivouacking. Most of the climbs found in this guide are Grade III or less in difficulty.

Free Climbing Difficulty Class

The Free Climbing Difficulty Class is based on an ascending scale from 1 to 5 and is then subdivided into an open-ended scale from 5.0 to 5.14 and beyond. This scale is designed to reflect the hardest free move on a pitch or the overall sustained character of the pitch. See the graph in Appendix B for detailed comparisons with other international ratings.

This open-ended scale allows for future routes of increasing difficulty. If a particular pitch contains a series of moves of the same difficulty, a higher rating is usually assigned. Further subgrading separates the easier 5.10's from the harder 5.10's by using the letters A, B, C and D (or as .10- and .10+). Some free-climbing routes at the local crags are underrated due to top-roping before leading. The best solution is to rate the climb according to an on-sight lead by a climber unfamiliar with the route in question.

Aid Climbing Difficulty

The art of modern nailing, Aid Climbing Difficulty or Class 6, is quite unlike its neighbor mentioned above. Both the technical severity of the piton or pro (protection) placement and the climber's security are linked to the same rating. In the sport of nailing, the letter A indicates aid climbing, while the number, (0 through 6 and higher), indicates the degree of nailing. The letter C indicates that it can be ascended clean without the need for pitons or other gear driven with a hammer. All of Class 6 aid climbing uses equipment as the means for progressing up the rock scarp to a higher point.

- A0   Pendulum, shoulder stand, tension rest, or a quick move up by pulling on protection.
- A1   Solid equipment placements.

- A2 Is more difficult to place but offers some good protection.
- A3 Involves marginal placements and the potential for a short fall.
- A4 Frequent marginal placements; will only hold body weight.
- A5 Pro supports body weight only; risk of 50-foot-plus fall.
- A6 Involves full pitch leads of A-4 and serious ground fall potential.

Modern nailing equipment has profoundly changed the way in which climbers approach a prospective route. Knifeblades, RURPs, Bird Beaks, and a variety of hooks and ultrathin wires offer new ways to aid climb at the extreme edge. Since free climbs are often maintained as free climbs, certainly some nailing routes should be maintained as nailing routes.

For those routes requiring a "seriousness" rating, they are as follows:
- PG: Protection may be adequate near the difficult sections, yet involve risky or runout sections which can increase the potential for an accident.
- R: A bold lead with a serious fall potential; may involve questionable or poor protection; serious injury is likely.
- X: Involves high risk of ground fall potential; very poor to no protection available; serious or fatal injury possible.
- TR: Indicates the route is generally a top-rope climb, although the climb may have been free climbed in the past.

The climbing difficulty class rating listed in this guide is not to be considered as absolute. All climbing routes are subject to unforeseen challenges that can quickly make the climb inherently dangerous.

Confidence, ability, intuition, and good judgment are crucial for managing the degree of risk that you and your climbing partner are willing to accept. Develop those invaluable skills so that you can foresee your risks or liabilities, because careless judgment becomes a harsh learning curve. Proceed with caution; climb at your own risk!

The "Star" or Quality Rating used throughout this book is designed to help climbers selectively choose the more aesthetic climbs. This is a highly subjective system, for many of the un-starred routes are worthy of attention. Do seek out the lesser-known climbs, especially if you have an extra hour.
- No Stars: An ordinary route.
- One Star (★): Good quality route, better than the usual.
- Two Stars (★★): Excellent route, good position with quality rock climbing, a highly recommended route.
- Three Stars (★★★): Superb position, a classic line on excellent rock, a must-do route on everyones list.

Of these starred routes, not all will be bolted face climbs. Some will be crack climbs, several will be short but worthy, and a few will be two routes connected together making an even better classic climb.

The star ratings for a climb at Broughton Bluff will vary from the quality routes at Beacon Rock or Smith Rock as they represent the favorable, interesting routes at that particular cliff.

EQUIPMENT AND SPECIALIZED GEAR

Both personal safety and your quality of enjoyment depend on your being adequately prepared with the appropriate gear when rock climbing at the crags. Essential equipment such as locking carabiners, belay-rappel devices, and even double ropes will help to ensure that your outing is a successful one.

In recent years, climbers have seen quality improvements in rock climbing equipment, both innovative and beneficial to the sport. Standard rock gear protection ("pro") such as spring-loaded camming devices (Camalots, Friends, TCUs, etc.), HBs, RPs, curved wired stoppers (I often refer to these as wires), bolts, and tailored rock shoes have contributed greatly to climbers' overall safety and climbing enjoyment . The following gear recommendations should be used as a broad list from which you can generally determine your needs for a specific climb. Gear sizes appear under each route name as a guideline, but choose your gear by analyzing your skills and needs for each rock climb *before* ascending it. Ask other climbers what they may have used for route protection, and be willing to take extra equipment and perhaps even larger-sized gear.

For traditional free climbing you will likely need a variety of the following gear: A single 60-meter rope, helmet, a set of 12–15 quick draws (QDs), wired stoppers up to 1½ inches, small camming devices like TCUs up to 1½ inches, and larger spring-loaded camming devices ranging from 1–4 inches.

It is wise to bring extra slings as well as some of the big stuff like Hexcentrics or Big Bro, especially if a particularly fine off-width crack is your challenge. Tiny specialized pro (like HBs, RPs, or Steel Nuts) may be useful on a few of the desperately thin routes.

Remember, wherever you climb, always exercise good judgment before and during the climb. Practice route analysis, ask for consultation and advice from others, develop foresight, and when you begin your ascent, climb with a reasonable degree of caution, fully aware of the risks of this sport!

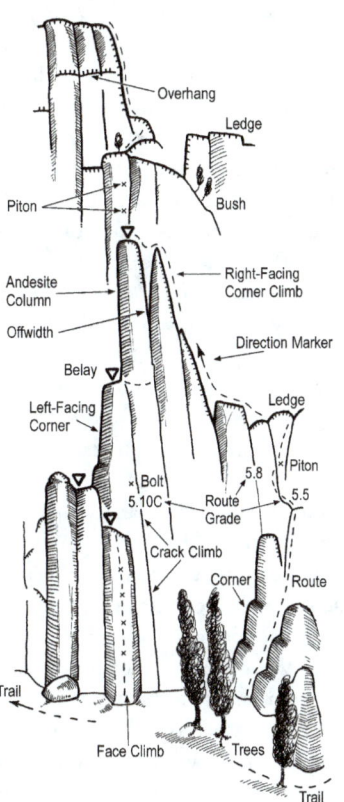

GPS GEODETIC DATUM

All GPS units of measure within this guide are based on GE (Google Earth) UTM geodetic datum. If you need to convert it from UTM to DD (Decimal Degrees) or DMS (Degrees Minutes Seconds) there are free websites or apps that can convert it for you. Or just change the settings in GE. Most cell phones have access to the GE free app. Different software programs may yield slightly different results so beware of the potential for slight GPS differences per software.

ABOUT THIS GUIDE BOOK

This books goal is to educate users about long-term stewardship

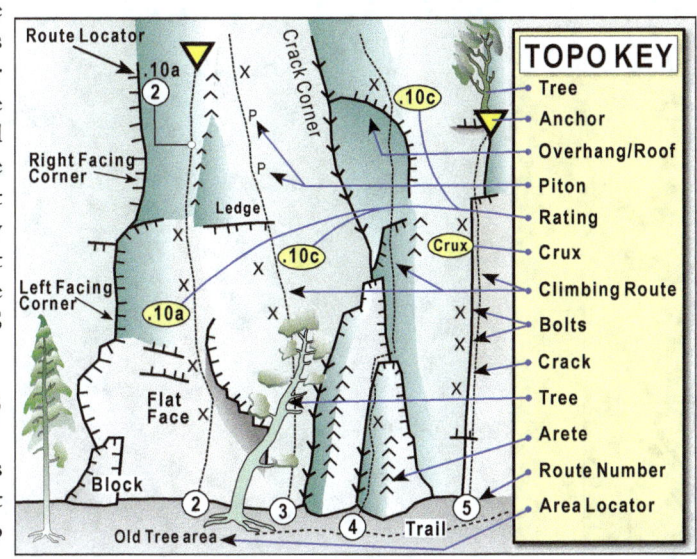

of our natural resources we enjoy climbing upon. Our purpose is to provide information that will help influence rock climbing for the public good. This guidebook aims to give insight about some of the nuances of each different climbing and bouldering site. This information helps teach us where to park our vehicle, seeks to identify the proper trail to the crag (avoiding a braided network of shortcuts), informs you if the site is not suitable for large groups (or if there is a site memorandum effecting guided groups), explains regulations such as seasonal raptor/flora closures, suggests where overnight camping options may exist, and points out basic community and emergency services at nearby towns.

The book expresses ideas on route development, site limitations, cliff flora factors, climbing ethics, bolting and anchors, and potential private property or ownership issues.

People involved in this outdoor sport should also be actively involved in a recreation based community interest user group that discusses and resolves various issues that effect access to our favorite crags and bouldering sites. Well designed guidebooks often play a crucial role by providing a communication bridge to rock climbers in the hopes of eliminating or reducing potential friction with area residents. We encourage recreational climbers to become involved in trail maintenance and other crag stewardship opportunities. Climbers are reminded to show respect for an owner of private land (adjacent to a sports crag site). Outdoor recreation enthusiasts should be cognitive of how to be essential yet articulate visitors while using various public lands, and about being courteous when using leased or privately owned timber entity lands where multi-use access is allowed. On state or federally managed lands, you are not merely a visitor, but a valued partaker with an interest in how these public lands are being managed.

We aim to broaden user interest throughout the entire region, encourage users to visit many different areas, seeking enjoyment from the adventure and seeking results that bring beneficial tourism-based stimulus to our local economies. This book is all about creating a good public resource that will be helpful toward preserving access in both public and private venues, and brings crucial reference material forward for public officials, and is highly useful with emergency response agencies for developing emergency rescue or evacuation plans.

Guidebook Support

If you develop new first ascent routes or boulder problems at any of this region's rock climbing or bouldering sites, take the time to contact us so we can successfully update the product information knowledge base for each climbing and bouldering section. Site data in this guidebook will become increasingly effective and more thorough when your new beta or insights are shared with the author of this book.

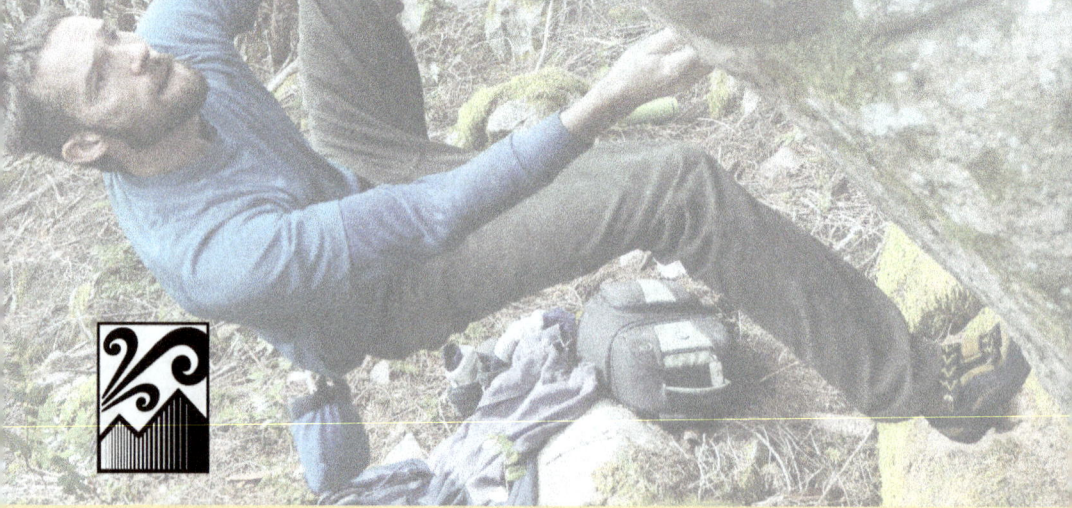

PART 1   Popular Rock Climbing Opportunities

ROCK CLIMBING

Climbers who journey into the Columbia River Gorge or along the back roads around Mt. Hood can experience great opportunities, not just to climb, but also to view the scenic peaks of our northern Oregon and southern Washington Cascade mountain range. This lengthy chapter details a brief selection of popular rural rock climbing sites, some near Hood River, and some near The Dalles, often within the general proximate vicinity to Mt Hood along either the U.S. Hwy 26 corridor, or U.S. Hwy 35 corridor.

This chapter provides a gateway to adventure with a selection of fine quality rock climbing places you are certain to find rewarding. Most of the crags in this chapter are nestled within the forested landscape of the Cascade mountain range, and are enjoyable little rock climbing cragging destinations. Yet we use the term 'destination' lightly, for in reality these crags provide a rock climbing experience on a small and less crowded scale.

FRENCH'S DOME

Though tiny in comparison to many crags, the merits of French's Dome should not be overlooked. Many Portland area rock climbers have discovered that this miniature crag's rare qualities give it an enduring appeal. A visit to French's is sure to spark your enthusiasm, as well.

This unique and easily accessible dome of rock lies amongst a tall canopy of evergreen trees along the lower west side of Mt. Hood. There are about two dozen climbing routes available ranging from 5.6 to 5.12+. Most of the climbs are fixed with bolts, practically eliminating the need for natural protection. The overall height is 160 feet from the longest side and 80 feet on the road face.

The dome itself is not visible above the forests of Douglas fir trees, but it is just a short, one-

minute walk to the crag. French's Dome is an interesting geological wonder of the Oregon woods and a perfect little area to escape from the city.

The Dome seemed to languish for years after the intial four original routes were established. In the 1980s local summer ski school coaches became enthralled by the place and sought to establish a string of new routes that has literally set the place on edge. Hermann Gollner, Vance Lemley, Pat Purcell, Tom Sell, John Rust, Joe Reis, Tymun Abbott and Dave Sowerby put considerable time into establishing the 5.11/.12 grade at the Dome. Their route development energy helped tremendously to make the Dome a premier climbing destination in the Mt. Hood National Forest.

Effective erosion control platforms have been built along the cliff base of French's Dome providing a long-term solution to a hillside that had been rapidly sliding away. With Forest Service trail building guidance and a volunteer workforce locals have built a legacy that will keep this place a perfect little Mt. Hood gem!

The routes at French's Dome are described symmetrically clock-wise, which you will find quite beneficial because the trail first encounters the crag at the routes facing the road. Beginning with the road face the list shown below details each rock climb as if you were to descend the perimeter trail around the crag to the left from the road face. Then from the lowest portion of the Dome the routes are described uphill past the Yellow Brick Road route.

French's Dome is a sport crag haven because the nature of the rock (crackless) lends itself to bolt protected climbing. If this is your first visit you are certain to enjoy the quality of this unique place, regardless of the climbing grade you typically send.

French's Dome is composed of olivine basalt and is a tall remnant of an old volcanic neck core after the surrounding softer material eroded away exposing the rock knob.

Season: Accessible for approximately 6-7 months of the year from early May till late October (or early November). When the weather has been rainy and cool, the crag tends to remain slippery for a day, due mainly to its location within a thick tall canopy of Douglas fir trees.

Directions:

Drive east from Gresham/Portland on U.S. Hwy 26. Continue through Sandy, Oregon until you are near the small community of Zigzag at the base of Mt. Hood. Turn north on the Lolo Pass Road. The crag is located 6¼ miles up the Lolo Pass road (NF 18) from its junction with U.S.

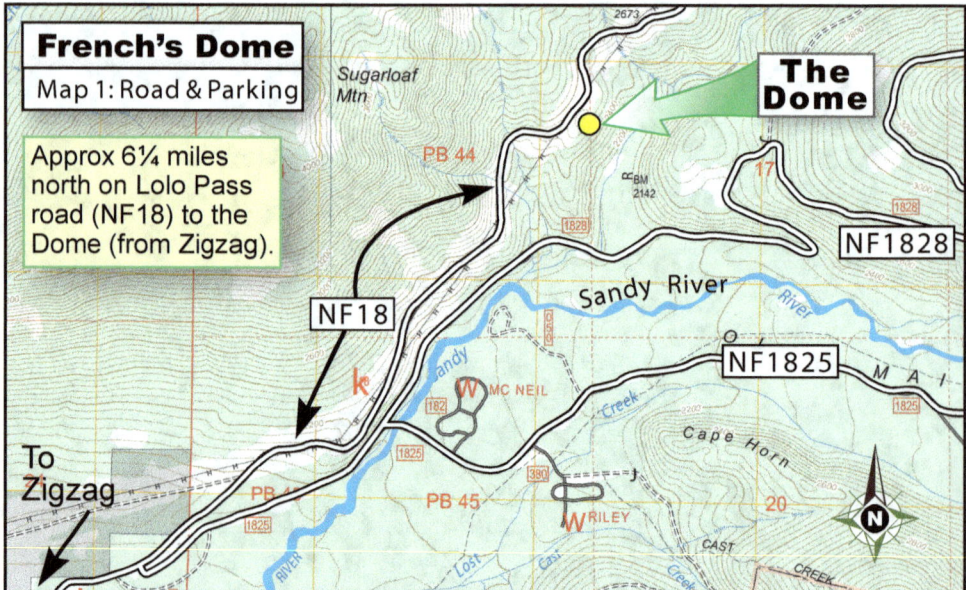

French's Dome ✦ ROCK CLIMBING   15

Hwy 26 at Zigzag. Look for an unobtrusive dirt pullout on the right and the NW Forest Pass sign. A vehicle parking pass is required for all users at this site. You can obtain a daily or annual Northwest Forest Pass parking permit at their office in the small community of Zigzag.

The following routes are numbered according to a descent made clockwise to the left from the road face area to the lowest portion of the Dome, and then up the south trail.

1. **High Voltage (aka Rhoid Rage) 5.12 b** ★★
   60' (18m) in length, 5 QD's
   This rock climb starts a few feet immediately right of the Road Face climb, which is located at the crest of the slope where the trail meets the pinnacle. The steepest hung route at French's, with large edges and sidepulls, pumpy climbing that leads up to a big overhung bouldery crux bulge that ends on a final finishing jug. Very good climb, considered one of the best climbs for its grade at French's. High Voltage was named by Hermann, while some Portlander's called it **Rhoid Rage.**

2. **Road Face   5.12a** ★★★
   60' (18m) in length, 6 QD's
   The trail meets the crag at this point. This is the second climb from the right. This route, originally done as an aid line, is now a popular and difficult free climb. The climbing has mod-

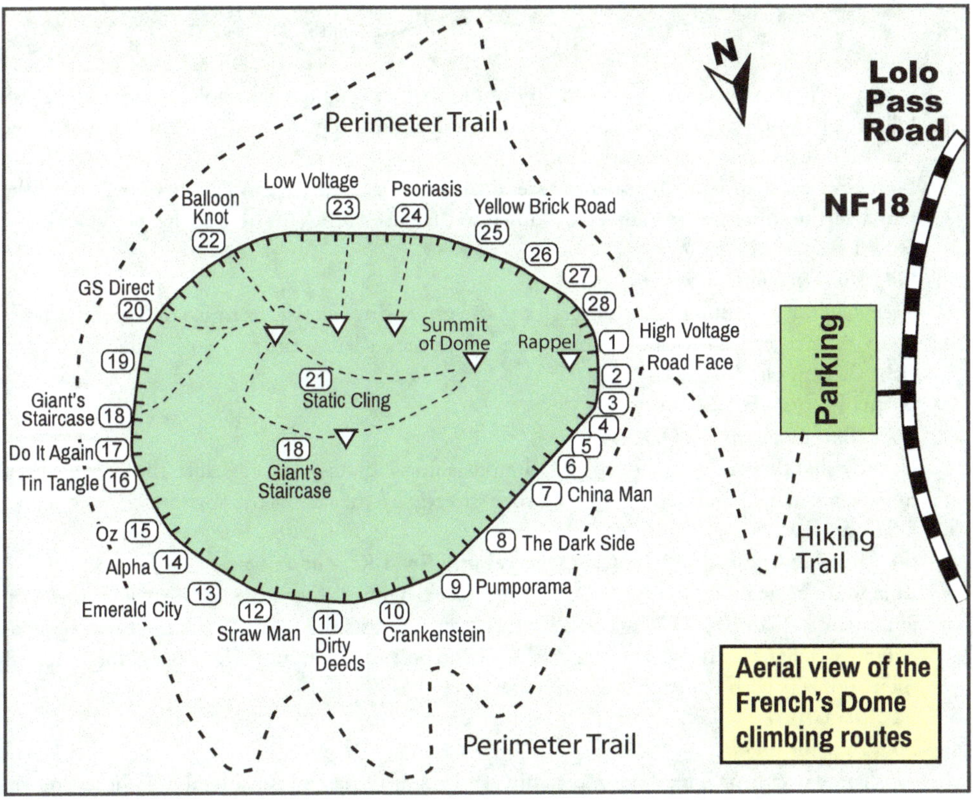

Alan leading at French's Dome

Aerial view of the French's Dome climbing routes

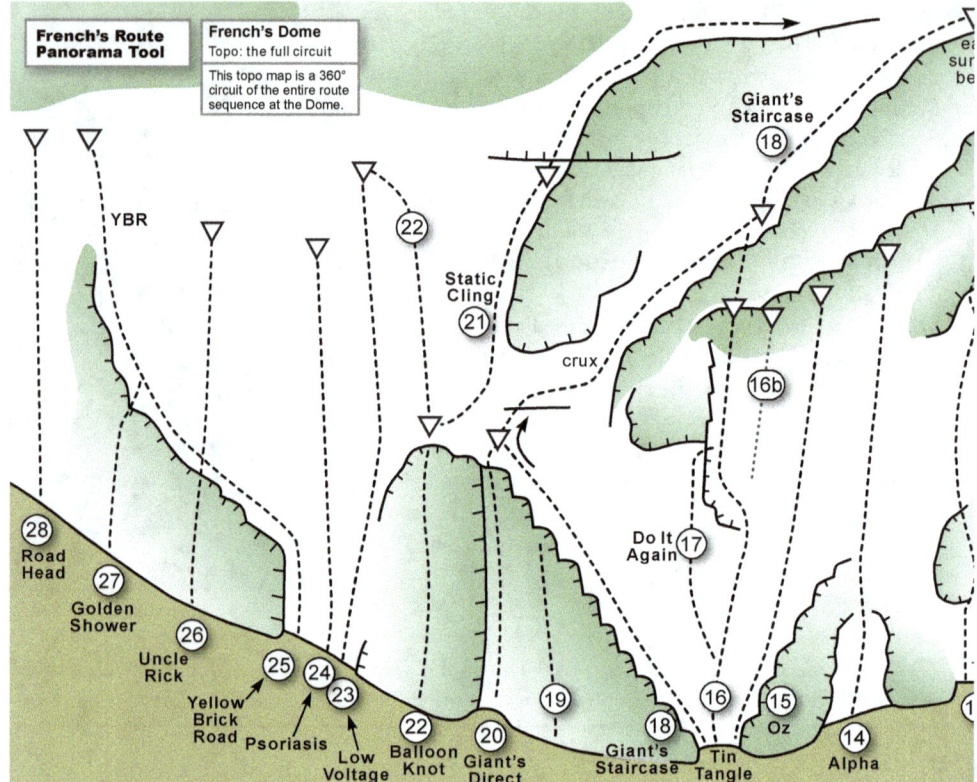

erately variety of powerful thin crimp movement, offering a full shake hold out at mid-height, followed by some stout movement at a crux overhanging bulge section near the top just below the belay anchor.

Note: For those of you who plan to ascend the Giant's Staircase (5.7) route to the top of the pinnacle, the summit rappel descends down to the base of the cliff here at the "road face".

3. **Road Kill   5.12a**   ★★

    60' (18m) in length, 5 QD's

    Techy slightly overhung face climb. This is the upper direct finish from Road Rage that leads up to its own separate anchor. Where Road Rage moves left at the jug, Road Kill goes up and right slightly. Grade may be 5.12a/b.

4. **Road Rage   5.12a**   ★★

    60' (18m) in length, 5 QD's

    Crimpy slightly overhung face climb. Climb the first 2 bolts of Road Kill to the rest jug, then move diagonally up left to a third bolt, then directly up the face to the anchor.

5. **BSD 5.12b**   ★

    60' (18m) in length, 6 QD's   (BSD merges into Road Rage at 4th bolt)

    This route begins on the uppermost Tier #9 (see diagram). A three bolt direct start variation joining into Road Rage. Using the BSD direct start boosts the rating to 5.12b. Initial sequential movement on thin techy crimps (risky second bolt clip) with numerous holds for about 18' till it connects with RR at the fourth bolt.

6. **Jackie Chan   5.12b**   ★★★

    60' (18m) in length, 5 QD's

    This route begins on Tier #8. A steep thin crimp climb entailing considerable technical movement and endurance. The route starts with a series of initial tough crux opening boulder moves to get to the first bolt, then easier freedom of movement to an odd natural feature at mid-height, then finish with a series of moves on steep terrain to an anchor. Note: You can clip the first bolt from atop the upper tier, or you can bypass the initial opener moves entirely via an 5.11d variation by cutting in from off the upper edge of the top tier.

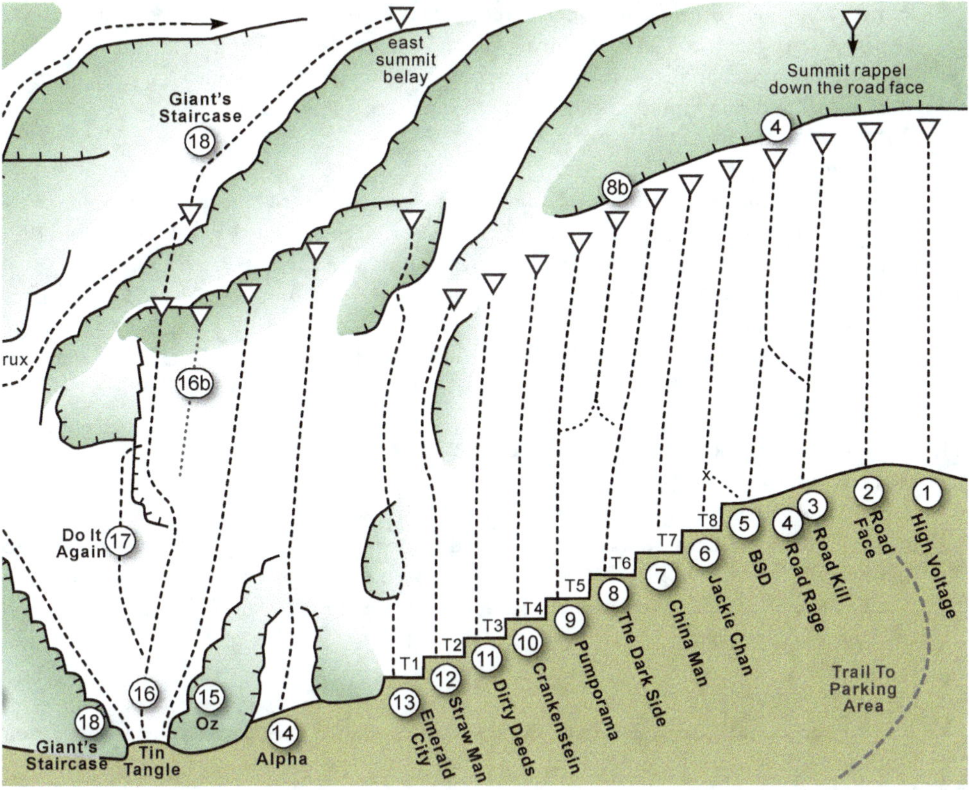

7. **China Man   5.11b   ★★★**
60' (18m) in length, 8 QD's
The route begins on Tier #7. An excellent climb on a slightly overhanging face with many small edges and finger holds. Powerful pumpy climbing on the lower section leads to a nice mid-height shake out rest point. More pumpy climbing on the upper section that ends with a good jug at the anchor.

8. **The Dark Side (aka The Siege)   5.12b   ★**
60' (18m) in length, 6 QD's
Initial moderate opening moves lead to a lower crux section, followed by a series of continuously pumpy climbing all the way to the anchor. This stout climb attracted a variety of interest in its development phase. It was bolted by Hermann Gollner, left untouched for several years, then further projected by Florian Jagodic (while strength training), but Hermann apparently completed an ascent before Florian could build endurance for the line. Dave Sowerby also found the climb of interest and began working the climb during this same brief period in history and succeeded in an ascent.

8b. **Philanthropy   5.12c**
60' (18m) in length, 8 QD's
A powerful variation that splits off from either Pumporama or TDS. Climb first 4 bolts of

Pumporama, then veer right and climb a steep bulge (4 more bolts) to a fixed belay station. Via the POR start gets you 5.11+. If starting via The Dark Side clip first 2 bolts (or clip 3rd bolt with long sling to minimize risk), go through its crux, then move left onto the steep bulge (4 more bolts) and climb up to a belay. Via TDS start gets you 5.12c.

9. **Pump-o-rama 5.12a/b** ★★
   60' (18m) in length, 6 QD's
   An interesting, well named route that offers challenging sequential movement up steep overhanging and pumpy terrain that ascends along an obvious black water streak. A series of thin holds low on the climb lead to a difficult sequence of moves at the 4th and 5th bolts.

10. **Crankenstein 5.11c** ★★★
    60' (18m) in length, 5 QD's
    An excellent climb and considered to be one of the best routes at the Dome. The technical crux is low on the climb, but the bulge near the end of the climb is surprisingly formidable to most people.

11. **Dirty Deeds (aka Silver Streak) 5.10c** ★★★
    60' (18m) in length, 6 QD's
    Superb (and very popular) climb to help you quickly grasp the nature of steep edgy face climbing at the Dome. The route was developed and named (Dirty Deeds) by Pat Purcell, and to those climbers from the Hood River area it has been known by that name. And, for those climbers from Portland it was always referred to as Silverstreak. In any case, its a stellar climb and well worth sending.

12. **Straw Man 5.7** ★★★
    65' (20m) in length, 9 QD's
    A very popular and classic rock climb that starts up easy holds, then passes a steep crux section near the 5th bolt.

13. **Emerald City 5.8** ★★
    75' (23m) in length, 9 QD's
    A steep enjoyable face climb located between Straw Man and Alpha. Surmount an initial bulge crux, then cruise up moderately easy terrain. The climbing steepens, then passes a pumpy lip section before the holds get bigger and difficulty eases near the belay station.

14. **Alpha 5.8** ★★★
    65' (20m) in length, 8 QD's
    A great climb with a variety of small ledges, face climbing, and positive knobby hand holds near the crux. Climb up easy steps in a gully, then continue up a steep face to a short vertical crux section on a knobby face. The original left start has been carved into the new Oz route.

15. **Oz 5.8** ★★
    60' (18m) in length, 8 QD's
    Ascends a ramp of large steps then embarks up and left on a steep face to a crux near the 4th bolt, and then large hand holds and edges on the upper portion near the bolt anchor.

16. **Tin Tangle (aka Tin Man) 5.8** ★★★
    60' (18m) in length, 8 QD's
    This excellent and popular route climbs directly up a subtle blocky flat buttress starting at the lowest point of the east face of French's Dome (where **Giant's Staircase** begins). Ascend up the initial big holds till the face steepens. Gingerly work up just right of the vertical flat rib. The best holds are situated on the vertical blocky flat rib, but the first three bolts are located a long reach out to the right. From about the third bolt angle slightly left onto the flat rib buttress then up easier terrain to the belay station.
    Note: a recent 2-bolt extension (**#16b**) continues up right-ish (from the third bolt) into a

French's Dome ✦ ROCK CLIMBING   19

French's Dome
Map 1: Giant's Staircase

weak corner ending at a belay station. You might use that variant but it's not the original route.

17. Do It Again   5.9   ★
50' (15m) in length,   8 QD's
This route travels up on the left side of the blocky flat ribbed buttress called **Tin Tangle**. Start at the same place as you would for **Giant's Staircase** at the lower eastside dirt landing but climb directly up to the first bolt, staying just to the left side of the inobvious flat ribbed buttress. At a small lip overhang, move abruptly right to merge in with **Tin Tangle**, then continue up easier terrain to the belay station. Rap or continue up to merge with **Giant's Staircase** route. This is a variation route left of Tin Tangle but is quite popular today.

18. Giant's Staircase   5.6   ★ ★ ★
Multi-pitch climb, and about 6 QD's per lead
This is a classic and original climb that ascends giant stone steps and ledges starting from the lower east side of the pinnacle. **P1:** Beginning at the lowest point on the east face, ascend up leftward on big easy steps (bolts) to a ledge and a belay anchor. **P2:** move up onto a thin stance immediately above the belay, then traverse rightward (bolts) to bypass (crux) a vertical section. A few brief steep moves quickly ease to large steps in a low angle ramp system and a belay anchor station. **P3:** Continue up the ramp system to the summit of the pinnacle and belay at the summit anchor. (Note: each pitch is roughly 60' per lead.)

Note: The Standard Rappel from the Summit:
To rappel from the summit of French's Dome, descend a few yards west down slope toward the road face where you can locate a fixed double bolt (80-foot) rappel station. This rappel descends down the road face, a section of cliff that is substantially overhung, and lands a few yards from the French's Dome historical plaque.

19. Park Her Here 5.4
30' (9m) in length, 3 QD's
Something minor tucked just left of the famous **Giant's Staircase** route. This lil' minor route jogs up a pile of steps to its own belay (just a few yards from the Giant's Staircase first pitch belay. Bring more quickdraws if you're going above it.

20. Giant's Direct 5.7
30' (9m) in length, 5 QD's (for first short lead)
This is a short vertical bolted direct start alternative route that merges with Giant's Staircase at the first belay station. Bring more QD's if you're climbing something above this route.

21. Static Cling 5.10b
60' (18m) in length, Pro: about 5 QD's (if doing it as two short leads)
Interesting route with a short steep crux right out of the gate. From the old westmost first belay anchor on the Giant's Staircase route, commence directly up right-ish into a vertical bolted scoop. Using the right side of the scoop will reduce the rating to 5.9. The climb eases quickly to another belay station, then climbs over a horizontal crumbly seam up a minor steep face to easier mossy terrain near to summit. The upper portion of the route is easier but a bit crumbly. Belay at the summit anchor. Bring about 8+ QD's if doing it as one single long lead.

22. Balloon Knot 5.9 ★
80' (23m) in length, 5 QD's (P1) & 5-6 QD's for P2
An initial steep section (5.9 crux) which soon lands at the belay ledge (used by Giant's Staircase). **P2:** step up left and climb airy 5.8 moves till it merges at the Low Voltage belay.

23. Low Voltage 5.11a ★
60' (18m) in length, 7-8 QD's
An interesting long climb which is a bit easier (.10-) if you are climbing on the big holds over to the right of the bolts. A bit gravelly on the upper section near the anchor.

24. Psoriasis 5.13a ★★★
60' (18m) in length, 5 QD's
This route and the previous share the same initial opening bolt. A true power-enduro route that lacks a comfort jug. The business begins at 3rd bolt so get your rests where you can find them. Crux between 4th and 5th bolt, but pumpy to the anchor.

25. Yellow Brick Road 5.10b PG ★
160' (50m) in length, QD's mostly, and minor pro to 1"
Less frequently climbed in the past, but with the addition of newer stainless bolts (and bolts added where there used to be odd gear placements) this route should certainly gain in popularity in the years ahead. Brief minor runout exists near the top of the route. Located on the southwest side of the Dome on a surprisingly overhang aspect of the wall. Begin at a vertical right facing corner, clamber up, then traverse left on a slowly rising ramp that also narrows the further you go up it. As the ramp fades to a vertical corner, ascend up a steep slightly hung section of cliff face (bolts at the crux) till the terrain eases to a belay anchor. The route is one single lead. Rappel.

26. Uncle Rick 5.12d ★
60' (18m) in length, 7 QD's
Begin to the immediate left of the initial start of the **Yellow Brick Road** route. Climb a series of difficult steep moves, then cross over the ramp of the YBR route, and continue to climb up a powerful and crimpy substantial overhung cliff face. Somewhat pumpy .11+ climbing gets you to the second to last bolt.

27. Golden Shower 5.11a ★
60' (18m) in length, 6 QD's

A direct start variant to the renowned **Yellow Brick Road** route. Ascend up a slightly overhung cliff face (3 bolts at 5.11-) by going up right till it merges onto the narrow YBR ramp. Continue up left-ish as the YBR ramp steepens to a vertical corner (3 bolts) taking you to the high belay doing some laybacking and pumpy climbing (YBR 5.10- crux is just before the belay).

28. Road Head 5.11d
60' (18m) in length, 6 QD's

Road Head is actually immediately right of High Voltage route which faces west toward the parking lot. This route is a powerline involving long moves between good holds, and pumpy climbing on a substantial overhung section of wall. The climbing is slightly right of the bolt line.

ENOLA (THE SWINE)

Beta from Jim Tripp and Tymun Abbott

The Swine (aka Enola, aka The Swinery) is a well-established crag holding a sizable selection of steep rock climbs on a bluff facing west overlooking the tiny community of Rhododendron.

The bluff is composed of Tertiary pliocene andesite and is surprisingly steep in places. The rock climbing routes and quality vary from small finger edge face climbs to sloping pocketed sections interspersed with larger edges. A variety of climbing routes exist such as pure face routes

Dave leading Burning Zone

while others are traditional crack climbs using natural/mixed pro. The climbing routes are typically 50' to 100' in length. The crag is well-suited for climbers who have solid 5.10 to 5.11 leading capabilities. The lesser traveled 5.9-and-under routes (and there are plenty) tend to be a bit mossy and dirty from lack of use. Jim Tripp and Paul LaBarge (and several other Govie' locals) were the primary original crag developers prior to 2008, followed by Mr Abbott and friends starting in 2009.

Seasonally the crag is limited to Oregon's reasonably good summer months (May to late October) as it receives the brunt of most weather systems arriving from the west. Yet a mild breeze rolls up through the trees from the valley below the crag keeping the temperatures comfortable all season while generally keeping various pesky insects away.

This guide sub-divides the entire wall into recognizable sections for easy reference. The initial upper wall at the overlook is called Sunset Wall. The popular middle wall (with its stellar classics) is the Moonshine Wall (the alcove). A hidden Bench Area branches up left from the alcove on a steeply zigzagging trail. The North Point Wall is located about 400' northward along a path from the second wall.

Directions:

Drive east of Rhododendron 1¼ miles, then turn left onto NF Road 27. Follow the paved portion east, then back up west on a very rough gravel road to the upper west most bend in the road at the 3000' elevation (total of 2⅓ miles from highway). Park on a small dead-end side spur road in a thick stand of fir trees.

From the forested parking area follow a level trail one minute west to a viewpoint overlooking the community of Rhododendron. Immediately below your feet is the Sunset Wall. Follow a narrow descending trail northward that zigzags down below the Sunset Wall.

SUNSET WALL (UPPER WALL)

The climbing routes are listed as if you are descending the trail. The first route described is the long arête climb on the left of the Sunset Wall.

1. **Pig's Knuckles**   5.11d ★★

    Length: 100', Pro: 8 QD's
    This is the bolted arête on left side of the wall. Great climb involving technical steep face climbing. Reachy mid section, and balancey on upper arête.

2. **Pigs Nipples 5.11a** ★★
    Length: 100', Pro to 2½" including cams & doubles
    This is a stellar crack that climbs a corner system to the immediate right of the arête. Route involves a tenuous layback through the middle crux section.

3. **Forbidden Zone 5.10a**
    Length: 90', Pro: nuts and

Enola
Map 1: Upper Wall

cams to 2"

This is the left direct crack leading up and right to merge with Tibbets.

4. **Tibbet's Crack 5.12a**
Length: 90', Pro: nuts and cams to 2"
A deceptively difficult crack system that starts under the left corner of a roof and powers up a tenuous thin crack. Merges with FZ.

MOONSHINE WALL

Continue to descend steeply down a narrow trail to the next wall. The first climb is next to a large maple tree. A short distance further lands at the main area. This wall offers a comprehensive selection of routes ranging from quality 5.9 routes, pumpy 5.10 routes, to stellar crimper 5.12 face routes. The alcove is the place where most first-time climbers come in order to experience the invigorating flavor of Enola.

5. **Calm Before The Storm 5.7**
Length: 40' Pro: 4 QD's
This is a nice climb on a fairly steep face that follows next to a minor crack on the upper part. Start behind a large maple tree.

6. **Granny's Got A Gun 5.12b**
Length: 75' Pro: 8 QD's
This climb is located to the immediate right of the toe of a minor sunny buttress that overlooks a boulder field. This climb zooms up positive holds to a 'knock-you-in-the-head' powerful crux move punching through the outer right edge of the overhang then merges into the classic Burning Tree route.

7. **Burning Zone 5.10c ★★★**
Length: 75' Pro: 8 QD's
This is considered to be one of the best routes at Enola. This stellar line gets plenty of sunshine in the afternoon hours. Climb starts at the toe of a minor buttress and ascends tricky face edges then angles up right above the lip of the large roof on good holds. Finish up a very steep rounded nose on interesting face holds.

8. **Samurai 5.10c ★★**
Length: 75' Pro: 8 QD's
This fine route branches up left from Burning Zone at the 3rd bolt, and continues directly straight up to its own belay. The crux is on BZ so this variant offers interesting face climbing that eases as you get near the belay station.

24 MT HOOD ZONE ✦   Enola

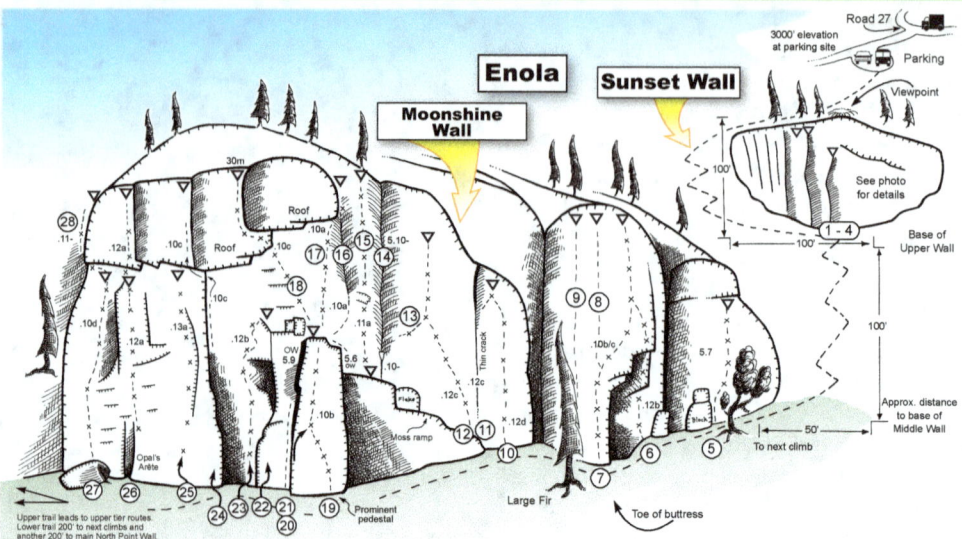

9. Meatloaf 5.10c ★★
Length: 75' Pro: 8 QD's
This high quality climb is completely independent to its anchor. Start just left of Burning Zone and climb up next to a bush, then gingerly surmount the wobbly block, and continue up sustained face climbing to a belay station.

10. Hillbilly Hot Tub 5.12c ★
Length: 45' Pro: 4 QD's
An extreme thin face climb immediately to the right of Scorpion.

11. Scorpion BBQ 5.12c ★★★
Length: 45'
Pro: #3 TCU, #1 WC rock, #00 TCU (opt.), #5 nut, #0 TCU, 1½" Cam
A powerful thin seam lacking in real holds this quality climb is composed of painful side pulls, smears, crimps and long reaches. The climb eases at the bolt so don't peel off during the last few moves. Just use a biner on each pro piece.

12. Fifty-seven 5.12c ★★
Length: 70', Pro: 7 QD's
As in AGE fifty-seven not Heinz. A fierce edgy face climb that powers up left from the seam. Merges with the next route. Starts at the base of the grass ramp. The rating is based upon avoiding the thin vertical seam of Scorpion BBQ.

Access the next three climbs on a long grass ramp ledge system by utilizing a belay anchor at a stance immediately above the large flake.

13. Serpentine Arête 5.10a
Length: 60', Pro to 2" then QD's
Scramble up the grass ramp past the large flake to a belay stance. Power up a vertical crack over the chock stone (crux) wedged in the crack, and then angle up RIGHT on the bolt line that ascends a vertical face. This route merges

Dave leading *Fifty-seven*

with the route Fifty-Seven.

14. The Easy Way 5.10a
Length: 60', Pro to 3" including small cams & nuts

Walk up the ramp and hop up past the large flake to a belay stance at a single bolt. Power past the initial chockstone (crux) wedged in the crack. Finish directly up the vertical minor crack corner system (5.9) on good edges and smears.

15. Calf's Gash 5.10c
Length: 60', Pro: QD's

From the same ramp belay stance power up past two bolts on a vertical flat face (crux), then power over a large block with a crack in it. Balance up a steep smooth face using delicate smears (bolts) to the belay anchor.

Access the next three climbs from the belay anchor on top of the prominent pedestal.

16. Mr. Hair of the Chode 5.10a PG
Length: 60', Pro to 2"

From the belay anchor at the top of the pedestal, step hard right and climb a poorly protected crack system with jug holds. The protection gets better the higher you climb. Exit past the right side of the roof to a belay anchor.

17. Jugalicious 5.10a ★★★
Length: 60', Pro: 5 QD's

One of the great quality routes at Enola totally worth doing. From the belay anchor at the top of the pedestal climb up RIGHT (bolts) using positive holds. Exit past the right side of the roof (crux) to a belay anchor.

18. SOTT P2 5.10c ★★★

Length: 60', Pro: 6 QD's & minor cams to 2"

This is P2 of Swine of the Times. From the belay anchor at the top of the pedestal climb up LEFT (bolts) on vertical terrain. Balance out left through the upper roof (some minor hollow rock) then continue climbing a vertical face (cam pro) to a belay anchor. A classic warm-up route when connected with the face climb on the outer side of the prominent pedestal.

The following two routes start at the base of the prominent pedestal at the 'Cove.

19. Jethro 5.10b ★

Length: 50', Pro: 6 QD's

Face climb on the outer portion of the prominent pedestal. Climb direct from the ground on vertical face edges (bolts) all the way to the belay at the top of the pedestal. The first move can be protected with a small cam if needed.

20. Swine of the Times 5.10b ★

Length: 50', minor pro to 2" & QD's

This starts up Fat Crack, then steps right to send the last 3 bolts on the outside of the pedestal. Continue up to the ledge on a pedestal. SOTT pitch two launches off the top of the pedestal up left through a series of overhangs. Last moves need minor 2" pro.

21. Fat Crack 5.9

Length: 50', Pro: 2½"

Climb the obvious off-width on the left side of the pedestal. Usually top-roped. Another top-rope on a flat face just left of Fat Crack is called **Prohibition** 5.12c (TR).

22. Tipsy McStagger 5.11d

Length: 50', Pro: gear to 1", including micro-cams

Climb the wide broken corner to a short left facing corner capped by a roof. Power over the lip and up a very thin crack (crux) till it eases onto a small ledge at a belay.

22b. Fortune Cookie 5.12b

Length: 50', Pro: 5 QD's

Climb a face immediately right of the previous route. Thin crux face sequence on upper ¼.

Enola
Map 4: Moonshine Wall

Brian in for another *Twenty Years* 5.10b

23. Grits & Gravy 5.12b
Length: 50'
A wild face climb that balances up delicate face moves to a slight lip. The 'gravy' portion is below the small lip. The grits potion ensues at the lip where you must pull on small rounded edges and non-existent foot smears (crux).

The very heart of the Alcove where most climbers congregate to plan for action.

24. Too Cool 5.10c ★★★
Length: 90', Pro: 3"
This is the stellar and obvious dihedral corner crack climb in the very center of this wall. The route powers directly up the crack on relatively holds, then launches into a small overhang. Move out and up left on precarious terrain to a tight stance, then out left again through the giant roof and then finish up a vertical corner groove to the anchor. Easy to get flamed out by the end of the climb at the top.

25. Psycho Billy Cadillac 5.13a ★★★
A powerful series of committing sequential moves utilizing the outer arête edge of a nearby dihedral. A strenuous series of crimps through the crux require excellent body core balance to connect the difficult string of moves.

26. Opal's Arête 5.12a ★★★
Length: 60' (P1), Pro: 7 QD's
Opal's Arête is considered to be one of the great classic routes at Enola. It is a tribute to the late Opal who owned what used to be called the "Food & General Store" in Rhododendron. Ascend an initial short slot then launch up on a vertical smooth face using tiny edges and sharp knobby pockets. Use one of the methods listed below to power through the crux, then from a nice stance move either up right or up left for one move then clip into the belay anchor. Rappel. Opal's Arête has several methods for ascent, so pick your style and go for it.
From the fifth bolt plant your right foot high onto a long narrow rail and using the right facing vertical rib pull up by rocking up onto your right foot.
Other option: From the fifth bolt plant an initial right foot on something, then reach out LEFT to the left arête. Slap up both blunt arêtes until you can stand on a narrow sloping right foot edge to clip the next bolt. Use the method that best suits your skill level, core body strengths and structure.
From the sixth bolt lean out left to use the left arête, or stay in close to the right rib.
Sea Hag Roof extension (5.12a) is the roof above Opal's Arête. Continue a few moves up from the belay anchor and climb out a large roof past 3 bolts.

27. Twenty Year Hangover 5.10d ★★★
Length: 60', Pro: 5 QD's
Twenty Year Hang-

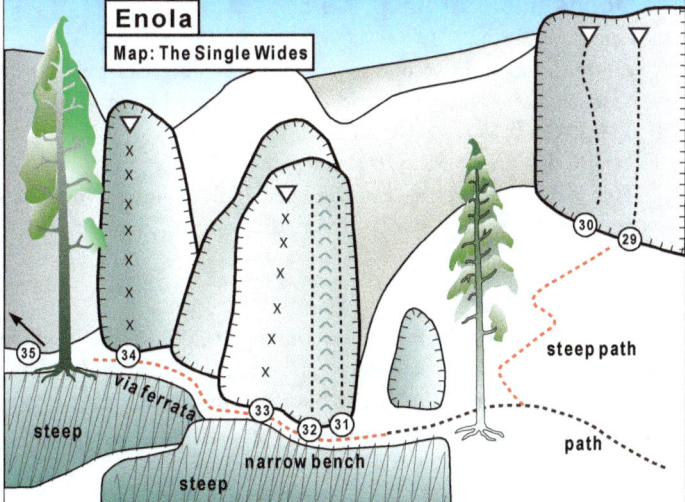

over is certainly one of the more popular climbs at Enola. The route uses a minor crackless corner immediately left of Opal's Arête. The route has many unique face edges and pockets.

28. _____ 5.11a
Length: 25', Pro: 4 QD's
This route launches out up left from the belay anchor on 20YH around the left edge of the large upper roof to an upper anchor.

THE BENCH

This section can be accessed by a steep trail which starts next to Twenty Year Hangover. The trail zigzags uphill to a shaded steep wall (80' tall) with the following two routes on it.

29. _____ 5.11 [?]
Length: 80', Pro to [?]
Climbs up steep face and crack corners, then powers through a bulge.

30. The Fang 5.10a
Length: 80', TR
Climbs up a steep face using minor seams, and then cruises up a crack on the left side of the overhang to the belay anchor.

THE SINGLE WIDE AREA

A string of routes along a narrow Via Ferrata ledge system are available by walking halfway up toward the Bench area and then stepping to the left. Each buttress along this ledge is tall like a bunch of single wide trailers stood up on end.

31. Shine 5.12d ★
Length 60', Pro: 5 QD's
A technical thin face climb on the right south facing aspect. The OW to its right has been TR'd and goes at 5.8.

32. White Lightning 5.11c ★★★
Length 60', Pro: 7 QD's
Climb past a prominent pocket up a rounded face through a techy thin crux at mid-height. Thought to be one of the best routes here. FA: TA 2012.

33. Single Wide 5.12a ★★
Length 60', Pro: 6 QD's
A difficult face climb on the left side of the first tall buttress along this narrow ledge system.

34. Moonshiners Arête 5.13b/c
Length 60', Pro: 7 QD's
A face climb on the second pillar along this ledge. Start next to a large fir tree. Ascends a series of strenuous wave shaped features on the steep buttress. FA: TA 2012.

35. Tailgater 5.12a
Length 60', Pro: mixed QD's and gear to 2"
This is on the far left end of the Via Ferrata. Climb corner crack, step left to ramp, climb up ramp to upper left corner of ramp, then around a corner crux to nice crack on left headwall, then up crack to belay.

NORTH POINT WALL

Walk north from the middle wall for about 200' on a flat trail that follows the base of a mossy rock bluff. The trail ends at a steep rock scarp (see diagram). It has a small selection of climbing options that guide you up to several belay anchors on a higher ledge.

Reach the next three rock climbs via 5.4 easy steps to a belay anchor.

36. King of the Moes 5.9 ★★
Length: 120', Pro to 2½" including cams
Dash up the easy steps to the ledge anchor. Embark up left (bolts) then move up right under a large nose-shaped prow, and continue up a right facing thin crack system to the top. Rap from anchor.

37. _____
Length: 60'
A potential route that can tackle the overhanging prow.

38. Dismantled Fears 5.10a ★★
Length: 60', Pro to 3"
From the ledge belay anchor launch up left on a face past 3 bolts to a crack, then climb up under a large roof (bolt). Power out the roof and up the double cracks above to an anchor.

39. _____
A potential thin seam starts up a right arching crack then punches up onto a steep blank face, but awaiting a potential buyer.

Access the next two climbs at the furthest point on this cul-de-sac trail.

Tymun on *Psycho Billy Cadillac*

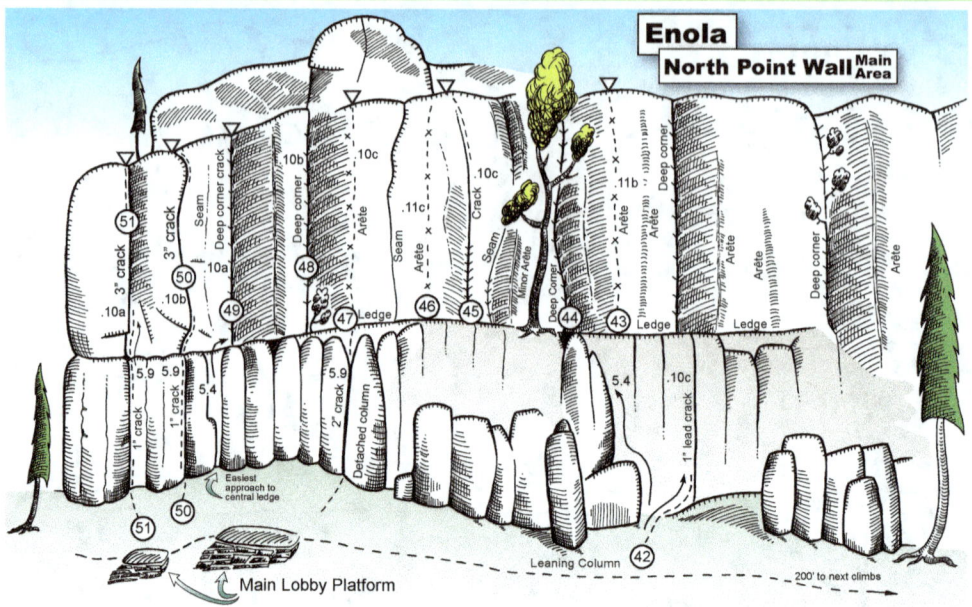

40. Tres Hombres P1 5.8 R (avoid), P2 5.10+

Length: 40' 1st pitch (avoid), 50' 2nd pitch, Pro to 3" including cams

The first 40' is a mossy runout 5.8 R to the ledge with an anchor. Avoid this first pitch until someone safely fixes and cleans the climb better. Best to use the next 5.8 route to access a midpoint belay ledge (see topo). From the belay launch up right in a stiff 5.9 flared crack to a stance, then onto an odd arête (bolt) over a crux bulge (bolt) to the anchor.

Access the next climb from a single bolt belay stance on the ground at the very end of a narrow trail.

41. Welcome to the Swine P1 5.8, P2 5.11b/c ★ ★ ★

Length: P1 40', P2 50', Pro: P1 has 5 QD's, P2 has 8 QD's

A stellar arête climb considered to be one of the better routes at Enola. Walk out to the very end of the narrow trail to an exposed belay perch stance at a single bolt. The belayer should set up a belay here. Ascend up a delicate steep 5.8 face climb (bolts) to a large ledge with a belay anchor. Power up left onto the arête (5.11a) to a tiny no-hands rest stance under the roof. The crux roof is a height dependent (5.11b/c) inobvious riddle to solve. After you surmount the roof continue to an anchor at the top of the cliff.

The trail descends northward at an angle for about 100' then continues horizontally another 100' to a main amphitheater.

NORTH POINT WALL - MAIN AMPHITHEATER

The base of this wall has an open slightly contoured amphitheater with a string of twelve steep crack and face routes to select from (see topo). This section is broken by a midway horizontal ledge system which is very narrow on the left but is a wider ledge system for the routes on the upper right. The routes on the upper right tier can be accessed by several gear lead starts (see topo).

42. PB Direct 5.10c

Length: 40', Pro to 2"

Start up a 2" wide jam crack (5.10c) on the lower tier to a ledge & belay. Or squeeze up behind some blocks (5.4) just to the left of the thin crack.

43. Plum Butt 5.10d
Length: 40', QD's
From the midway ledge climb the quality bolted route on a double arête.

44. Thin & Lovely 5.10b
Length: 40', Pro to 1"
A thin seam crack corner system near a large maple tree.

45. This ain't yo momma's five-nine 5.9
Length: 40', Pro to 2½"
A vertical crack corner system.

46. The Plum Arête 5.10d
Length: 40', Pro: 5 QD's & gear
A bolted arête face climb with minor gear placements at the last move near a tree belay.

47. Plumberette 5.10+
Length: 40', QD's
A nice bolted climb on a minor rounded prow.

48. _____
Length: 60', Pro ___
A steep crack corner system.

49. _____
Length: 60'
A deep corner crack system immediately above the initial rock step. Not developed.

50. EMF middle 5.9
Length: 60', Pro to 3"
This line ascends a thin 1" crack to a minor stance, and then launch into a slight bulge following a wide crack corner.

51. EMF left 5.9
Length: 60', Pro to 3"
A nice long wide jam crack on the left side of the main arena that ascends a thin 1" crack then powers into a wider crack on a vertical wall.

PETE'S PILE

Written by David Sword

History of the Area:

    It was the summer of 1984, and I was on the hunt for a job before ski season rolled around. I was sitting on the porch outside of the Mt. Hood Country Store when a baby blue '67 Nomad rolled up. A friendly faced Newfoundland stuck his head out the passenger window, and a stringy blonde haired man with Popeye sized forearms jumped out, fired me a quick handshake and said, "Pete's the name, and danger's my game." Two things I quickly learned about Pete Rue were that he was always game for climbing, and he was rarely seen without his dog, Andy.

    Pete's early explorations took him all across the Hood River valley in search of climbing possibilities. One day he asked me along to explore a crag across from Pollalie creek. The rock here was messy and frightening. Broken, fractured, and unstable basalt was the norm, but plumb sections of pure joy offered a respite from the pain. Many near misses came during these initial outings, with both emotional and physical scars to prove it. During one first ascent, Pete lead through a tough vertical hand crack. "Watch the loose flake!", he yelled. Even twenty five years later I can see that flake buzzing past my head as my girlfriend climbed ahead of me. We finished the route at sunset and rappelled to the ground without headlamps. As with many of our early ascents, the route itself still stands, but the quick sketch topo made on the inside of a matchbook on the car ride home was lost long ago. Most of the early ascents were never recorded, and many of the original lines lay in repose, awaiting new motivations and adventurers to make their mark.

Later, we continued to the south and began to explore the vertical columns of what we now know as Pete's Pile. Any vision for an accessible climbing area came from Pete, and his obsessive bond with the Pile became almost legendary. Pete single-handedly put the crag on the map while most of us were driving to Smith Rocks or doing crack laps at Beacon Rock. Establishing a climbing area can be an arduous task. For some time Pete did much of the laborious work himself, including hauling in secretly quarried rock for the stairs. Eventually he found he could motivate locals by offering up lunch and beers in return for physical labor; and sometimes even a shot at a new FA. The name Pete's Pile became the local's reference for the outcrop, but other names, such as Pollalie Crags, Sunset Dihedrals, and East Fork Columns were discussed in the early development stages.

Surely ascended before the mid 1980's, climbers from the past left only tattered slings and a handful of fixed pitons; not exactly a clearly marked road map. There were rumors that some famous names had stopped by, and we wondered if perhaps Fred Beckey or Yvon Chounaird ever graced the crag. Most likely however, the fixed remnants were left by local pioneers who used the outcrop for aid climbing and rescue practice.

We taught ourselves how to aid climb and to rope solo from a well worn copy of Robbins' Advanced Rockcraft. Where the book fell short we would fumble around with the intricate de-

David Sword leading at *Pete's Pile*

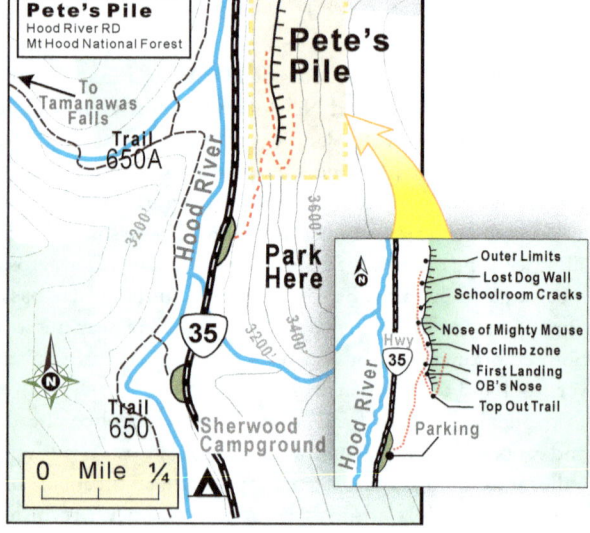

Pete's Pile
Route analysis for the upper cliff face

tails until it felt good. When a solid stance was reached, or when we ran out of rope or motivation to continue the grind, piton and stopper belay stations were built. As the sport climbing movement in America was still young and extremely controversial, most all the early ascents were accomplished from the ground up. The first permanent top anchors were placed at the top out of Pop Bottle (.10a), by Pete using a 22 ounce framing hammer and a handful of Rawl bolts poached from a construction job. Pounding anchor bolts into the hard Oregon Basalt led to severely blistered hands, but the man would not be swayed by such trivial set-backs. We taped over the wounds so Pete could top-rope the route later that same day.

As is common at climbing areas, there were controversies at the crag. When talks of further crag development evolved, area naturalists were worried about the effect it would have on a plant species known as Suksdorf Violet Rock-Brake (Suksdorfia violacea). At the time, the violet flowers were only found growing on a handful of northwest facing rock abutments. Active local climbers met face to face in an attempt to find common ground, and in conjunction with local USFS personnel, a climbers association was developed. One of the main tenants of the now defunct group, was to protect this rare flora. Even greater alarm developed when locals devised a powerful route cleaning technique for the dirt and moss choked dihedrals. By securing a fire hose to a seasonal drainage atop the crag, new routers could quickly pressure wash the rock, virtually eliminating the gargantuan efforts required previously. Clearer thinking, and more ecologically forward minds prevailed, and only a few routes sprouted from the Firehose era.

Climber's from the past and present who helped shape the crag include Pete Rue, Dr. Roger Stewart, JD Decker, Stewart Collins, Emily Kohner, Jim Thornton, Susan Nugent, Jim Opdyke, Deno Klein, David Sword, Reed Fee, Elmo Mecsko and the late Jeremy Flanigan. With the continued efforts of USFS personnel, and the continued adherence to local

MT HOOD ZONE — Pete's Pile

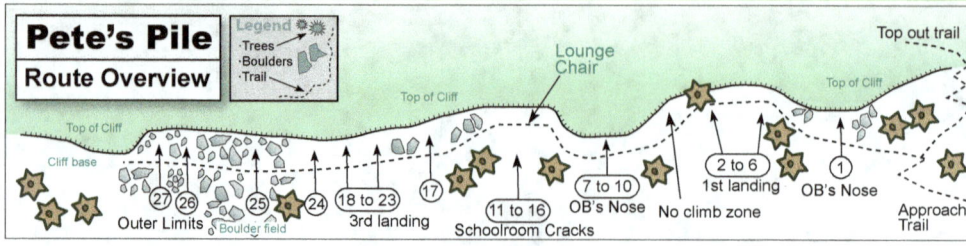

guidelines from the climbing community, the balance of recreation and preservation has been created and continues to move forward. As of today, the Suksdorf Violet Rock-Brake at Pete's Pile is growing stronger than ever, and has botanists reviewing its status as a sensitive species.

Crag Scope Info:

Pete's Pile is a hidden gem and one of only a handful of traditional climbing areas in the region. The crag is an excellent multi-season climbing area generally free of snow from April through October. Kept secret for a few decades, only recently has Pete's seen much traffic from outside the local community. Even today the crag remains a quiet place to get your crack climbing skills up to par, and the scenic beauty is well worth the price of entry. Amazing views of the eastern and north slopes of Mt. Hood await you while climbing here. As the base of the crag sits a couple of hundred feet above the East Fork of the Hood River, once you climb to tree top level, the sense of exposure is spectacular. Most of the current routes are moderate (5.10 and under), and the potential exists for dozens of more climbs of various grades.

Guidelines for climbing here are straightforward and simple; 1) If you pack it in, you pack it out. This includes cigarette butts, food wrappers, TP, and tape; 2) Do not remove dirt or vegetation from cracks unless it is necessary to provide safe hand-holds, steps, or for placement of protection. The Suksdorf Rock-brake has continued to grow for years even in some of the established climbing areas because climbers have left the soils surrounding the plant intact. Suksdorfia violacea is found throughout the climbing area, and is most easily identifiable by it's puffy, round violet flowers that are reminiscent of something from the pages of Dr. Suess; 3) Stay on the established trail system to avoid soil erosion. This includes the access trail, the base area trail beneath the climbs, and the descent trail from the top of the cliff.

Geology Of Pete's Pile:

The exposed cliff line making up Pete's Pile is basalt made up from ancient flows originating from the Cloud Cap area of Mt. Hood. Geologist refer to the columnar formations as olivine-bearing basaltic andesite, which is common on the northern flanks of Oregon's largest volcano. Although vertically sliced, the broad band of basalt has many features conducive to climbing. The steep and sustained nature of the rock is softened slightly by incut edges, ledges and pockets, and the soaring cracks accept a multitude of traditional protection. Adding to the challenge are overhanging roof sections, which become more prominent as you move northward. Sections of loose rock exist and necessary precautions should be followed. A 60-meter rope is standard here, but 70m ropes are handy. A standard free climbing rack is sufficient for most climbs. Don't forget a nut tool for the gear gobbling cracks, and long runners or cordelette, which are useful for belays and top anchors.

Some routes can be approached from the top of the crag by setting up rappels and top ropes. The top of the crag is sloped and tiered, and anchors are neither marked, nor necessarily convenient for setting up top ropes. Extreme care should be taken for your own safety and for the safety of those below you! Route numbers begin at the right most portion of the crag (OB's Nose) where the approach trail first meets the rock, and proceed northward (left).

Directions:
Drive south from Hood River on Hwy 35 for 23¼ miles toward Mt. Hood. Park at a dirt pullout on east side of the highway (the pullout is ¾ mile south of the Cooper Spur Road and ¼ mile north of the East Fork Trail #650).

From Portland follow Hwy 26 to Government Camp. Take the Hwy 35 exit towards Mt. Hood Meadows ski area and Hood River. Park at a dirt pullout on east side of the highway located 0.6 miles north of Sherwood campground.

Parking and Approach:
At a small pullout on the east side of the highway access a parking area made from an old section of roadway. An unmarked trail ascends towards the crag. As you near the cliff, sign posts directs you to the left (base of the crag) or to the right (top access). Once at the base of the crag, the trail follows the cliff band, terminating at the northern end of the established climbing area (Sandbox). The climbing routes are listed from right to left as you first encounter the cliff.

SOUTH END

The first climb you encounter on the approach trail is the Beer Garden located on a minor nose of rock at the sound end of the main bluff.

1. Beer Garden 5.8 ★★
Length: 80' (30m), Pro to 2½"
Beer Garden is a clean blocky route punctuated with plenty of steps and edges on the lower portion, and ending in a steep crack corner for the finale. It is a well traveled climb and rightly so because it protects reasonably well.
Belay from the trail or 3rd class to a higher platform. Wander around on slabby moves until it gets steep, and then stick to the right side. Anchors at top sit back from the lip so bring cordelette for a TR or be mindful for rope cuts.

THE FIRST LANDING
As you ascend the trail northward you first encounter the cliff scarp at a large dusty land-

ing spot at the base of a series of popular rock climbs.

2. **For Pete's Sake 5.8** ★★★
   Length: 92' (28m)
   Pro to 2½" including cams
   Another great moderate climb whose attention is well deserved. Although it starts up odd blocks and steps it quickly fires into a superb steep corner crack that jams well and protects very well. This route is entertaining all the way to the very end with diverse moves on steep basalt with a crux section up high on the route.

3. **Guillotine 5.10a** ★★
   Length: 92' (28m), Pro to 2"
   A brilliant climb that tackles a steep dihedral and small roof resembling a guillotine, A great rest on the left welcomes you about 35' up the route, just before you pull over the roof and climb up the smooth surfaced crux section just above. A long section of sustained climbing with great jams takes you to the top of the bluff.

4. **Temptation 5.9** ★★
   Length: 92' (28m), Pro to 2½"
   With a crux close to the ground this steep 'niner is another gear gobbler worth its weight. The

triangular roof visible from the ground is the crux. Diverse and challenging climbing all the way to the anchors.

5. **Even 5.7** ★★★
   Length: 92' (28m), Pro to 3"
   A high quality moderate and certainly a must do route for every visitor. The route offers good protection with ample rest stances between the crux sections. Belay tree marks the beginning of the right facing book. Be mindful of some minor loose rock below and left of the belay bolt anchor.

NO CLIMB ZONE

Between the route called 'Even' and the route 'Mighty Mouse' but before you reach the Schoolroom Cracks, there is a protected riparian zone that is set aside for flora preservation purposes. The Suskdorf Violet Rock-Brake grows well in this dark water stained cliff scarp. Signage placed at both ends of this section reminds climbers that this is preserved as a 'no climb zone'.

NOSE OF MIGHTY MOUSE

A prominent feature at Pete's Pile is a buttress formation that dips low along the entire stretch of the trail just before you reach the Schoolroom Cracks area. This is the Nose of Mighty Mouse which provides a haven of classic lines that will surely challenge the crack climbing aficionado.

6. **Mighty Mouse 5.10b** ★★
   Length: 165' (50m), Pro to 2"
   This is a long steep sustained crack corner climb starting at the base of a sunny buttress of rock. Start up steps and launch into a long crack system to a bolt belay at mid-height. Continue up another crack system to the top of the cliff. Rappel from anchors. Originally given a sandbag rating of 5.9.

   Mighty Mouse Rappel
   The Mighty Mouse rappel is a single 60-meter rope rappel for descending down from the top of Pete's Pile. A cliff top anchor and a mid-point anchor offer a convenient means to rappel if you have only one rope and you have topped out on a nearby route.

7. **Stinger 5.10b**
   Length: 82' (25m) TR
   A wild top-rope problem on the nose of MM buttress. Start at absolute toe of the buttress and work thin moves up to the protruding arête. Climb the arête using smears and side pulls for 70'. Access to the black painted rappel anchors by climbing nearby routes or from lowering in from top of cliff.

8. **Tribes 5.10b**
   Length: 165' (50m), Pro to 2"
   Long steep sustained climb.

9. **S.T.A.R.D. (aka Pedestal) 5.10a**
   Length: 82' (25m), Pro to 2"
   STARD is an acronym for short, thin and hard. An apt description for this seldom traveled route. Begin up the shallow left facing dihedral with the pencil thin detached flake.

10. **Bottlecap P1 5.10a, and P2 5.10c** ★★★
    Length: 165' (50m), Pro to 2½"
    You can recognize this route by the dark 'bottlecap' shaped overhanging roof 35' up the initial

part of the climb.

An old slider nut left during the FA remained fused under the crux roof for over a decade; a testament to both its difficulty and few ascents over the years. Bottlecap is the first 5.10 route established at the crag. This climb can be done in one long 165' lead to the summit anchors.

Pitch 1 (82') 5.10a: Begin by climbing up a steep crack till you are under the bottlecap shaped roof. Move right to surmount past this feature, and then continue another 20' to a stance. A belay anchor exists to the right on the next route if you choose to bail over that direction.

Pitch 2 (82') 5.10c: Continue up left to another smaller roof. Pull through this second roof and continue up very steep sustained crack with great finger and hand jams. If done in one long pitch it is a full 165' long. A great welcome-to-the-crag route with solid power packed punch to the entire climb.

11. Doctors Patient 5.10a
Length: 82' (25m), Pro to 2"
Start in mossy corner left of the Bottlecap roof. Ascend a mossy corner to the bottlecap roof,

step left and climb a dirty crack to a cluster of broken roofs. Power through this roof and continue via jug holds and crack climbing to the belay anchors.

SCHOOLROOM CRACKS

The Schoolroom Cracks is the second large flat dirt landing area, and this section provides the most popular selection of climbs at Pete's Pile. A large wooden bench is available here to sit on while you are relaxing between climbs. The belay anchors (three total) for the next six climbs are located 70' up the cliff face. You can access all three belay anchors by leading up the route of your choice and traverse left or right to access the other anchors. By far the most ascended zone at the crag, many of these cracks were climbing in the 1980's, and have been named and renamed more than once.

Pete's Schoolroom Cracks
Map 8

Pete's Schoolroom Cracks
Topo B

12. Pop Quiz 5.7
Length: 70' (21m), Pro to 2½"
Though very dirty it is a seemingly viable method to the schoolroom cracks bolt belay anchors. Follow low angle crack up and left to anchors above Smokin'.

13. Smokin' 5.8 ★★★
Length: 70' (21m), Pro to 3"
A superb moderate climb that is totally worth leading. Though most first time climbers start with Dunce, Smokin' is an optimal warm-up climb with a plethora of edges, great jams and good protection placements. A second pitch ascends the slightly overhanging left facing dihedral to top of the cliff. It's rating is unknown, but is certainly a couple of grades harder.

14. Not For Teacher 5.9R ★★
Length: 70' (21m), Pro to 2"
Though less often led this shallow open book crack climb is great even as a top-rope. The route is unusually tricky with odd smears and small featured edge holds that keep climbers challenged all the way to the anchors.

15. Times Tardy 5.10a
Length: 70' (21m) TR
An eliminate top rope effort between Smokin' and Not For Teacher. Edge, smear, pinch and layback up the arête. Using crack on either side lowers the grade to 5.8

16. Schoolroom 5.8 ★
Length: 70' (21m), Pro to 2"
Schoolroom is no less challenging than its immediate neighbor to the right (Not for Teacher). A challenging shallow open book crack climb filled with jams, smears and tiny edge features. A route that will challenge your balance.

17. Dunce 5.6 ★★★

Length: 70' (21m), Pro to 3"

The most frequently climbed route at Pete's Pile since most visiting climbers head straight to the Schoolroom Cracks area first. Wander up a crack 15' and pull past the small roof, and then zen your way through a few tenuous moves to easier terrain and a wider crack. Large edges and steps make the last few moves a cruise to the bolt anchors. Climbers often traverse from this bolt anchor over to the next bolt anchors to set up a top-rope for all the Schoolroom Cracks routes, but if you do watch out for rope drag!

18. Dirt In Your Eye 5.9+

Length: 165' (50m), Pro to 4"

Though seldom ascended this is a unique climb with great history and character. The earliest route established to the top and Pete Rue's favorite. Begin by jamming up a crack corner to the left of Dunce targeting the obvious right facing chimney capped with a chockstone. Once you near the small roofs step over to the RIGHT side of the detached pillar and continue climbing a wide crack (beware the chockstone) on the

Pete's Escalade Third landing Map 9

right side of the long column to the top of the cliff. Fun and diverse movement.

19. Eye Of The Needle 5.9+
Length: 165' (50m), Pro to 3½"
EOTN takes the same start as Dirt in your Eye up to the roofs. From there it stays on the LEFT side of the detached rock pillar using hand jams and edges to ascend a wide crack dihedral system to the top of the cliff. Use a tree for a belay anchor.

THE SECOND LANDING

A few yards further along the trail past the Schoolroom Cracks is another large flat dirt landing area. A series of fine quality routes begin here including the classic and popular Escalade. After Ramble One the trail dips down a bit past another small cluster of routes before aiming north out onto an open boulder field slope below the Sandbox Area.

20. Unknown
Length: 70' (21m), Pro to 2"
Ascending a crack between Eye Of The Needle and Escalade, a 2 bolt anchor awaits those willing to roll the dice on this mysterious climbed route.

21. Escalade 5.8 ★★
Length: 70' (21m), Pro to 3"
A fun and challenging route also known as Abandonment Issues. Start on the right side of a large tall detached block. Stem up the corner, place wide pro to protect the slight bulge, and then slide out up left onto the top of the detached block to a nice stance. Continue to cruise up steep terrain with great pro and good edges to the bolt anchor. An alternative 5.6 start is on the LEFT side of the block which protects better and with smaller pro.

22. Reckless Abandon 5.10a
Length: 70' (21m) TR
This is the direct start to Escalade (outside face of large block). The bolts were removed by angry locals shortly after the first ascent. Climb a series of thin, bouldery moves past two bolts to the stance atop the large boulder, and then continue up the route Escalade.

23. Ramble On 5.7R
Length: 70' (21m), Pro to 1¾"
Another fun route that needs more traffic. A bit runout with some dirty sections, lead climbers should take caution. Begin up a short crack corner to a small overhanging roof, step left and continue to climb up the slabby column. Amble up left from the crack to reach the rappel anchors on a flat face.

THE THIRD LANDING

A few yards further north along the trail is a third flat landing platform. Pumpin' for the Man begins here.

24. Pumpin' For The Man 5.9 ★★★

Multi-pitch 195' (59m)
Pro to 2" on P1, to 3" for P2, and to 5" for P3

Pumpin' is a quality three pitch lead with energizing technical pitches from bottom to top.

Pitch 1 (60') 5.9: Begin out of the gate with a crux move off the deck by powering over the initial bulge to a stance under the larger roof. Carefully place some pro, then balance right and up into the long steep crack corner system. The first lead takes good small cams and nut protection. Power past a second small triangular roof, and then exit up left to a bolt belay anchor at a small perch.

Pitch 2 (50') 5.8: From the anchor continue up right in a crack past a small roof and 20'+ to a large ledge and belay at a bolt anchor. You are standing next to a long detached pillar.

Pitch 3 (90') 5.9: From the belay ascend a long sustained offwidth by climbing on the left side of the huge columnar pillar of rock. This lead is very wide and requires large width protection devices. Tremendously exposed! Belay anchor at

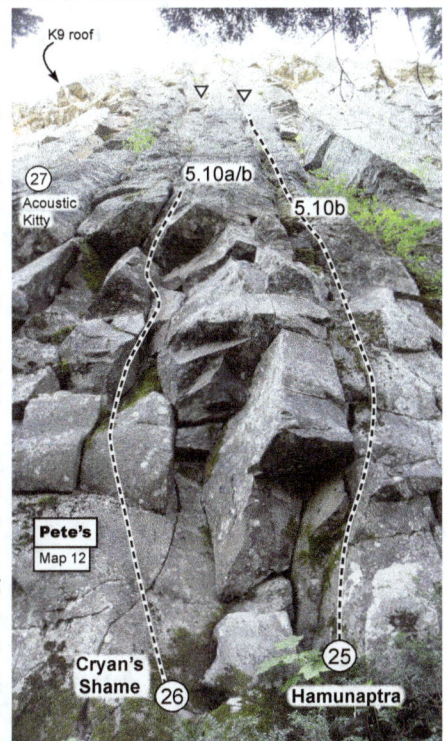

summit.
Rappel route, walk off, or descend down the Might Mouse rappel.

25. Hamunaptra 5.9 A2
Multi-pitch 200' (60m), Pro to 3"
Originally climbed by aid and top roped, this multi pitch outing awaits insitu belays. Ascend left facing corner surmounting roof on the left side. Continue up ever-steepening crack to the cliff top.

26. Cryan's Shame 5.10b (2 pitches)
Multi-pitch 200' (60m), Pro to 2½"
Pitch 1 100' (30m): Start by climbing up on edges and thin finger jams below a broken series of small roofs. Surmount the small roof and climb up to a bolt anchor on a sloping ledge.
Pitch 2 100' (30m): Follow shallow open book to top of cliff. Use tree for anchors. A great route that could use some cleaning.

27. Acoustic Kitty 5.9 A3
Multi-pitch 200' (60m), Pro to 2½"
Another steep outing that awaits permanent belays and an all free ascent. Begin in crack system to the right of the large, red roof complex which houses K-9 Shanghai. Zig zag leftwards

over a series of roofs with jams and footwork.

LOST DOG WALL (aka SANDBOX)

A large open boulder field is at the extreme north end of Pete's Pile. A vast sweep of vertical cliff scarp here provides some of the most challenging climbing at Pete's Pile, including the stellar K9 Shanghai route. Jeremy Flanigan nailed 5-6 unrecorded routes on the long crack systems, but little record remains of the original ascent.

28. K-9 Shanghai   P1 5.11a, P2 5.12a, P3 5.10a ★★★

Multi-pitch 240' (73m)
Pro to 3½" including cams, doubles small & medium cams P1
FFA: Elmo Mecsko, Reed Fee 8-2008
K9 is one of the newer challenging climbs at Pete's Pile , putting into perspective the vertical possibilities for the ultra-initiated. The route is long, sustained and technical with demanding crux sections. The classic crux second pitch punches OUT and over a massive improbable looking yet surprisingly well featured overhanging double tiered roof.
Pitch 1 (100') 5.11a: The first lead is technically thin but fun with interestingly steep crack climbing that increases in difficulty the higher you climb. Climb past a small overhanging crux near the anchor.
Pitch 2 (60') 5.12a: From the belay ascend steep thin jams and smears, then launch out the double tiered overhanging roof using a variety of face holds and a finger-hand jam crack. Strength and pure thuggery gets you through the giant roof crux. Use a 3½" cam for crux (A2).
Pitch 3 80') 5.10a: From the belay anchor above the crux pitch, move right and climb the steep arête upwards with mixed gear. Finish through a small overhang moving up left to bolted anchors on a big ledge. An outstanding climb with unmatched position!
Rappel with two ropes only…or walk south and descend via another standard rappel.

29. Dunlap 5.9
Length: 80' (25m), Pro to 1½"
Follow the shallow face between 2 steeps cracks. Left crack accepts protection more readily. Sustained climbing eases as you near the anchors. Dunlap and its neighbor Outer Limits were developed by a gregarious and prolific local outdoorsman, the late Jeremy Flanigan…Good on ya' mate.

30. Outer Limits 5.10a
Length: 80' (24m), Pro to 1½"
The left most climb at Pete's Pile located at the northernmost end of the Sandbox area.
Begin on the right side of a series of stacked blocks and ascend up easy terrain to a crack immediately above the blocks. Power up the short flat face via a nice jam crack and exit left to the belay bolt anchors. Rappel the route.

BULO POINT

The rocky crag of Bulo Point is a fascinating group of steep bluffs with quality rock climbing opportunities for leading and top-roping from mid-May to late October. Located roughly ten air miles east of Mt. Hood and a few miles south of road NF 44 this site offers enjoyable climbing from 5.6 to 5.11+. The site qualifies as one of the better backcountry climbing crags nestled in the ponderosa pine covered eastside crest of the Cascade mountains incline.

Nestled on the sunny eastern facing slopes overlooking the Fifteen Mile Creek watershed west of the small town of Dufur, Bulo Point offers visitors a quality selection of routes on a surprisingly steep 40-70' high rock bluff.

Although many of the rock climbs are sport routes, a fair selection of routes are traditional natural gear routes. Bring an adequate selection of cams and wires if you plan to lead any of the traditional climbs. Most of the climbing routes have fixed belay anchors which can be accessed from above for top-rope purposes.

Geological characteristics:

The rock at Bulo is composed of heavily-weathered course-grained rock from old lava flows originating from the vicinity of Lookout Mountain. The outcrop is revealed later when the surrounding softer earthen layers are eroded away, leaving exposed bedrock that experiences chemical and mechanical decomposition from the principal reacting agents oxygen, water, and carbon dioxide.

The rough surface texture of the rock provides positive smearing friction opportunities along with numerous hand or finger edges. Moderate routes from 5.6 to 5.10 are plentiful, but the cracks

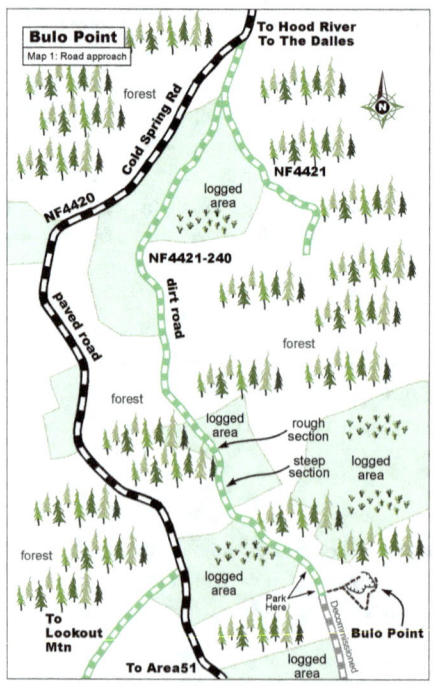

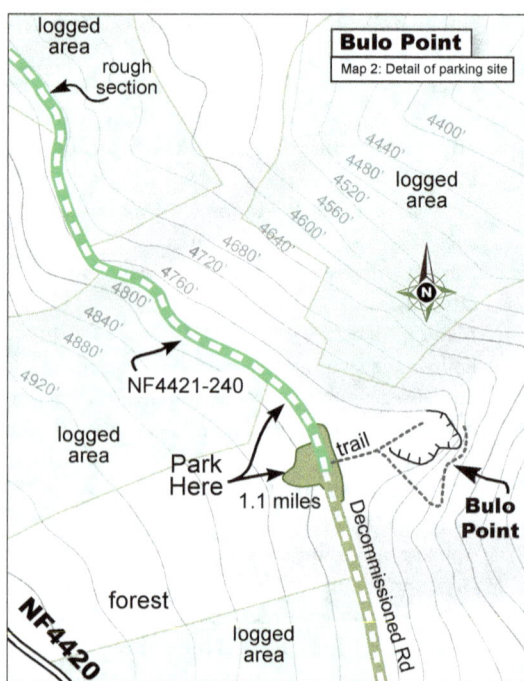

Bulo Point ✦ ROCK CLIMBING

tend to be shallow and flared, which can be challenging while placing protection on lead. The Point is a good place suitable for moderate to expert climbers.

These forested slopes provide recreational opportunities for hunters, hikers, mountain bikers, as well as rock climbers who find the Ponderosa pine covered Dufur watershed a delightful haven far from the madding crowd.

Many individuals were dynamically instrumental in developing this climbing site. Bulo Point has long been an established historical climbing site prior to the 1980s and a number of the routes were top-roped and some were lead climbs long before the era of fixed bolts. Do your part to keep this site a rare treasure for all climbers by packing out what you pack in.

Directions:

To visit Bulo Point, drive south from Hood River, Oregon on Hwy 35. Drive east on NF 44 for 8¼ miles and turn south (right) onto NF 4420. Follow the paved road initially for ¾ mile. At the Dufur Watershed sign take a gravel road left onto NF 4421-240, which is a narrow dirt road. This road splits again within a few hundred feet. Take the right fork and drive for 1 mile to Bulo

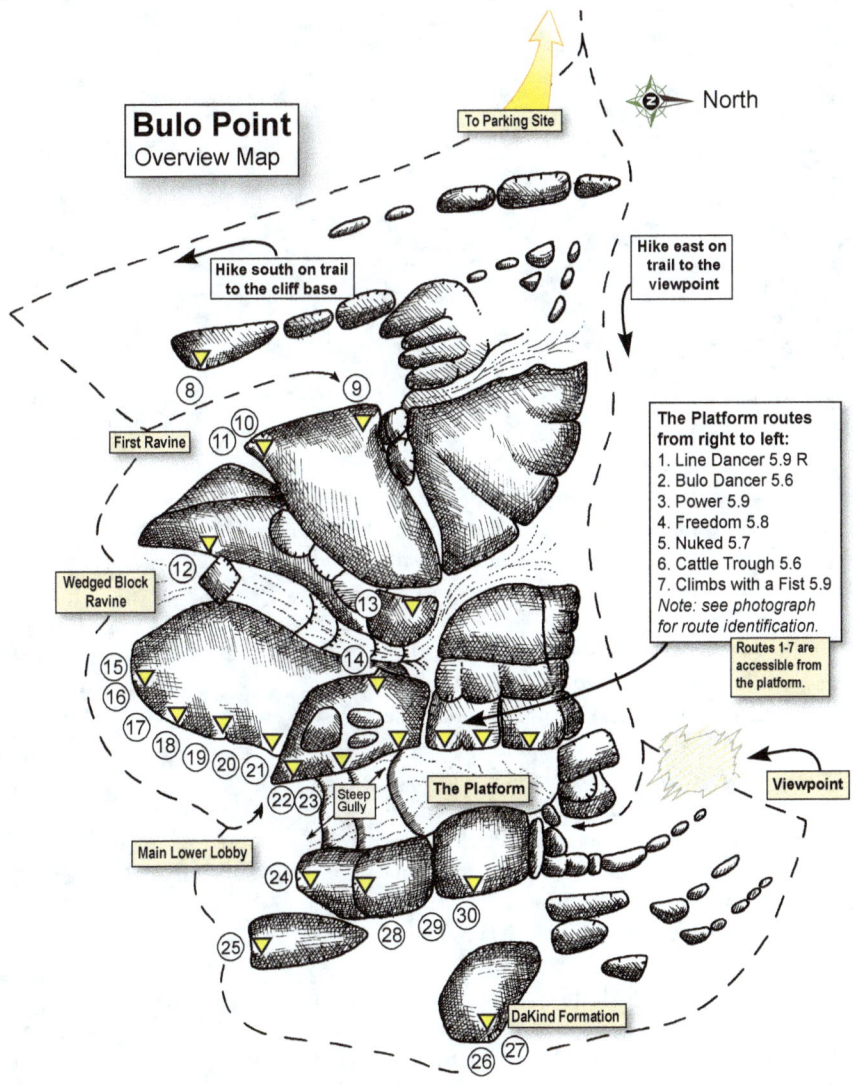

48　MT HOOD ZONE ✦　　　　　　　　　　　　　　　Bulo Point

Point. Park at the roads end (being decommissioned beyond this point), and walk east down a footpath that leads out through the forest to the top of the crag. The crag is a one minute walk from your vehicle to the bluff top viewpoint.

The Viewpoint:

The first string of routes begin at the Platform which is a common starting place where people arrive on their first visit to Bulo. Take the main trail out to the scenic viewpoint at the top of the bluff. Immediately downhill on your right side is an alcove platform with a short vertical east-facing wall. The routes at the Platform are listed from right to left. Only routes accessible from the Platform are listed here. **Jet Stream** and **Jet Wind** are listed in the Main Lower Lobby area.

To access the Platform routes scramble down exposed 4th class ramps to the alcove. Or climb up onto the top of the higher bluff, set a top-rope and rappel down to the Platform. Be cautious if scrambling down to the alcove platform as it is surprisingly steep.

1. **Line Dancer 5.9 R** ★★
   Pro: Thin gear to 2"
   A sustained tricky thin crack on the upper right end of the Platform. This is the nearest route to the scenic viewpoint at the top of the bluff.

2. **Bulo Dancer 5.6**
   Pro: Behemoth gear to 5" or 6"
   This is the fat wide crack which is easier to just TR.

3. **Power & Politics 5.9** ★★★
   Pro: Gear to 2"
   Starts the same as next, but launch up into the right thin finger crack. This line is a bit more difficult to lead. If you clip just the first bolt to protect the initial starting move off the ground the remainder of the climb can be done on natural gear.

4. **Cattle Guard. 5.8** ★★★
   Pro to 2"
   One of the best short face climbs at Bulo Point. Climb the steep edgy face past a bolt then up to the left jam crack. Only the first bolt is necessary. The remaining portion of the climb protects well using natural pro and does not need the other bolts.

5. **Nuked 5.7**
   Pro: QD's
   A minor face climb on the extreme left end and facing toward Cattle Trough.

6. **Cattle Trough 5.6**
   Pro: Behemoth gear
   A large chimney separating the outer buttress from the main flat faced wall.

7. **Climbs with a Fist 5.9** ★★
   Pro: QD's
   A face climb on the outer buttress immediately right of Jet Wind and facing Cattle Trough.

FIRST RAVINE

First Ravine offers four routes. You can access this ravine as you descend the hiking trail before you reach the Lower Lobby.

8. **Silence of the Cams 5.9** ★★
   Pro: QD's
   Located on the immediate left in the First Ravine as you descend the hiking trail. Climbs a short vertical face using small edges and finishing on jug holds.

9. **Inversion Excursion 5.10a** ★
   Pro: QD's
   Located at the upper end of the same ravine as Silence of the Cams. Begin up an initial steep off-width crack, then step up right to finish up a low angle face to the belay anchor.

10. **Awesome Possum 5.11+/.12-**
    Pro: QD's
    An improbable face climb ascending the arête and ending at the same anchor as Separated at Birth. Located on the right side of the First Ravine. A powerful climb using small sloping holds on a substantial overhang. The upper bulge has another thin crux section on small edges just before you reach the anchor.

11. **Separated at Birth 5.10b R**
    Pro: QD's
    Located in the First Ravine on the right and utilizes the same anchor as Drawin' a Blank. This route stems up the large deep chimney using positive face holds. Move up left on good face edges to a short hard steep face just before the belay anchor.

WEDGED BLOCK RAVINE

As you descend the hikers loop trail to the lower lobby you will see a narrow ravine with a massive wedged block in it. Atomic Dust Buster is next to the wedged block.

12. **Atomic Dust Buster 5.10c**
    Pro: QD's
    Starts on the left next to the huge wedged chockstone. Climb the short vertical face past a small lip to the anchor.

The next two climbs are visible uphill behind the giant wedged block. You can access both routes from several different places.

13. **Barking Spider 5.8**
    Pro: QD's
14. **Slice of Pie 5.9**
    Pro: Nuts to 2"
    This is a crack climb located up left of Nook and Cranny on the upper west side of the buttress with a belay anchor at the top.

Main Lower Lobby is the primary destination for climbers because the popular Jet Stream is a must-lead route of stellar proportion.

15. **Alice 5.9**
    Pro: Some gear and QD's
    Located on the far left side of a lower lobby. Climb a flat face broken with cracks to a boorish one-move wonder over a bulge.
16. **JRat Crack 5.8** ★
    Pro: Wires and cams to 4"
    The broad face is broken by a wide zigzagging flared crack. That's it.
17. **Raiders of the Lost Rock 5.9** ★
    Pro: Nuts to 2"
    Immediately right of JRat is a low angle bolted face. Ascend easy steps to first bolt, then smear delicately up small sloping edges till it eases.

LOWER LOBBY

18. Fat Rabbit 5.12b/c
Pro: 3 QD's
An very difficult route on a short vertical face.

19. Plumbers Crack 5.6 ★★★
Pro to 3"
An enjoyable deep corner crack system and a suitable lead for everyone.

20. Return of Yoda 5.10c ★★
A great balancy face climb with thin sloped edges that will keep you gripped. The final crux moves use some of the Nook & Cranny holds so in essence it is a bit squeezed at the end.

21. Nook and Cranny 5.8 ★★★
Pro to 2" including small cams
A popular crack climb immediately left of the long vertical arête. Rappel from belay anchor. Or if you are inclined step up around the corner to access an upper 5.8+ crack lead (Slice of Pie) that ends at the top of the bluff.

22. Jet Stream 5.9 ★★★
Pro: 10 QD's
Jet Stream is considered to be the best route at Bulo. When standing at the main Lower Lobby you can easily spot Jet Stream because it is the long bolted arête route on the tallest buttress.
Ascend the prominent arête on small but positive face edges. Power through the first over-

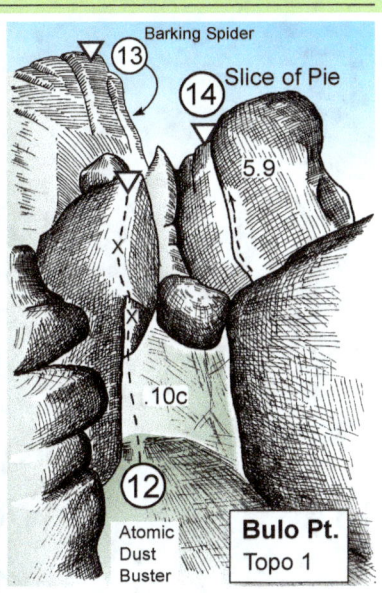

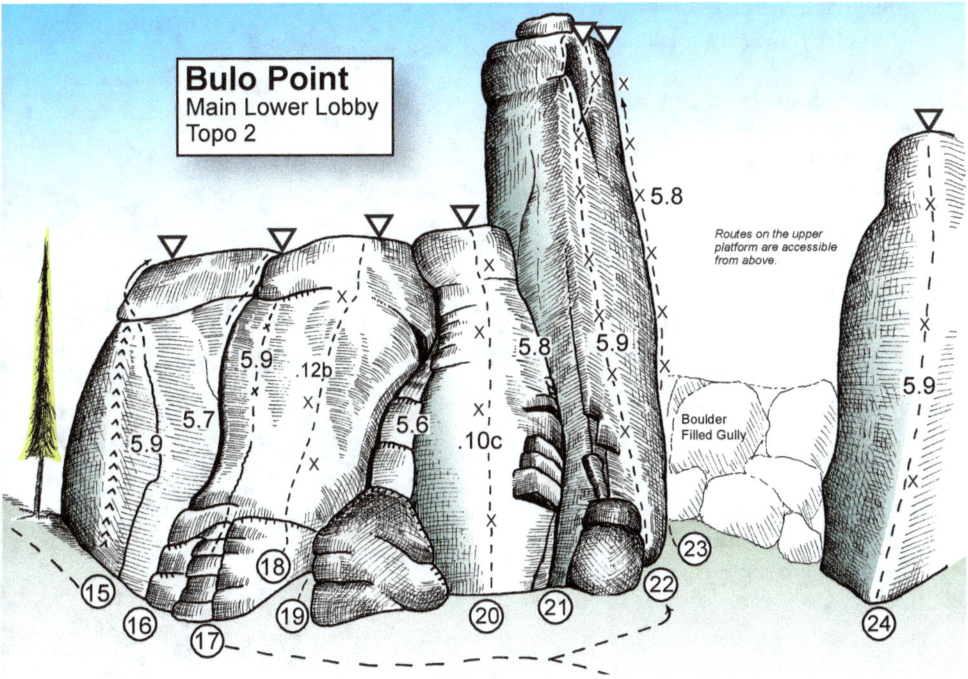

Bulo Pt. Topo 1

Bulo Point
Main Lower Lobby
Topo 2

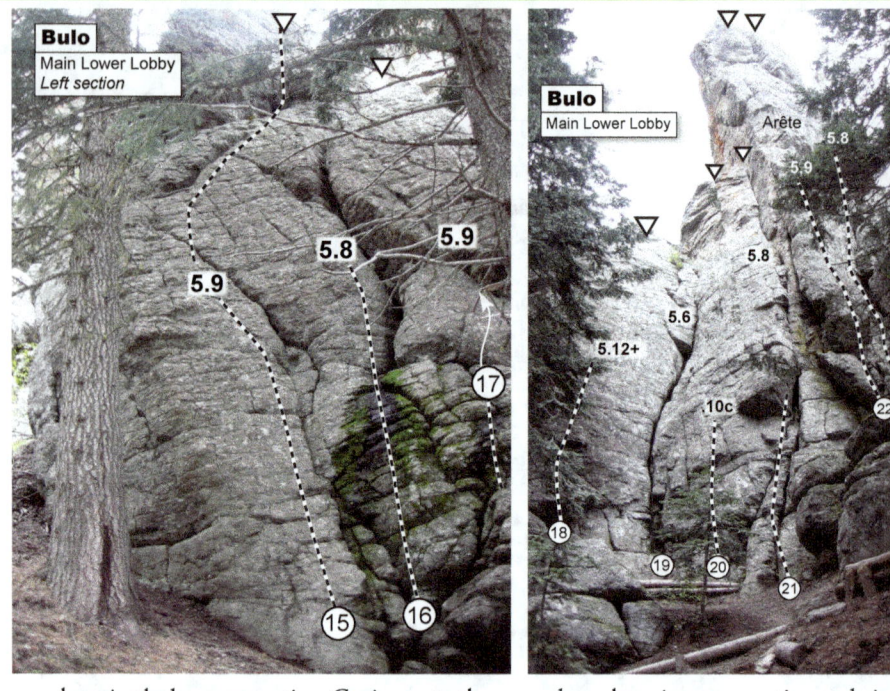

hanging bulge crux section. Cruise up to the second overhanging crux section and aim right to get through this bulge (avoid the variation exit crack on the left). Finish on easier holds to the anchor at the top of the cliff.

Alternative route ending variation: If you plan to exit up *left* using the upper left exit crack variation it is called **Jet Stream Variation** (5.10a). Bring minor gear to 2" including cams. Climb Jet Stream, but at the second overhanging crux bulge jaunt up left in a minor crack to the top.

23. Streamlined (aka Jet Wind) 5.8 ★★★

Pro: 10 QD's (minor gear to 2")

A stellar long climb immediately right of Jet Stream on the same tall buttress formation. Start up a corner to a short crack (minor gear to 2") on a face, then continue to face climb up right (bolts) around a minor bulge on positive holds to the top of the cliff formation.

24. Black Market 5.10a

Pro: QD's

A insignificant climb on a minor arête on a minor bluff. The first several moves are awkward, but the rest of the climb is basic and in some ways a bit runout.

25. Don't Call Me Ishmael 5.11b

★★

Pro: QD's
At the far lower right end of the Lower Lobby is a wildly overhanging formation leaning out over the trail. This is a short but stiff seam/face climb that often gets free climbed, but also frequently gets 'dogged' by pumped climbers. The belay anchor clip is difficult.

DAKIND BUTTRESS
26. Scene of the Crime   5.10 C
★★★

Pro: QD's
Located on the left side of the DaKind Buttress formation, which is a large rock formation separated from the main bluff. Power up into a vertical short crack using face holds, then balance up right (crux) under an overhang. Attain better hand edges past the roof and cruise on up the belay anchor. Shares the same anchor with the DaKind route.

27. DaKind 5.9 ★★★
Pro: Minor gear to 3"
Located on the right side of the DaKind Buttress formation. Step up under an overhang using a crack, then lean out the slight bulge (pro) to grasp the edges above the overhang. Power past this initial overhang to better holds, and continue up slightly right on steep terrain with good holds to an anchor.

The last three routes are located uphill behind the DaKind Buttress formation. These routes are seldom climbed.

28. Who's the Choss? 5.9
Pro to 2"
This and the next two routes are located to the right and uphill on the east side of the same bluff of rock. Scramble up a steep dirt gully around DaKind to approach these routes.

29. Big Al 5.7 TR

30. Rock Thugs 5.9
Pro to 3"

AREA 51

Beta written by Kay Kucera and Paul Cousar
   Area 51 is a great climbing crag that packs an energetic list of powerful rock climbs, all on a convenient south facing bluff. The site boasts unique advantages over other east side crags; it is great for early or late season climbing, and is conducive for rock climbers who are seeking a place to expand their skill level into the solid 5.11 range. The site tends to be dryer on overcast cold cloudy days when Bulo Point is too damp after a brief summer shower.
   Area 51 is cast in a similar light as Bulo Point (proximity and seasonal temperatures) nestled in a forest of pine trees at the 4100' (1250m) elevation. Its southern exposure is advantageous in

early Spring or late Fall. Area 51 is definitely a step beyond in terms of leading ability because the site has no easy routes under 5.9. Many of the climbs range in difficulty from 5.10c to 5.11+ and beyond, all on a very steep 80' high bluff. Many of the routes are mixed-sport routes in that you do need some specialized equipment (cams, nuts, etc.) to ascend the route without undue risk. The upper fixed belay anchors are not accessible from the top of the bluff so avoid trampling the fragile soils on the top of the bluff.

Area 51 was initially tapped as a climbing resource in the late '90s by several regional climbers. Others soon followed. Finding the site suitable for steep relentless climbing, they and friends quickly embarked onto creating a cliff where they could refine their climbing skills while enjoying the sport with friends. Paul Couser, Kay Kucera, and Jim Anglin were the primary route developers. They refined and enhanced the trail network, created stabilized platforms at the base of many routes, and placed an importance on climber awareness toward the ecological biodiversity of the Area 51 site.

Individuals who helped carry the dynamics of climbing into the 21st century were Dave Boltz, Jai Dev, Steve Mrazeck, Reed Fee, Matt Spohn, Adam McKinley, Kent Benesch, Elmo Mecsko, and other Portland area climbers.

With your dedication the following steward designed guideline yields a partnership of low impact rock climbing activity which continues to be an ecological legacy. Several Area 51 reminder points are:

1. Utilize the well-developed foot trails (no short-cutting). These user trails are well marked with stone steps and belay platforms to minimize the erosional impact.

2. The top anchors are not accessible from above so avoid walking on the fragile soils at the

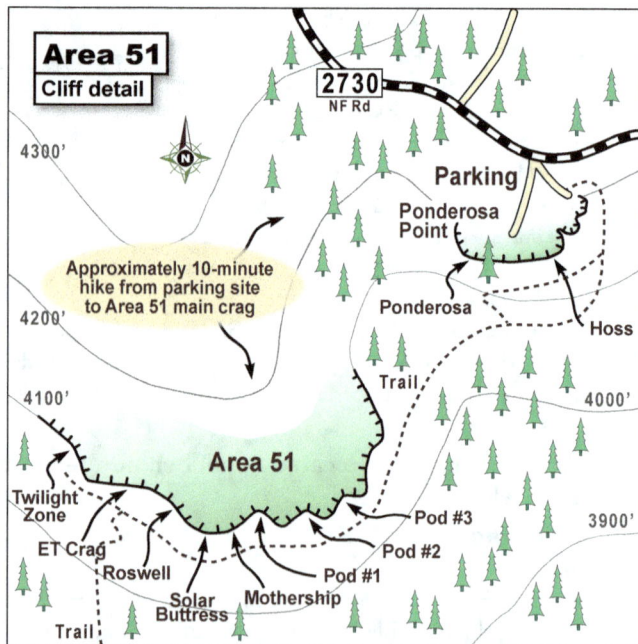

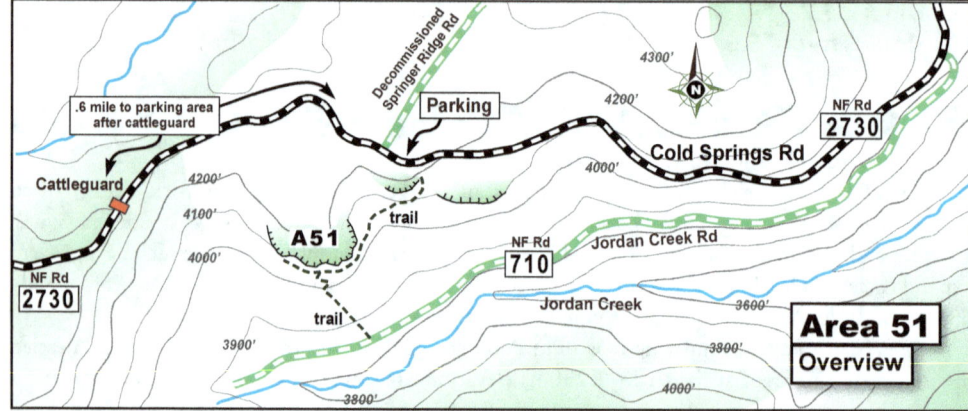

top of the bluff. Avoid unnecessary trampling of the local plant species. Do not remove indigenous flora from the cliff, from the rock climb, or along the cliff base.

3. Seriously consider leaving your pets at home. A loose, rowdy dog is not everyone's best friend. It can cause more damage in five minutes than twenty climbers in a month, thus it is best to leave the pup at home.

4. Pre-inspecting routes via rappel is normal business, so rappel bolting is the usual method (though not always) for route development here. Refrain from chopping fixed gear, chiseling or altering holds, retro-bolting existing lines without permission, placing bolts next to quality gear placements, avoid developing 'R' or 'X' rated routes.

5. It is recommended to wear climbing helmets while leading or belaying.

Directions:

Area 51 has good paved road access to the trail parking site. The site, though nestled in a pine forest at an elevation of 4,000' is often dry on cool rainy overcast days of Spring or late Fall.

Directions from Hood River: Drive south from Hood River, Oregon on Hwy 35. Drive east on NF 44 for 8¼ miles and turn south (right) onto NF 4420. Drive south on paved road NF 4420 past the Bulo Point turnoff. At a three-way junction drive south on NF 2730 past Fifteen-Mile Campground. The road descends eastward several miles and will cross a cattle guard. Continue for ½ mile and park in a large pullout on the south side of the road at Ponderosa Point. Take the descent trail as it drops downhill south below the parking site and aim west below Ponderosa Point. A ten minute walk will take you to the east end of the main A51 formation.

Directions from The Dalles: Area 51 can also be approached by driving south from The Dalles through Friend, Oregon and drive west on NF 2730 (see overview diagram).

Trail Approach: A fast ten-minute walk down below Ponderosa Point and along a path to the west will bring you to the east edge of the main A51 wall. An alternate but lesser used lower trail approach begins on NF 710 road and hikes uphill in 5-10 minutes to the base of the routes called Friend or Alien.

THE TWILIGHT ZONE

1. **Young Jedi 5.10a**
   Pro: 3 bolts and assorted gear
   Furthest west climb located 12' right of the "colonette cave". Start in crack left of Dreamland. Head right out crack through bolted bulge to common anchor.
2. **Dreamland 5.10b** ★
   Pro: 8 QD's
   Farthest left (west) bolted route on crag. Face climbing finishes out crack through bulge.
3. **War of the Worlds 5.11a** ★
   Pro: 7 QD's
   WOTW is 15' right of Dreamland. Follows right side of slab to steeper overlaps up higher.
4. **Men in Black 5.10b**
   Pro: 6 QD's
   MIB is 25' right of Dreamland. Funky face climbing with a slab finish.
5. **Crash Landing 5.12c** ★
   Pro: 8 bolts, and gear to 1.5"
   CL is 15' right of MIB. Start left of wide crack. Increasingly difficult face climbing with overlaps that leads up to a 'crash landing' finish (.11d AO).

Mackenzie Jones leading at A51

56 MT HOOD ZONE + Area 51

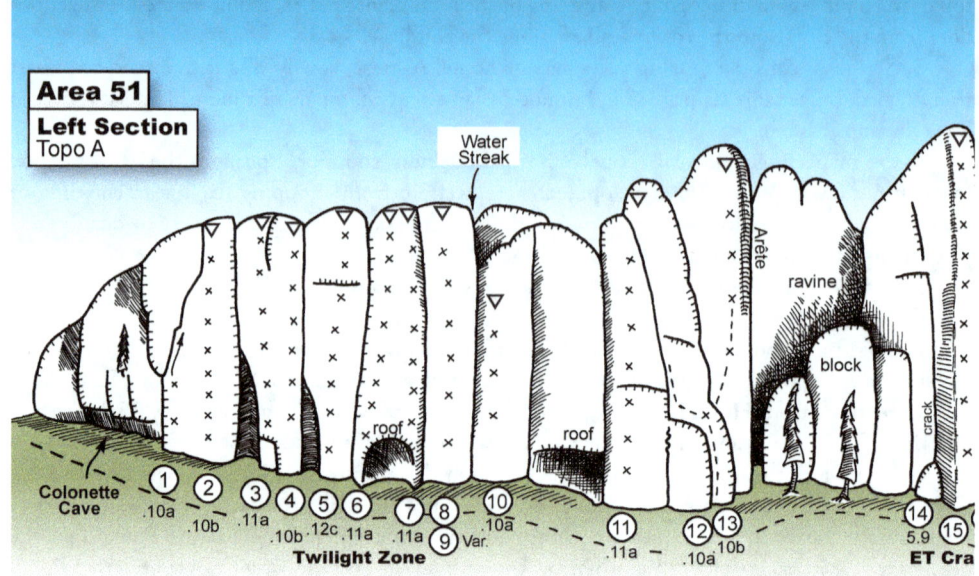

6. **Earth First (we'll log the other planets later) 5.11a** ★
   Pro: 8 QD's
   Pocketed face right of crack. Begin in overhanging corner, and move right to face. Finish up steeper bulge.

7. **Shape Shifter 5.11a** ★
   Pro: 6 QD's
   Obvious right facing dihedral with steep start and involves technical stemming.

8. **Alien Lunacy 5.11b**
   Pro: 6 QD's
   Contrived variation of Luna. Stay left of bolts, and the crack is out of bounds. Crosses to right on upper face.

9. **Luna 5.10c** ★★
   Pro: 6 QD's
   Face climb 10' right of Shapeshifter. Balancy crux at bolts #3-#4.

10. **Take Me To Your Leader 5.10a**
    Pro: 3 bolts, and gear to 2"
    Description: Broken arête and crack system right of wet streak. Mixed ice in winter.

11. **Cattle Mutilation 5.11a** ★★
    Pro: 7 QD's
    About 60' east of TMOYL. Crimp up sunny face with ledge midway.

12. **The Eagle Has Landed 5.10a**
    Pro to 3" [?]
    About 10' right of CM is a sharp edged left leaning crack. Ends at CM anchor.

13. **Erased Memory 5.10b**
    Pro: 5 bolts, and gear to 1.5"
    About 12' right of CM. Start on 'eagle' crack, move up and right to finish on a narrow pinnacle.

ET CRAG

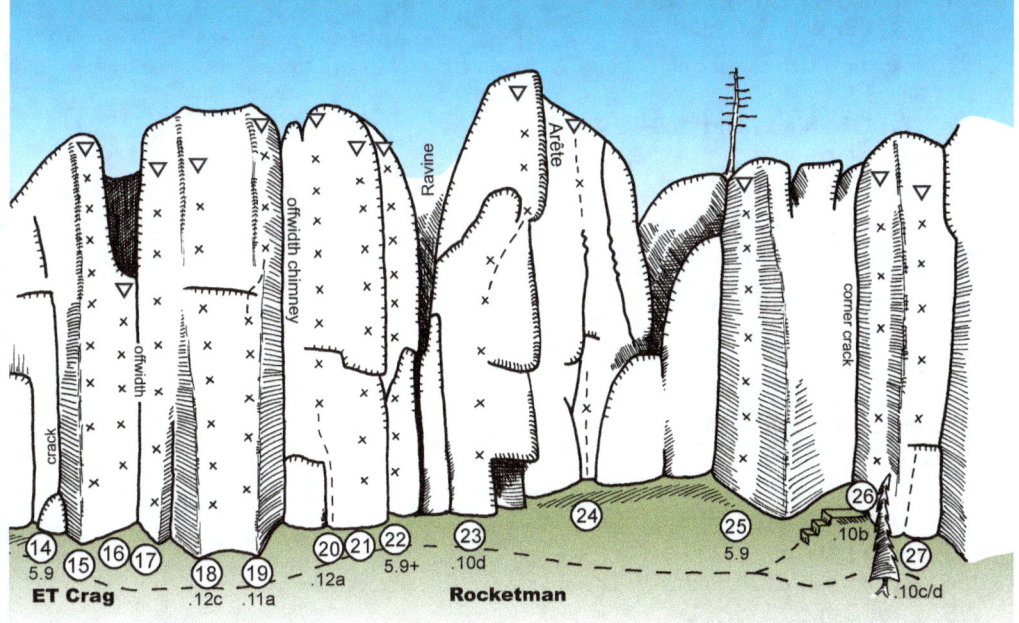

Photo courtesy of Paul Couser

14. ET (Extra Trad) 5.9
Pro to [?]
Start from top of boulder 5' left of Phone Home. Follow the crack system.

15. Phone Home 5.12b ★★
Pro: 9 QD's
Striking red arête. Steepening crimps to obscure finish.

16. Little Gray Men 5.11b ★
Pro: 5 QD's
Short face between Phone Home and Mars.

17. Mars 5.10d ★★★
Pro: 7 QD's
Beautiful red face on the right wall of open book that is broken by large horizontals. This route is west facing and involves 5.10d stemming, and offers a 5.11b direct finish.

18. Crop Circles 5.12c
Pro: 8 QD's
Located 6' right of Mars above lower approach trail. Start on left arête with smooth blank band. Stick clip past missing first bolt.

19. Friend or Alien 5.11a ★★
Pro: 8 bolts and gear to 2"
At the top of lower approach trail and 12' right of CC. Has some height dependent reachy moves.

20. Trouble With Tribbles 5.12a ★
Pro: 8 bolts and gear to 2"
Easy crack to bolted face with small overlaps.

Jim Anglin leading at Area 51

Tomma on *Alien Observer*

58 MT HOOD ZONE ✦   Area 51

21. The Cover Up 5.12a/b
Pro: 8 QD's
Start up a slab 5' right of Tribbles. Move up right and work through bulge to featured face above.

22. Out Of This World 5.9+ ★★
Pro: 9 QD's
Located 7' right of 'Cover Up'. Climb 20' of wide fist crack to heavily featured slab above. Route is best accessed from off of the Rocketman platform.

ROCKETMAN FORMATION

23. Rocketman 5.10d
Pro: 8 QD's
Located 45' left of First Contact above and right of the 'Cover Up'. Climbs slabby face, then moves right to a wide crack up to a pedestal. Step right and finish on fun arête.

24. Major Tom 5._ [?]
Pro: [?] bolts [?]
Discontinuous cracks to the right of a steep arête to a thin face.

25. Cosmic Debris 5.9
Pro: 6 QD's
A minor face climb on the left side of a steep rounded rock slab.

26. First Contact 5.10b ★★★
Pro: 6 QD's
Short stairs just behind a huge stump takes you up to a platform at the base of this route.

27. UFO 5.10c/d ★
Pro: 5 QD's
Located 10' right of First Contact. Climb up a hand crack left of some ledges and up to balancy

moves on a bolted face above.

28. Roswell 5.9+ ★★
Pro: 5 bolts and gear to 2"
Located 20' right of UFO. Start up a 25' tall finger crack. Move left, and face climb to a bivy ledge, and then continue up the small pedestal to a chain anchor.

29. Uranus Has Rings 5.10c ★
Pro: 4 bolts and gear to 2"
Located 8' right of Roswell. Balancy moves down low on the lead, but casual climbing up top.

30. It Taint Human 5.8
Pro: 5 QD's
Located 8' right of UHR. Climb a slabby face on the right up to a dihedral using juggy crack holds. A bit dirty but will improve with use.

SOLAR BUTTRESS FORMATION

31. Journey To The Sun 5.13a
Pro: 6 QD's
Steep route in a short cave follows a bolt line to pull the lip and onward to a slabby face finish. There is an easier variation right of the bolt line.

32. Solar Flair 5.10b ★
Pro: 6 bolts and gear to 3"
Climb arête 15' right of JTTS. Finish on a steep face which quickly ends at the Sunspot belay anchor.

33. Sunspot 5.10d ★
Pro: 5 bolts and gear to 2"
Located on a sunny face 10' right of Solar Flair. Follow up some discontinuous cracks to cruxy face climbing above a ledge. The climb is a bit easier if you are tall.

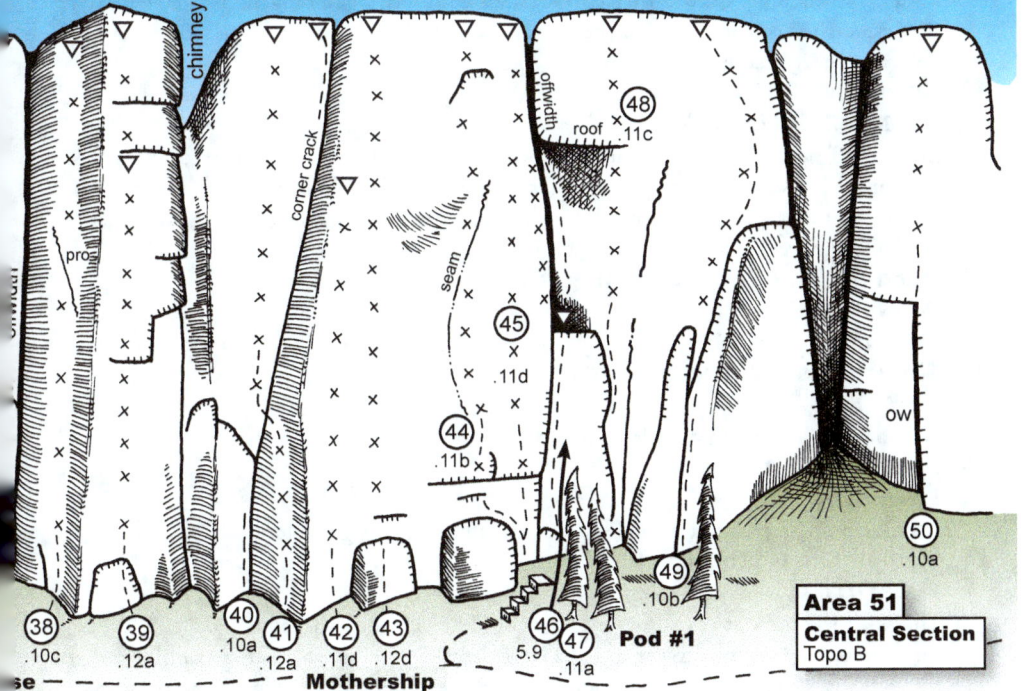

Area 51
Central Section
Topo B

THE ENTERPRISE

34. Vulcan Mind Meld 5.10b

Pro: 9 QD's

Located to the right of a drainage gully. Climb up large blocks to a roof. A vulcan mind meld might help with the perplexing moves above the roof. Finishes with adventurous climbing through questionable rock on blunt arête. Belayer should stay alert for flying objects.

35. To Boldly Bolt Where No Man Has Bolted Before 5.10c ★

Pro: 8 QD's

Located 5' right of VMM. Follow discontinuous cracks to finish on a blunt buttress. Route may be more difficult if you are short.

36. Live Long and Prosper 5.11b ★

Pro: 7 bolts and gear to 3"

Located uphill about 6' left of AA. Climb to the right of a vegetated crack up to another hand crack. At the 'Y' continue straight up on crimpy orange face holds to end at the belay anchor for TBBWNMHBB.

37. Captain Jim 5.10+

Pro to 3"

Start as for LLP but follow up a right trending crack to the anchors.

MOTHERSHIP ZONE

38. Alien Autopsy 5.10c ★★★

Pro: 7 bolts and gear to 2.5"

Located on an obvious west facing wall. Bolts and gear will protect a delicate series of face moves between discontinuous cracks.

39. Close Encounters 5.12a ★★★

Pro: 12 QD's

Located 10' right of AA. Multiple crux sections with varied climbing. It takes 10 clips to reach the first anchor, or continue past the first anchor by climbing through the roof past two more bolts to a short headwall to the upper anchor.

40. Black Ops 5.12a ★★★

Pro: 11 bolts and gear to 2"

Located 20' right of Close Encounters. Locate HAL which is the long right leaning crack corner. Black Ops start on a steep technical slab immediately right of HAL, and then cross over the crack onto the left where Black Ops powers up a vertical slightly hung bolted face with reachy, fun moves.

41. Open the Pod Bay Door HAL 5.10a ★★

Pro to 3"

This is the obvious long right leaning crack corner system starting next to the trail.

42. The Truth Is Out There 5.11d ★★

Pro: 7 QD's

Fun shallow dihedral that leads up to technical moves above a good rest.

43. Death Star 5.12d ★★

Pro: 11 QD's

Attacks multiple crux bulges on left side of a tall face with light colored rock.

44. Mothership 5.11b ★★★

Pro: 9 QD's

This is THE classic at A51. Located 18' right of HAL and to the left of Pod #1 at the base of the stairs. Clamber up onto the top of a large detached boulder. Step up to a bulge and power through an awkward crux mantle move. Delicate face climbing leads up left to a thin seam. Follow the vertical seam (crux) past a slight bulge to juggy holds. A few final face moves lands at an anchor.

45. Even Horizon   5.11d ★★★

Pro: 9 QD's

Start at the top of the stairs which leads to Pod #1. Climb far right side of light colored face just left of the blunt arête. Stay left at the 7th bolt for the full tick. Short aliens might not achieve liftoff.

POD #1

46. The Wormhole 5.9 ★

Pro to 3" (possible gear to 4" on upper part)

Climb a wide crack immediately right of EH to a large ledge called Denial Pedestal. Continue up the deep overhanging offwidth corner system up out left to an anchor at top of Stargate.

47. Stargate 5.11a ★

Pro: 7 bolts and gear to 2"

Walk up the stairs to Pod #1. Climb the first part of Wormhole to the large ledge. Stargate powers up a deceptively pumpy thin face off the ledge side of the ledge and merges in with the upper part of the wide Wormhole near the anchor.

48. Lies and Deception 5.11c ★★★

Pro: 7 bolts and gear to 3"

Walk up the stairs to Pod #1. A bolt protects the opening moves to an easy crack on the right side of Full Denial flake. Avoid Denial Pedestal, and climb a vertical reddish face to pass a roof on the right. Finish on technical crimps to an anchor.

49. Alien Observer 5.10b ★★★

Pro: 6 bolts and gear to 2"

Locate the Pod #1 area by walking up the stairs to the right to the landing. Start up a 30' hand jam crack that quickly widens as you near the flat top of a minor pedestal. Power off from the top of the pedestal up overhanging jug holds up right, and then up left to the anchor.

50. Probe 5.10a

Pro: 4 bolts and gear to 4"

Located on the right side of Pod #1 via the upper belay platform.

51. Dilithium Crystals 5.11b ★

Pro: 8 QD's

Crystal crimping up an obvious blunt face/arête. Start on main trail.

POD #2

52. Alien Invasion 5.10b/c
Pro: 5 bolts and gear to 2"
Located 9' right of DC in a right facing dihedral. Initial awkward moves lead to a finger crack passing a small roof on the left and ends on a fun slab above.

53. Abducted 5.10c ★
Pro: 6 bolts and gear to 1.5"
Begin on the highest platform between two wide cracks. Climb face and chimney (runout).

54. Taken 5.11d
Pro: 6 QD's
This is the direct no-stemming variation of Abducted. More difficult if you are short.

55. Glue Me Up Scotty 5.11b ★★
Pro: 8 bolts and gear to 2"
Located 30' right of AI. Usually starts from the low belay platform on the main trail. Climb a hand crack to the 'transporter' hold. Will Scotty beam you to the anchors? Stay tuned...

POD #3

56. We Are Not Alone 5.10d / .11a ★
Pro: 7 QD's
Located 5' right of 'Glue Me Up'. This route is the other side of the arête. Stay right of the bolts by using the pockets at start for the full value 5.11a stylin'.

57. The Borg 5.11a PG
Pro: 3 bolts and gear to 2"
Start on lower belay platform about 7' right of WENA. Belay on the trail. Starts in the crack/flake and ascends the bolted face above.

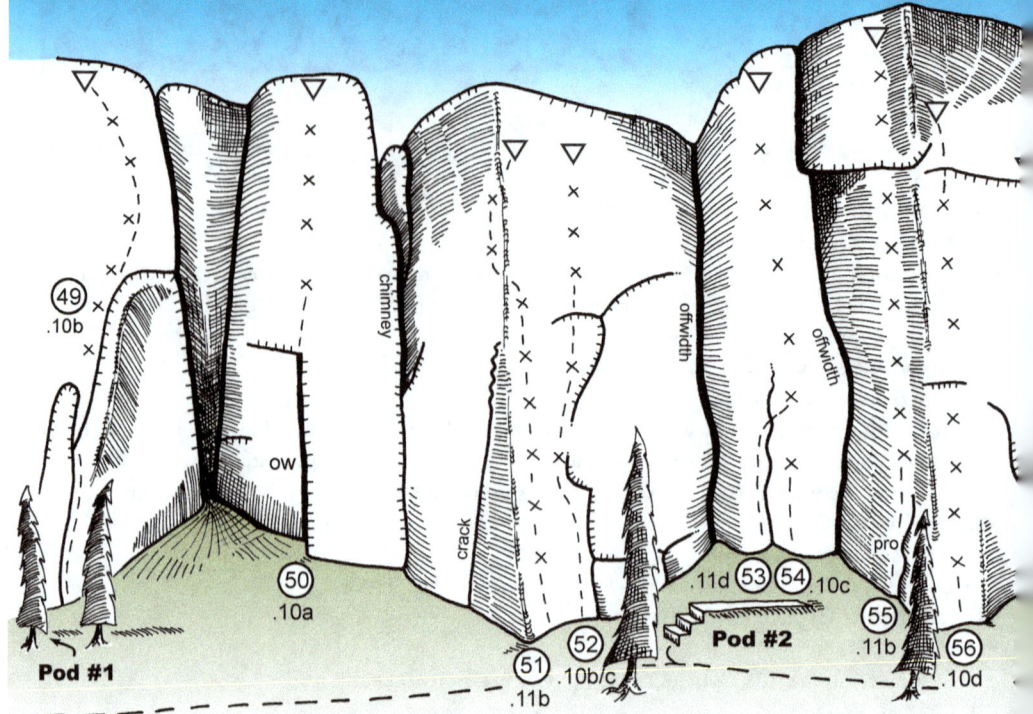

58. Lights Over Phoenix 5.12b ★
Pro: 7 QD's
Start on the upper belay platform 10' right of The Borg and left of the chimney. Technical climbing up a blunt arête.

59. Resistance Is Futile 5.11c ★★
Pro: 7 QD's
Located 8' right of LOP, but right of a mossy chimney on the upper platform. Mantle onto ledges leading up to a discontinuous crack system on a slightly overhanging face.

60. Covert Research 5.12b ★
Pro: 7 QD's
Located 14' left of Conspiracy Theory between two wide cracks. Surmount sloping ledge to a blank face above. Dude, if yo 6' or taller take off a letter grade!

61. Groom Lake (top-rope)
Pro: Top-rope
Located 5' right of Covert Research, and 5' left of Conspiracy. Power up a crack at the start which quickly leads to a hard boulder problem and micro flakes to an anchor.

62. Conspiracy Theory 5.12a ★★
Pro: 9 QD's
Begins on the far right wall in a steep, yellow dihedral. Climb up left past a small blocky roof to balancy moves on a blunt arête.

63. Conspiracy Lake 5.12c ★★
Pro: 7 QD's
Follows the initial part of Conspiracy Theory to the 5th bolt. Then it crimps out left and up a blank face past 3 more bolts to finish on the Groom Lake anchor.

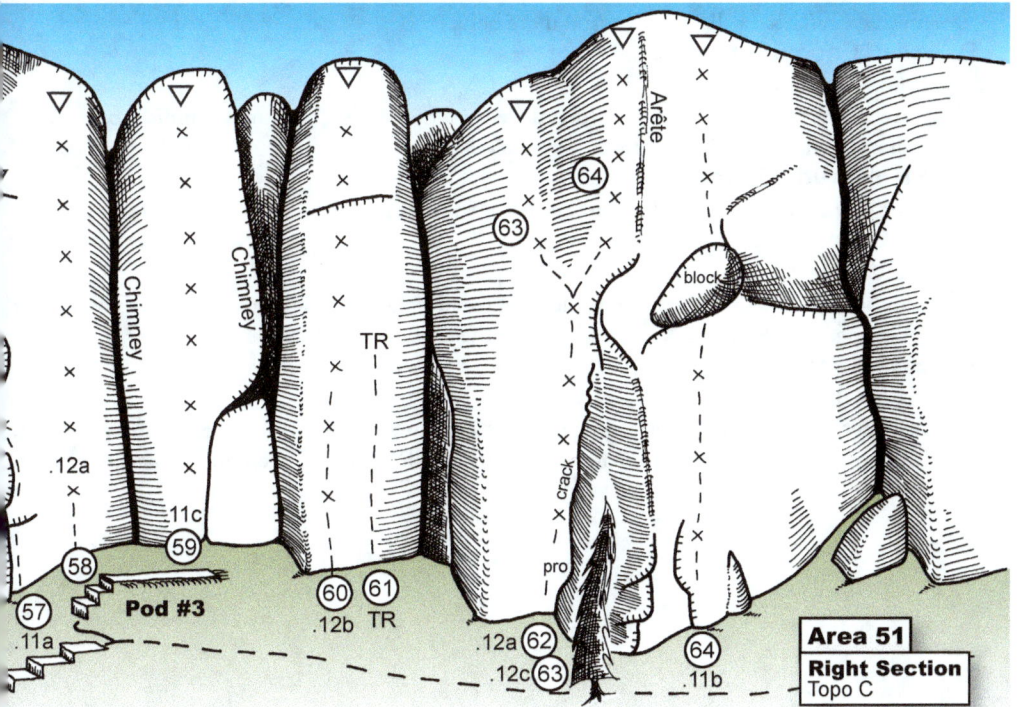

Area 51 Right Section Topo C

OUTER LIMITS
Only one route, but with cleaning there could be more.

64. Dark Side of the Moon 5.11b
Pro: 6 QD's and pro
Furthest climb at the east end of the main crag.

PONDEROSA POINT
Four known climbs, but the wall is extensive enough to see a few more.

65. Ponderosa 5.10b ★
Pro: 6 QD's
This is the right route on the buttress behind the BIG ponderosa pine. Climb up a shallow, featured dihedral and move up right around the flake.

66. Adam 5.10b
Pro: 6 QD's
Adam is the left climb on the right end of the formation. Shares the belay anchor with Hoss.

67. Hoss 5.10b ★
Pro: 6 QD's
The first climb encountered on Ponderosa Point approach trail (the right-most of these two). Pull through a fun bulge at the start. Follow discontinuous cracks and finish with exciting moves on slightly overhanging face moves near the top.

THE LINK-UPS
Here are some wild link-ups to mix some flavor into your venue on your next visit to A51.

A. Men Are From Mars 5.11b ★
Pro: 7 QD's
Climb up 5 bolts on Little Gray Men, clip the anchor with a long QD, and then step right to finish on fun headwall of mars past 2 more bolts.

B. Alien Encounter 5.11b ★★
Pro: 8 bolts and gear to 2"
Climb to 5th bolt on the Autopsy, then traverse right to Close Encounters. Finish through the roof to the headwall clipping three more bolts.

C. Black Truth 5.11c ★
Start on Black Ops slab (.11c), and finish on 'The Truth' as belay anchors.

D. Starship 5.11b ★★★
Pro: 11 QD's
Climb past 4 bolts on Death Star, and then trend right onto Mothership. Long slings reduce rope drag. Clip 7 more bolts on your way to the anchor on Mothership.

E. Event Gate 5.11c ★★
Pro: 9 QD's
Start at the top of the stairs leading to Pod #1. Follow 'Event Horizons' route to the 7th bolt. Move right onto easier terrain to finish on Stargate. Short stature aliens may not achieve liftoff.

Columbia Gorge climbing sites

RAT CAVE

The Rat Cave is one of Northwest Oregon's rare little gems in that it sports some of the highest concentration of difficult rock climbs within a reasonable proximity to Portland metro area.

The Cave is an unusual basalt rock feature with a wildly overhung 30' horizontal cave roof surrounded with a 50' steep overhanging outer face. The routes provide an intense opportunity to experience beta-intensive rock climbing requiring endurance, power and movement. The routes are beta intensive, because every single knob looks like a hold. An initial foray might leave you with a sense of being sandbagged but local climbers who know the routes very well can provide great guidance to each climb. The grades are based on a red-point lead, not an on-sight lead, because of the difficulty to identify which is a real hold and which is not. The listed ratings are 2-3 letter grades harder based on this red-point method.

Seasonal variables:

Climbing at the Cave is feasible for 12-months of the year, but the best time to climb here is generally from September till February. March and April bring considerable rain showers and warmer temperatures that allow steady seeps to occur along portions of the walls of the Cave, hindering access to certain climbs. June through August is typically humid (not like the east coast) and can lower your ability to effectively cling to pinches and tiny grips. Yet even during the long sultry days of summer you can find many days where climbing at the Cave is great and summer lighting colorfully photogenic. *Directions:* Drive east on I-84 exiting onto the old scenic U.S. Hwy 30 at Bridal Veil. The Rat Cave is located about ¼ mile west of the Wahkeena Falls parking lot directly across from Benson Lake at a small gravel pullout.

1. **Project**
   Starts on the outside wall of minor buttress and merges with the next route at anchor.

2. **Pissfire (aka Warm Up) 5.11d** ★
   Length: 70', Pro: 8 QD's
   This route has been cleaned up considerably and is a viable initial route to warm-up lead. Start on the far right side of the cave. Climb through a hard move to start then continue on big holds to a rest. Climb past a second hard section to reach the anchor.

3. **Sombrero 5.12a**
   Length: 60', Pro: 7 QD's
   Clip first 3 bolts of warm-up route, then aim up left (4 more bolts) in a groove to the anchor.

4. **Burrito (aka Warm Up) 5.12b** ★★
   Pro: 7 QD's, Usually fixed draws on the second half
   This route is still considered to be the original 'Warm Up' route at the Rat Cave. The crux comes at the beginning which is a long lock-off utilizing an under cling pinch to another pinch which continues up left through more pumpy climbing. The route follows a small left leaning channel to the first set of anchors in the middle of the face.

5. **Chicken Burrito 5.12d** ★★
   Start on Burrito and end at the top of the wall on Super Burrito.

6. **Dorkboat 5.13a** ★★
   Length: 70', Pro: 9 QD's
   This route starts just left of Burrito on the same start as Held Down, and climbs straight to the top of the wall. Punch through an early crux move after

Dave leading *Dork Boat*, Rat Cave

The Rat Cave

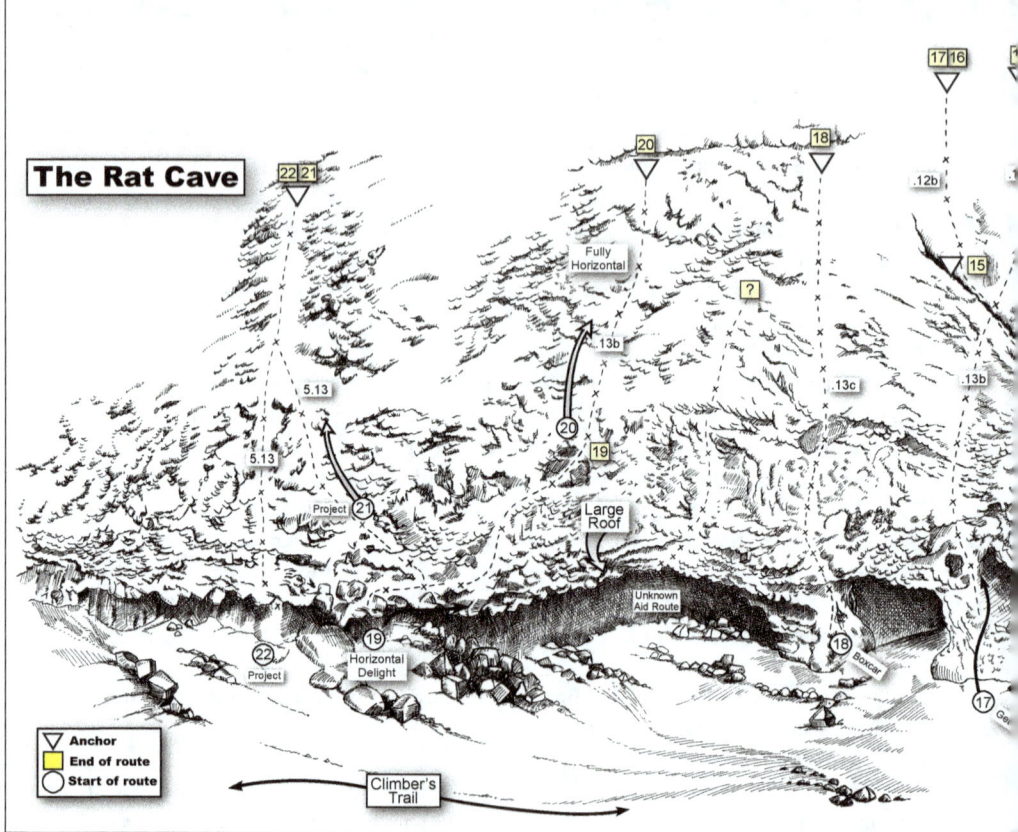

the first bolt, which involves a tricky sequence of pinches utilizing a well placed drop knee. Hard moves continue until the 4th bolt where the Warm Up route crosses at the good pinch jug rest. Continue straight up using decent pinches and under clings passing through a crux at mid-height. A small Gaston at the 7th bolt lets you get just enough strength back to push through the next two clips. Endurance is the key to sending this line.

7. **Held Down 5.12c ★★★**
Length: 70', Pro: __ QD's
Held Down is the next logical route to climb after the Warm Up route. It starts the same as Dorkboat moving left at the first bolt to finish at the anchor in the middle of the wall. Begin up a small pillar to the face. Punch through a couple of long moves to set up the crux, which is a long lock-off to the second bolt followed by a reach to a small triangle and undercling requiring a back-step and lock-off. Expect another under-cling lock-off before you reach the anchor.

8. **Conquistador 5.12c ★**
Start on Dorkboat and end on Held Down.

9. **Super Burrito 5.12d ★★★**
Start on Held Down. After clipping the anchor for Held Down continue on up the top of the wall with a surprise waiting at the end.

10. **The Stiffler 5.13b ★**
Length: 65', Pro: __ QD's
The business begins early on this route. Start just left of Held Down. Climb through a small roof past a horn which entails a knee-bar followed by tenuous lockoffs. Continue through a

Rat Cave ✦ ROCK CLIMBING 67

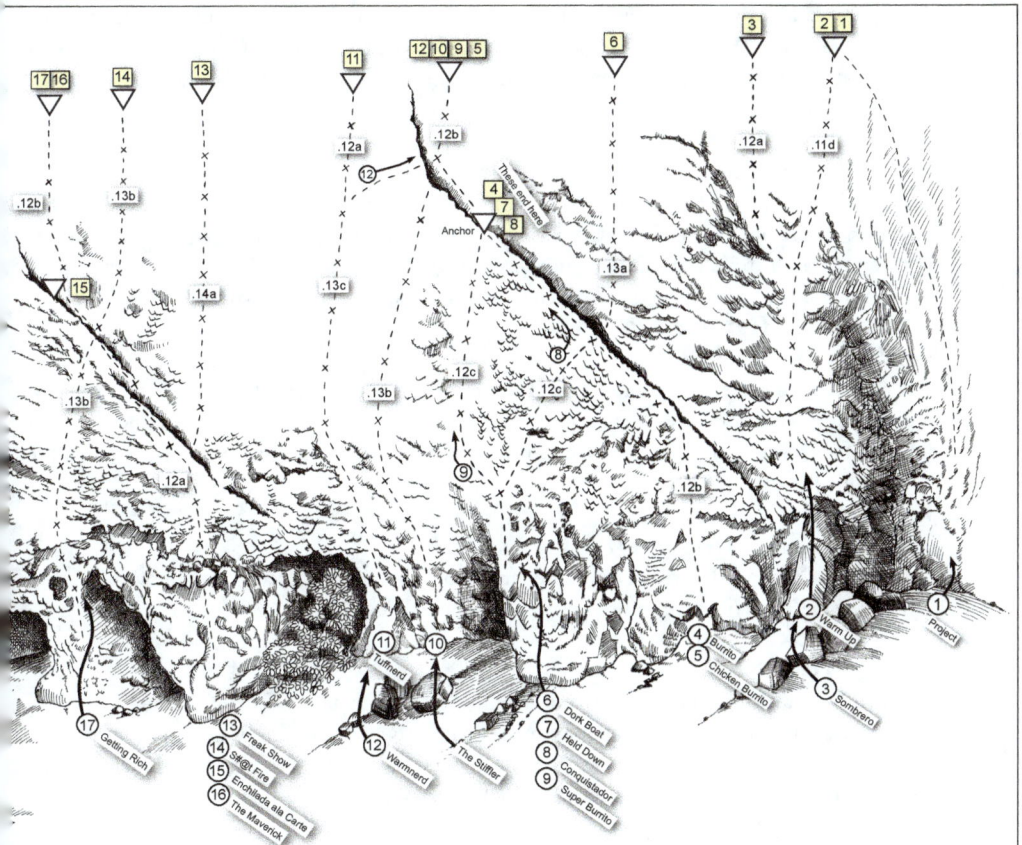

series of sloped holds, lockoffs and pinches to the anchor.

11. Tuffnerd 5.13c ★★★
Length: 70', Pro: __ QD's
Start just left of The Stiffler under a small roof. Begin with double hands and double heels on a hanging block-shaped rock feature followed by a series of side pulls using reasonable edges. The crux is moving off of two sloped holds at midway to a reasonable under-cling, followed by a series of lockoff Gaston moves. The climbing remains very sustained all the way to the anchor. You can find several useful knee-bar placements on this route. Some have the guns to make it to the end…some don't.

10. Warmnerd 5.13d ★★★
Length: 70', Pro: 8 QD's, mostly fixed Quick-Draws
This route starts on Tuffnerd and finishes on the Chicken / Super Burrito anchor. Pull the first three cruxes of Tuffnerd which take you to the 7th bolt. At the 7th bolt bust hard right by traversing through a series of sloped holds till you reach the last few bolts on the next route to the right. Make a powerful transition onto the under-cling to clip, then fire through a powerful pinch to sloped side pull crux and finish to the anchor.

13. Freak Show 5.14a
Length: 65', Pro: __ QD's. There is a midway anchor at the 5th
Start up Enchilada ala Carte for the first three bolts (.12-), the head straight up instead of following the left leaning weakness. The first few moves off the seam involve a tough sequence of powerful crimper lockoffs to a desperate toss to a marginal sloped hold (V7ish). Make a clip

off an OK under cling, and then enter the crux. A series of desperate pulls off sloped holds on a 30° overhang. This follows for two bolts (roughly V8). Unlike Tuffnerd this route lacks a decent rest before its pumpy headwall. Finish on sustained 5.12 for the last 5 bolts. This follows the second left leaning weakness from the right.

14. S#@t Fire 5.13c ★★
Length: 70', Pro: Some QD's. The second half has fixed quick-draws on it

Begin up Enchilada ala Carte and climb along the left leaning ramp/channel. At the 5th bolt transition to the upper wall. The climb kicks back dramatically here involving intense power climbing through three consecutive bulge sections. Expect long reaches in spots to marginal holds; however the occasional good pinch or crimp appears just when you need them most.

15. Enchilada ala Carte 5.12a ★
Length: 50', Pro: ___ QD's

This route provides access to one of the rat caves finest routes (S#@t Fire). Start just left of Tuffnerd and climb out a short but powerful overhang crux section, and then angle up left along a left-leaning ramp/channel. The climb is roughly 5.11- climbing for the last part to the RC mid-height anchor.

15b. Kings of Rat 5.13b
Length: ___', Pro: ___ QD's (fixed)

From the Enchilada belay, reach right and clip a bolt, then climb directly up a series of underclings and steep dynamic climbing till you reach a belay jug.

16. The Maverick 5.12b ★★
Pro: 10 QD's

Start just left of Tuffnerd using the same start as for Enchilada ala Carte. Climb out the roof and follow a left-leaning ramp/channel to the 6th bolt where the climbing eases near the anchor at mid-height. Continue past this anchor by making a long high clip, and then engage in a series of powerful pinches (2 bolts total) to the upper anchor.

17. Getting Rich Watching Porn 5.13c
This line punches out of the right edge of the main overhanging roof of the cave.

18. Boxcar 5.13c ★★★
Length: 45', Pro: Sports long fixed draws

Boxcar is a wildly overhanging route that begins at the very back of the cave. Move up on hanging blocks of rock using marginal pinches, and then climb horizontally for 30' out the roof using a variety of crucial opposition hand holds and knee-bars. Power past a 'pod' at the lip of the cave roof, then finish by climbing up the outer upper wall without getting too pumped.

18b. Boxtop 5.13d ★★
Length: 70', Pro: 16 QD's

Start on Boxcar, and climb out to the lip, then continue directly up after pulling the lip ending at a new set of belay anchors (left of Maverick belay).

Note: An unknown bolt line exists just left of Boxcar in the very back portion of the cave, but it is generally not used for free climbing purposes. Boxcar is the right bolt line.

19. Horizontal Delight 5.12d ★★★
Length: 35', Pro: 6 QD's, two bolt rap

Wolfgang leading *Horizontal Delight*

anchor

A stellar route that begins on the far left side of the cave. Climb out horizontally toward the center of the cave using a variety of oppositional counter pressure and knee-bars to finish in a 'pod'. Lower off here for just the .12d portion. Bolts have fixed chains and carabiners for the first 6 bolts to facilitate efficient climbing. The upper portion ascending the outer wall to the upper anchor is 5.13+.

20. Fully Horizontal 5.13b ★★★

This is the continuation of Horizontal Delight and it ascends the outer face past six more bolts with a crux at the upper bolt anchor. Has one reasonable rest point on the upper wall, but beware when clipping the anchor, especially if you line up backward for it.

21. Project 5.13?

This project branches directly up from the third bolt on Horizontal Delight.

22. Project 5.13?

This project is located at the very left edge of the cave.

ROCK CREEK CRAG

This small yet quality west-facing climbing crag (aka Clif's Crag) is great for afternoon warm sunny climbing in early Spring or late Fall seasons. Though limited in scope this site is an idyllic example of back woods cragging on a 40' to 65' tall cliff that has both trad and sport climbs.

Directions:

Drive north from Stevenson, WA on Red Bluff Road at the upper west end of town. It quickly turns to gravel. Shortly ahead the road splits (go right) on CG-2000 forest road. This road follows alongside the Rock Creek stream. Cross a small bridge at six miles with a pretty waterfall on the left. At 8½ miles the road turns sharply left to cross another small bridge. Instead you will go right just before the bridge on road CG-2060 and park in a wide area below the crag. Way uphill perched like a castle overlooking the valley is this tiny little west facing andesitic crag. A steep narrow path starts just past the flat open area and angles up right into the forest to the right of the landslide. The steep climbers path ascends directly uphill till it is even with the upper tier of rock and then walks leftward to the base of the upper tier.

1. Northern Pearl 5.8 R ★

Pro to 4"; length 45'

A continuous crack that varies in size from fingers to fist. The crux is near the top; don't be tempted to bail left into the easy but loose blocks.

2. Pearl's Jam 5.9 R ★

Pro to 4"; length 45'

Start on the same jam crack as Slow Dance. When the crack ends, traverse left four feet and finish via the top half of Northern Pearl. Detached, but seemingly stable blocks form the left side of the crack on the top half of this and the following climb; because of this, all gear placements through this section are suspect. SS chain/ring anchor.

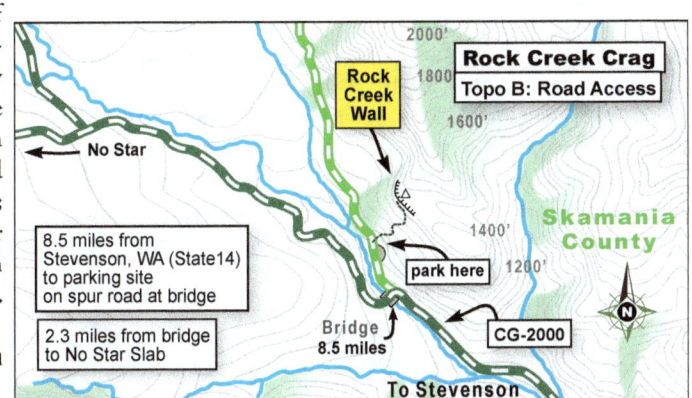

3. Slow Dance 5.10a

70 COLUMBIA GORGE   Rock Creek Crag

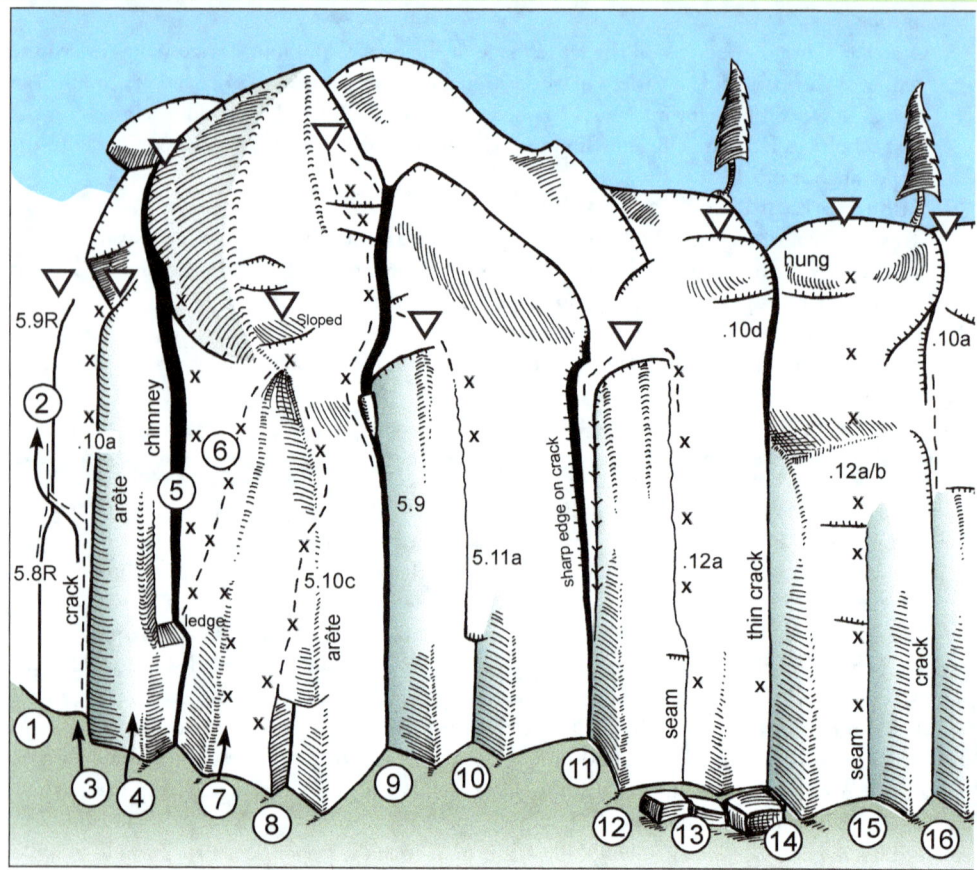

★★★

Pro: 3 QD's & #1, #2, #3 Cam

Jam up the sweet hand-crack located in a shallow dihedral. A small pedestal allows for a rest once the crack ends. Angling slightly right onto the face via a sequential blend of side-pulls, smearing, and crimps will get you near the top. If you've made it this far, a mantel move below the anchor won't throw you for a loop.

4. **Bearhug 5.11-**

Pro: QD's

A "double arête bearhug" climb with problematic stance positions. Falls are going to be *de rigueur* on lead. Ends at an anchor with Metolius rap hangers (shared by **Slow Dance**).

5. **Inner Sanctum 5.10c** ★★

Pro: 5 QD's and a #2 Camalot for the beginning; length 60'

The obvious off-width/chimney with several lead bolts lining the right side. Start by scrambling up a couple small ledges to the start of the off-width. Employ whatever trickery necessary to work your way up to several rests in the widening crack. Wiggle up the final 15' fully immersed in the bowels of the climb. SS chain/ring anchor. Could use some more cleaning.

6. **Bottle Rocket 5.10c** ★★

Pro: 4 QD's and a #2 Camalot for the beginning

This climb shares the start and first bolt with Inner Sanctum but avoids the off-width by angling right onto a fun and exciting face. A final perplexing move will put you at the anchor

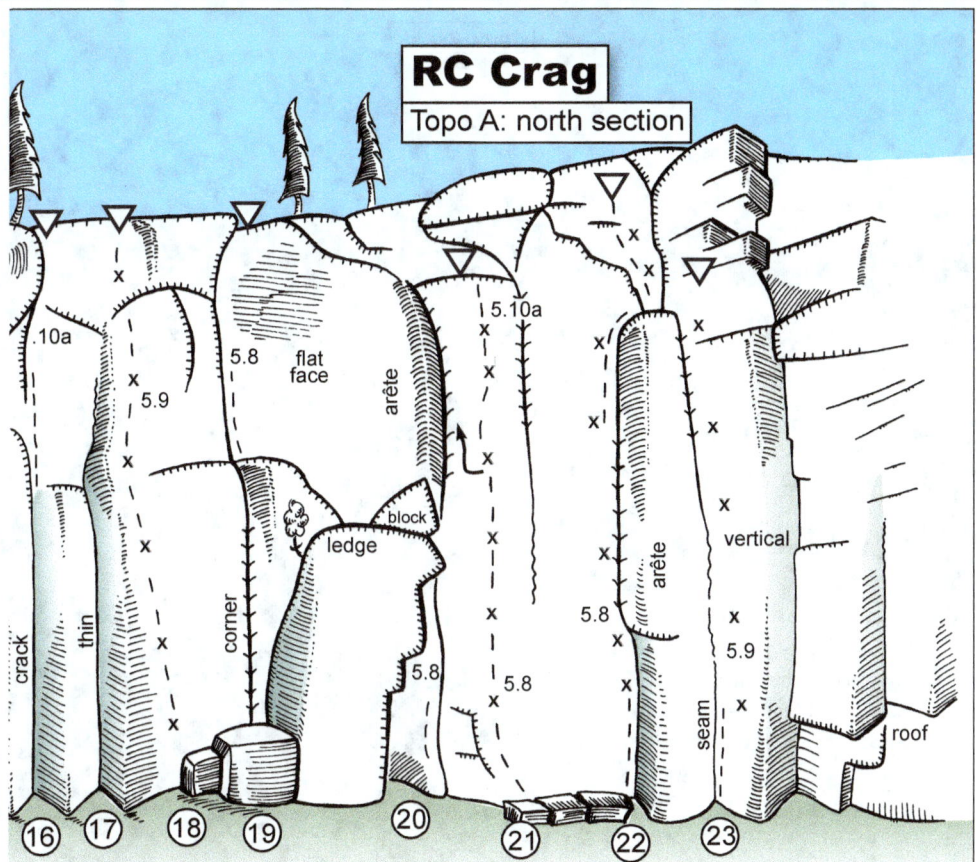

which is shared by The Watchman.

7. **Mists of Time 5.12a**
   Pro: 6 QD's
   A face with a thin seam running up it. A stout direct start that merges into the Bottle Rocket route. Shares the anchor with The Watchman.

8. **The Watchman 5.10c ★★★**
   Pro: 6 QD's
   A stellar arête climb. This is the first route encountered immediately after turning the corner on the north end of the cliff. Look for the first bolt under a light-brown mini-roof on the left side of the arête. A deceptive and tricky climb that won't let you off the hook until rounding the arête near the top. After you finesse the balancy crux switch to the right side of the arête then finish with a sloped mantle to the anchor Perhaps the best, moderate sport climb on the cliff. Carabiners installed at anchor.

9. **Motional Turmoil 5.9 ★★★**
   Pro: 4 QD's, nuts to 1", cams to 5" (4" feasible); length 60'
   The standard and classic warmup at the crag with a bit of ye ol' punch to it. Place good pro in the initial moves then power through the steep crux till it eases at a large wedged block. The remainder of the crack widens to 18' (and fatter) but is pre-fixed with several bolts on the upper part for your convenience and pleasure.

Chad leading The Watchman

10. Butterfinger 5.10d ★★
Pro: 2 QD's and pro to 1", and small TCU's recommended; length 45'
Quality climb that starts vertical and packs a healthy punch to it. Start climbing up a narrowing crack until it disappears. Continue on up the face making use of the arête to the left. A finishing mantel brings you to a sloped ledge where the climb moves left and continues up the final moves of Motional Turmoil. A variant exists on the upper right face has been lead.

11. Wyde Syde 5.10a ★
Pro to 2" including two C3 #00. A 12" Valley Giant is optional
A wonderful off-width that is a great introduction to the world of wide. The seam to the right takes small TCU's. SS chain/ring anchor.

12. Electric Blue 5.12a ★★★
Pro: 5 QD's
An arête to the right of the off-width that offers tricky sidepulls and crimper holds. Shares the same anchor with the next & previous route.

13. Sands of Time 5.11d ★★
Pro: 5 QD's
Unusual opening moves lead to a very powerful crux section. This is the clean face with the seam in the center. Shares the same anchor as Electric Blue.

14. Naked 5.10d ★★★
Pro: Thin nuts and TCU's, and cams to 4"
A stellar crack climb with powerful opening moves on a steep relentless thin corner seam that lands on a sloped slab at midway. A few moves up a fat crack ends with a wild ride up a sharp edged layback overhang crux to finish. This is a proud test of endurance and ingenuity. Stays

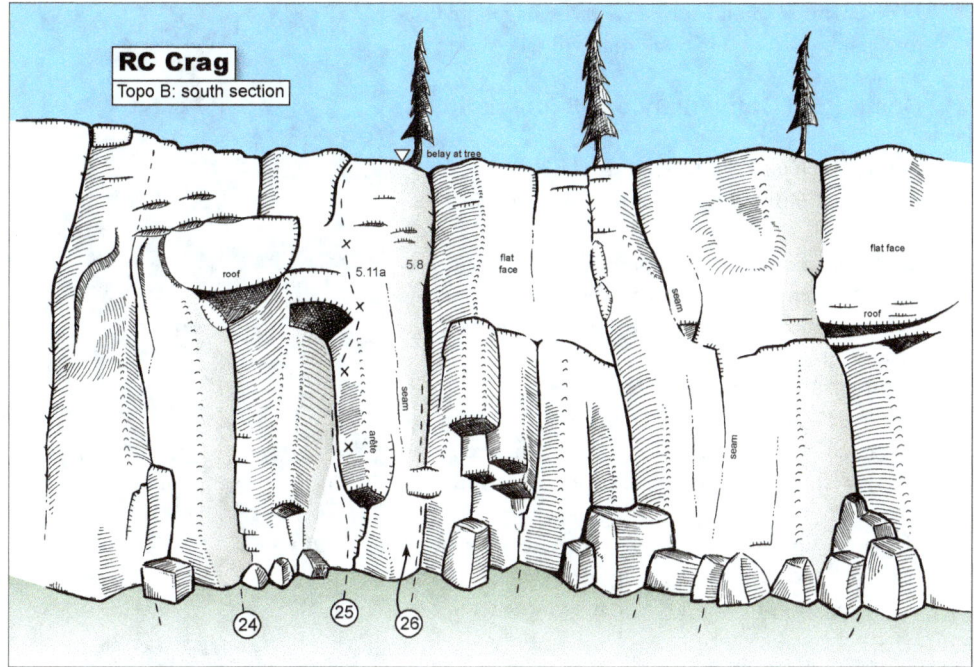

wet longer than most of the climbs at Rock Creek because the crack corner faces left on the lower portion of the climb.

15. Blue Highway 5.12a
Pro: 6 QD's
Powerful line with several technical bulges to surmount.

16. Mighty Mite 5.10a ★
Pro to 2" including small TCU's, doubles on #0.4, #0.5, & #0.75 Camalots optional
Begin in a small dihedral directly in front of the large fir tree. A tricky starting sequence is harder yet for those on the short side. After a good rest at the mid-point, the top half keeps you working right up to the (tree) anchor. Could use some more cleaning.

17. _____

18. Airtime 5.9
Pro: 6 QD's
The buttress on the right side of a blunt arête with numerous edges. A quality climb with tricky crux and a surprise crux ending.

19. Niceline 5.8 ★
Pro to 2"
This crack is never too difficult and consistently fun. Start by climbing up several large steps to get into the corner. SS carabiner anchor.

20. Plaidtastic 5.8 ★
Pro to 3"
Start in a blocky alcove with numerous edges.

Chad leading *Bottlerocket*

Halfway up, a small roof needs to be negotiated before gaining a pleasant crack that will take you to the anchor.

21. Committed Convenience 5.8 (crack finish) ★★

Pro for crack finish: 4 QD's, nuts and cams to 2"
Rating is 5.9 if staying on the face and using just the 6 bolts

Tricky opening moves combine pzazz with punch to make a worthy climb. Fairly fun but the face needs to cleaned better. Anchor is shared by this climb and the Plaidtastic crack.

22. Progressive Climax 5.8 ★★★

Pro: 7 QD's, length 55'

Awesome climb that ascends a large dihedral sporting numerous small horizontal edges. At the fifth bolt, step right (or move up to the jug then right) onto the airy arête and finish on easy jugs. Great warm-up. Webbing anchor. A high quality steep face climb that seems to put a smile of satisfaction on the face of every climber.

23. Scorpio 5.8+ ★★

Pro: 5 QD's

A fun romp up an open book loaded with edges. The difficulty starts early but quickly gives way to easier climbing. There are two possible ways to finish Scorpio: The harder option is going straight up to the obvious ring anchor. Alternately, one can clip the last bolt on Scorpio with a runner and step left of the rock fin to finish on Progressive Climax (two more bolts).

Note: Approximately 100 feet separate the previous two climbs from the next climbs.

24. _____

25. Black Ribbon 5.11a ★★

Pro: 4 QD's and a #3 Camalot for the finish, length 40'

Directly in front of a leaning snag is a clean dihedral with a large roof at mid-height. After two intense cruxes, moving up the dihedral and clearing the roof, scamper up the relatively easy face to the tree anchor (shared with Bungee's Crack). Consider clipping the 2nd bolt with a single carabiner.

26. Bungee's Crack 5.8 ★★

Pro to 3", length 40'

The southern most climb at Rock Creek is this enjoyable well protected crack climb. Stemming on the numerous edges allows for several rests and casual gear placements. A crux near the top needs to be surmounted before reaching the (tree/chain) anchor. Could use some more cleaning.

MONTE CRISTO SLAB

The MCS is an impressive diorite slab tucked along the west slope of a minor forested ridge crest overlooking a broad sweeping panoramic plateau of the fir tree covered South Prairie region near Trout Lake. The rock slab is a good example of the kind of granitic slab rock climbing you typically find at places like Leavenworth, Washington, but this crag is just a few hours from Portland.

Though not nearly as steep as you typically find at most major granite climbing sites, the MCS none-the-less is a quality destination for locals who relish low angle slab climbing. The steeper sections of the slab vary from 40°-55° overall angle (with a few near vertical steps). Considering its mid-Cascades Range locale, as expected the crag does have some minor moss and lichen, yet the slab does gets thoroughly scoured each winter by the snow pack buildup as it avalanches off the low angle slab. The west-facing aspect of the slab receives considerable hot summer sunshine, while the dioritic rock structure lacks micro-sized pockets between the crystalline matrix, thus tending to minimize moss growth. The crag is encapsulated in a forest of Douglas fir, cottonwood, alder, and willow brush thickets, yet the slab offers broad sweeping scenic view of the entire region to the west from the top of the wall.

The core emphasis for route grade ratings on this slab commonly range from 5.3 to 5.9 (the fun range), though a few short sections of several routes have slightly higher ratings.

One of the prime benefits about the MCS is to start warm-up leading on the short 100' climbs, then bust into a series of long 200' leads on the main wall of the South Dome. These long routes provide lead climbers with a distinctly unique opportunity to hone calf-burner sharp-end of the rope long slab leading skills, sending you home at the end of the day with a smile of satisfaction.

MCS is suitable for a certain general skill level of rock climber. Considering all factors, from the 4th class descent runnels, to good rappel stations, to the 9'-25' runout sections between lead bolts, to the large array of entry level routes, the MCS is quite suitable as a beginner to moderate climbing area. Most of the beginner routes (5.2-5.6) are well bolted. The youngest person to climb here was 3 years of age (little Davey). The site is especially well suited to the old-timer (and

the young) generation climber who have no desire to climb much beyond the 5.9 range. The slab is not a hardman climbing site for dedicated 5.11/.12 (and higher) climbers pushing the 'number' game. Thus, a .12+ climber here is like a fish out of water burdened by a subtle incongruency [like an intentional under achiever].

In addition, the crags numerative square-foot usability factor is quite small, yielding about sixty rock climbs maximum (considerably less than Broughton Bluff), while 50% of the visible slab is simply too low angle for any 5th class climbing purposes. The MCS distance from the city, its general isolated locale on back-country gravel roads may naturally limit overall user interest.

Road Directions:

From Portland, Oregon drive east on I-84 freeway to Cascade Locks. Cross the Bridge of the Gods bridge. Continue east of Washington State Route 14 (through Stevenson, WA) for 14.5 miles (passing Dog Mtn Trailhead). Turn north onto Cook-Underwood Road (CR86) and drive 5.1 miles (through Mill A community). Turn left (north) onto Willard Road and drive 2.1 miles (passing through Willard). Willard Road becomes Oklahoma Road at Willard. Just north of the community of Willard turn left onto NF 66 road (South Prairie Rd). Drive north on paved road NF 66 for 12.7 miles (becomes gravel), then east on gravel road NF 6610 for 2.2 miles. Turn right on NF 6610-030 and drive 1/10 mile, then left on NF 717 a narrow old logging grade for 2/10 mile. Park at a circular loop turn-around sizable enough to hold perhaps 6-8 cars. Driving time from east Portland is about 1¾ hours (from Hood River about 50 minutes).

Several alternate driving directions to MCS for non-AWD vehicles.

From South Prairie Pond (for 2WD vehicles): Continue north on NF 66 past South Prairie Pond for several miles, then cut east on a rough road NF 8820 for 1.5 miles, then south on NF 070 for 1 mile, then west on NF 6610 for .5 mile, then south on NF 030 for .1 mile, then on final narrow decomm road NF 717 for .2 miles to loop parking spot.

From White Salmon (for 2WD vehicles): At highway SR14 at the White Salmon River (where it meets the Columbia River) drive north on SR 141 (the Bypass) 2.1 miles to a junction. Continue north on SR 141 for 19 miles to Trout Lake, then go through town and west on SR 141 for 4 miles, then turn left (southwest) on NF 86 (gravel) and drive 1.8 miles. At a 'Y' go right on NF 8620 (Cave Creek Road) and drive 4.9 miles west uphill to a 'T' intersection. Drive south from the T on NF 070 for .5 mile to a 'Y', then drive west on NF 6610 for .5 miles. Turn left (south) on NF 030 for .1 mile, then on final narrow decomm road NF 717 for .2 miles to loop parking spot.

Path Info:

Two paths exist to reach the crag (the north path and the main path). Both start the same, but split in about 40' from the parking spot.

North Path: At the northeast end of the parking spot the primary foot path cuts northward. In about 60' you will reach a dry creek drainage. Cross the dry creek drainage, then gently gain elevation for several hundred feet, then cut directly sideways along the base of a minor rock outcrop to reach the North Nook Landing, a nice sunny gravel landing with a fat string of quality climbs. From the north nook walk south a few yards along the base of the 2nd rock lobe, then up onto a wooded minor ridge crest. Follow up this wooded ridge crest for about 200' (at 100' a brief short path cuts over to the base of the 1st rock lobe to access a string of rock climbs there) to reach the Middle Landing. This landing has a plethora of easier routes conducive for basic and beginner type rock climbing on a low angle slab environment. You can reach this section of the crag easily by taking either the north path or the main path.

Main Path: At the northeast end of the parking spot the primary foot path cuts northward. In about 40' just **before** reaching the dry creek drainage, the main path cuts directly eastward and cruises uphill to the cliff, landing just below the main south dome headwall section. A connector path exists along the entire base of the wall from the south end to the north end.

Rock Surface Nuances:

Textural nuances of the rock vary from low angle to moderate angle slab, mostly flared rounded pockets (1"-5"), various water grooved runnels, delicate techy smears, and lots of undulating wave-like terrain offering rounded palm friction surfaces. The site is basically un-like any other Northwest Oregon or southwest Washington climbing site, so be prepared to relearn your footwork technique, especially if you are not accustomed to a slab climbing environment. The crystalline mineral surface friction is excellent (light to medium grade sandpaper) giving an ease for smearing on all surfaces.

Descent Options:

About 80% of the routes are setup as 90'-100' lead climbs and all those routes are frequently ascended on lead or top-rope, and rappeled.

The steep solo descent runnels are mostly 3rd or 4th class, but you still may not like solo descending a steep slope of rock. Alongside the Dark Water Streak at the south end is a series of assistance or emergency rappel (ER) stations that you are welcome to use for rapping down that runnel. If you are really hard pressed, its possible to walk into the forest at the north end of the crag and descend a midst the trees.

South Dome Main Wall: Avoid rappelling down the long 200' routes on the steep main south

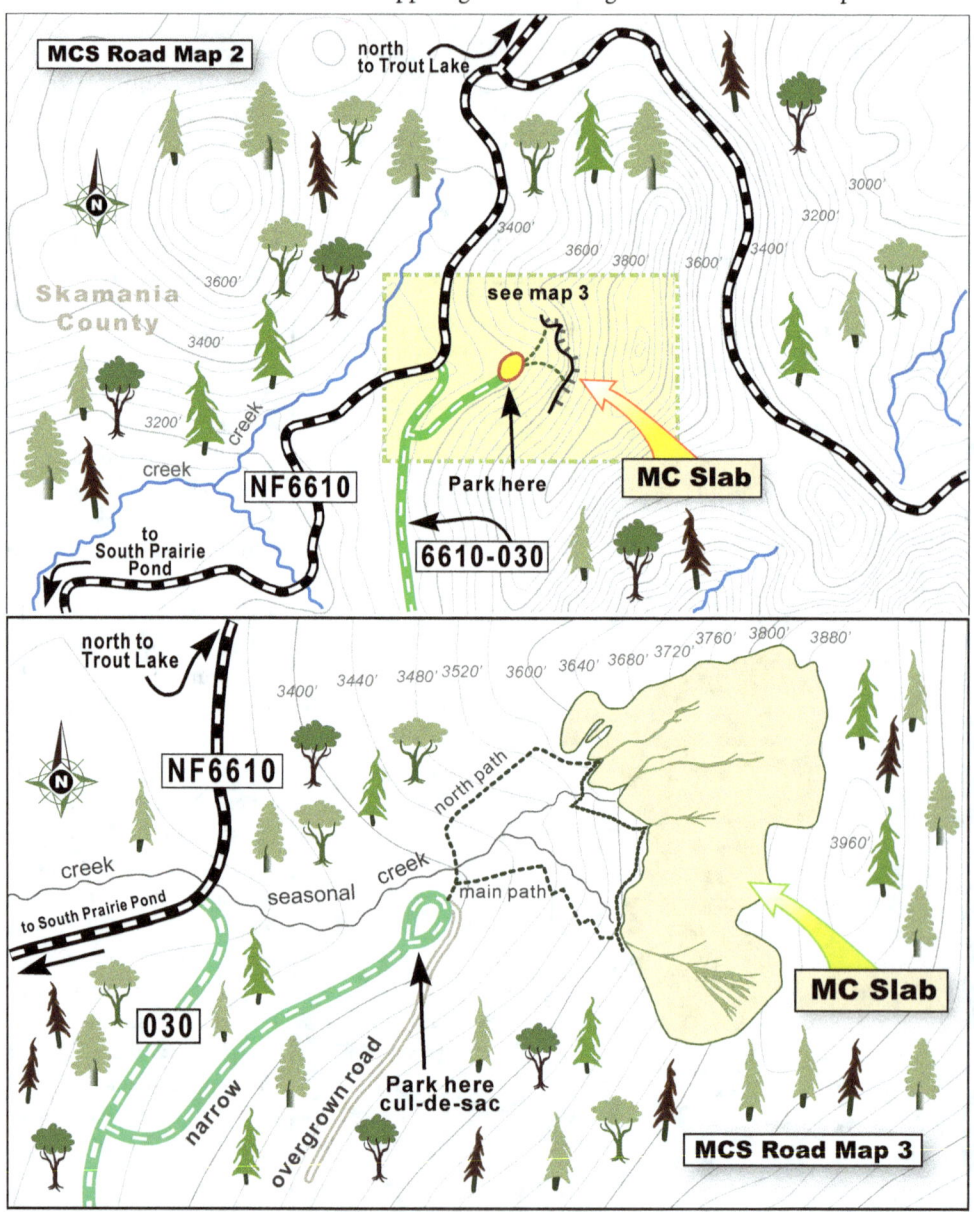

dome headwall. Why not? **1.)** Because other climbers will likely be climbing on a route directly below or next to you, or perhaps even starting on the route you just finished (you cannot see them from above). **2.)** When you rappel your knot will get snagged on a bolt hanger on the upper part of the wall and you will have a hernia trying to unsnag it. **3.)** To pull down 200' of rope on a rounded slab lets the rope snag every little pebble. **4.)** The rope may get entangled with another nearby climber and cause an incident. **5.)** Its very difficult to pull two ropes across 200' of rounded slab. **6.)** Its much faster to walk off.

So, coil up your rope and walk off south (or north) to the 4th class descent water runnels. Both walk-off options are steep yet fairly basic (provided you don't slide). Or, use one of the specifically arranged 100' rappel stations descent methods explained in the beta section.

Gear Needs, and Other Site Awareness Factors:

Bring just quick-draws (or expandable loop quick-draws) because there are no cracks on the entire wall (leave all your stoppers and cam devices at home).

A 60-meter rope works for most routes, but the lead length of two routes require a 70-meter rope. A few routes are a bit over 60-meters in length (about 204' long), but can still be done with a 60-m rope provided the leader knows that when reaching the belay anchor they should tie in with a sling or daisy chain. The first six routes on the South Dome area are best ascended with a 70-meter rope.

If it begins to rain heavily while you are rock climbing, stop immediately and lower off from the nearest bolt hanger (or from the nearest belay station). The diorite slab can become slick very quickly during rainstorms, and the common 4th class walk-off descent methods may not be an option, so when need use the ER's near the Dark Streak.

If you are unfamiliar with slab climbing technique and its your first 1-3 visits, try not to get too bold on lead. Learn some foot smearing methodology on high-angle friction first before tackling a bold lead. If we all lived in the land of granite this would not be a lesson to relearn.

If you skate or grease off a slab while on lead you will slide and scrape your way down below your previously clipped bolt so perhaps long pants might be beneficial in this instance. Since bolts are 9' to 25' apart its best to build up your smear leading confidence gradually.

Technically speaking, there are no R/X rated lead climbs at MCS, though this parameter is based entirely on logical anticipatory preparation factors and skill level in dealing with slab climbing technique, which is all foot technique and not finger crimping. Some routes may still feel bold, but most crux sections are well protected. When the terrain angle eases on the upper portions of many longer routes, the bolt spacing increases to usually 15'-25' apart as the grade difficulty eases.

There are several sections (see diagram) at the top of the slab with some square-ish flat stones (2"-6") in diameter lay scattered along the edge of the forest. Do not drag the rope through these areas. A helmet may be beneficial when leading or belaying. If you accidentally dislodge any rocks while at the top of the crag, let us know you did something dumb, and yell loudly to any persons at the base of the slab. Due to the rounded curvature of the steep slab a tumbling stone may take perhaps 3-5 seconds to reach the bottom of the cliff, hopefully enough time for others to react quickly. Much of the slab is

Lisa Rust climbing *Uluru*

generally void of loose material, though the slab has some loose 1" flat rock chips that exfoliate a bit seasonally (typical of granitic rock).

The black lichen (mostly at the top of the slab) and the minor areas of moss can become very slick during rainstorms, and on cold October days (when the humidity is high), so use caution.

Etiquette:

Friendly climber social interaction is indispensable here at MCS, primarily because communication helps each climbing team to coordinate its next climbing route goal, especially if a plethora of teams are actively climbing on the same day.

Kari leading Aero Cognition

There is no poison oak, no ticks, no nearby water source (the ravine dries out quickly), and no cell phone reception. Car camping exists along NF 66 road at several fee based campgrounds with water and toilets. There are plenty of pullouts along various nearby gravel roads for free overnight car camping. Avoid car camping at the turn-around loop (limited space for vehicles). Refrain from setting up campfires at this site, because it's a fire risk with no nearby emergency water to put it out.

Parking space is limited, so plan to carpool. Park your vehicle so as to allow enough space for other vehicles to use the turn-around loop, too. There is minimal space for about 7-9 vehicles at the turn-around loop. Consider limiting your total group team size to 1-15 persons. Instructional guiding, commercial, clubs, and organization activities in this Forest Service district are permit regulated. Some advisory recommendations within the stewardship framework promote effectual continuity goals.

At present, the open square footage maneuvering space along the cliff base is narrow due to the encroaching brush thicket. There are 3-4 common spots along the cliff base where climber's tend to congregate and most of those are quite small (its more like rubbing shoulders in an escalator). The entire length of the cliff base is mostly a thicket of dense brush which makes it difficult for human or dog to step off the path to go potty pooh. So, the answer should be obvious (i.e. not on the path). Walk away from the cliff base a fair distance if you need to find a pooh spot. Consider leaving your pet at home. If you bring it here keep it fully controlled (e.g. leashed). Do not leave non-degradable trash strewn along the base of the crag.

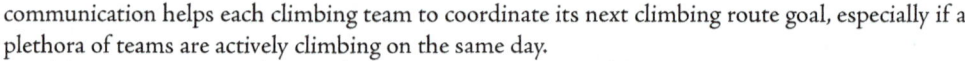

Seasonal Factors:

The MCS is generally accessible from late-May through late-October. Hot mid-summer temperatures can be a challenge, especially when the temperature reaches 90°F (or higher) in Portland, which is about 80°F at MCS. During July and August, when

Laila climbing *Bronze Whale*

there is little or no breeze, its best to get there early and climb until it gets too hot. On hot summer days (1-4pm) when the afternoon sun is directly facing the slab it can be unbearably sultry along the base of the crag. Some tall trees and minor shrubs grow along various parts of the slab base providing some shade (not at the North Landing or Middle Landing). During the summer months most west side rain systems forecasting 40% rain simply do not effect the crag much, primarily because of its slightly easterly locale in the high Cascades Range.

In early May and late October the slab can be damp with morning dew, or it may be damp with narrow water seeps all day, especially when the weather remains cool and cloudy, or had recent rainfall, or is well below 60°F at the slab. Shaded portions of the rock slab tend to remain damp during this part of the season making certain routes unclimbable. In summation, heavy rains in Spring or Fall season, excessive dew, and high humidity will effect the climbing options.

Limitations:

Leave the power drill at home; all the hard work is done, and all the routes are developed. Do not strive to 'squeeze job' climbs between the existing climbs. The present routes are identifiable as lead routes, because of the slight separation (a factor lost through further condensing).

Though some of the routes may start a bit wider at the base of the slab, when a set of climbs reach the top of the slab they tend to get much closer together, primarily because the climbable portions of the slab have a dome-shaped aspect (like the top of an egg). Even smaller portions of the slab have additional mini dome-shaped curvatures, such as the first ½ dozen routes at the south end, and the string of routes on the 2nd, 3rd and 4th rock lobe at the north end. Some routes meet at the same belay station (varies from 1-4 routes per belay).

Most of the routes follow some form of natural nuance, be it a series of natural pockets, a fat rib, or a skinny water runnel. These characteristics give the route its sense of natural flow and intrinsic value. This goal enhances the leading experience without a potential tangle of grid pattern bolt lines that loose the essence of each routes characteristic qualities.

Stewardship at MCS:

The view from atop the slab provides a stellar

Steve, Hugh, and friends climbing at *MCS*

captivating scene of distant Lemei Rock in Indian Heaven, the South Prairie Pond, the Big Lava Bed, Huckleberry Mtn., and (on a lucky day) very compelling peaceful silence, all wrapped in an extensive fir forest. Its thoroughly rewarding just to rock climb up to the top of the slab to sit and partake of the vast scenic beauty. Visit and enjoy the rock climbing here and experience the unique qualities and value of this Washington state natural resource.

Stewardship ideals emphasize user group diversification options, site maintenance needs through organized efforts, anchor program, and other practical site recreation goals.

MCS site stewardship ethical continuity ideals are coordinated through an advisory committee that works with various regional entities. MCS primary development phase is through the efforts of Mr O & Mr B (plus positive effort by friends). See the MCS CCA page for stewardship and general climbing info. Ethically based stewardship brings value, incentive and inherent harmonious quality toward use of this crag. Enjoy the serene experience and enjoy the climbing.

Rock Structural Characteristics:

MCS is geologically known as Miocene Intrusive Diorite (Mid) of a granitic stock family with medium-grained dark minerals (1-5mm), lacking quartz minerals, roughly a porphyritic pyroxene diorite. The entire structure is likely the top exposed portion of intrusive diorite stock, formed originally as a subsurface congealed marginal portion of magma stock from a larger, deeper diorite mass. The west-facing exposure of the slab likely reached its present visibility when the upper layers of softer detritus materials eroded away, or

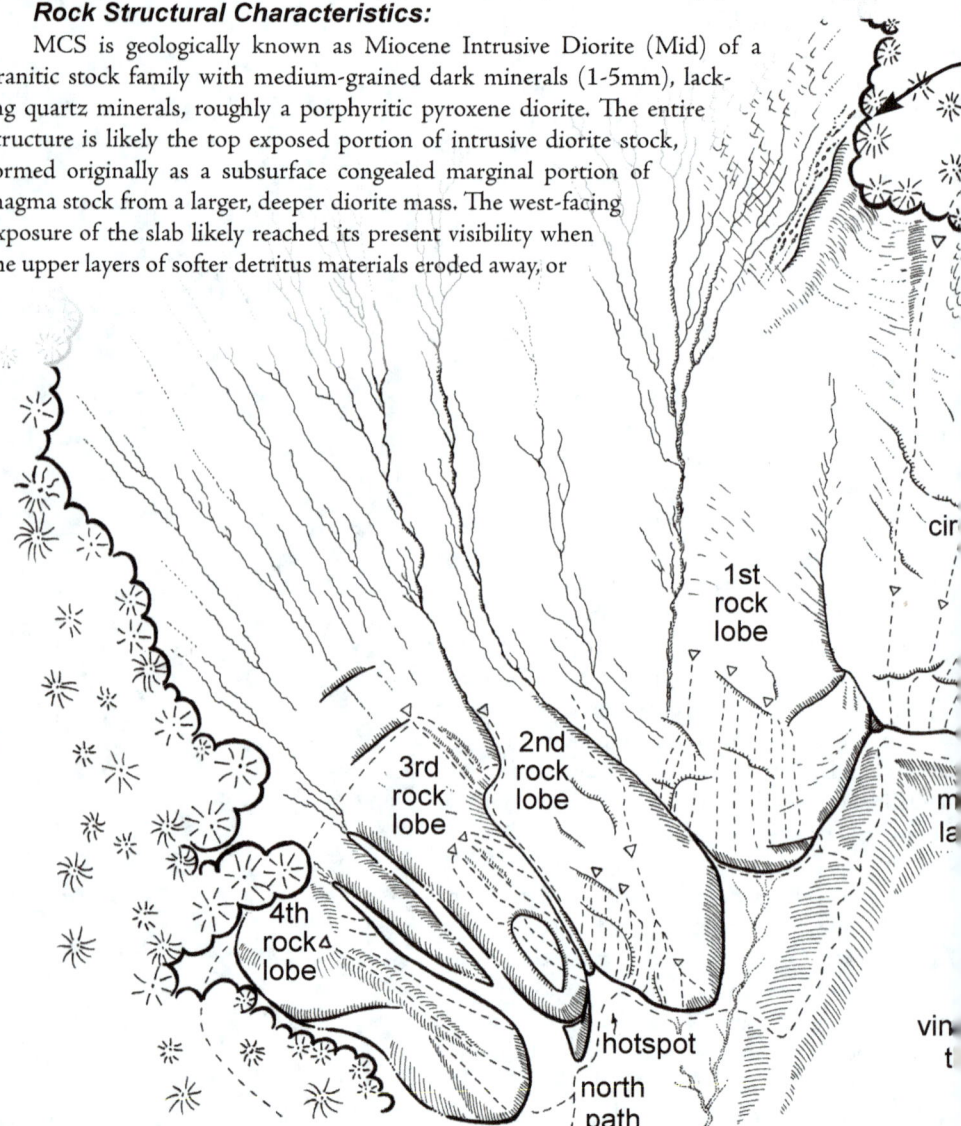

possibly when the surrounding slopes abruptly sloughed off downhill westward sometime in the past millennium.

The northern portion (with the lowest angle) of MCS shows very distinct heavy snow loading and avalanche impaction features, mainly long scratch lines (top down), a total lack of moss, and sections of unusually smooth surface rock where the natural rock curves were partially scoured for 200'+ down the slab. These factors match similar characteristics as those found on worn rock

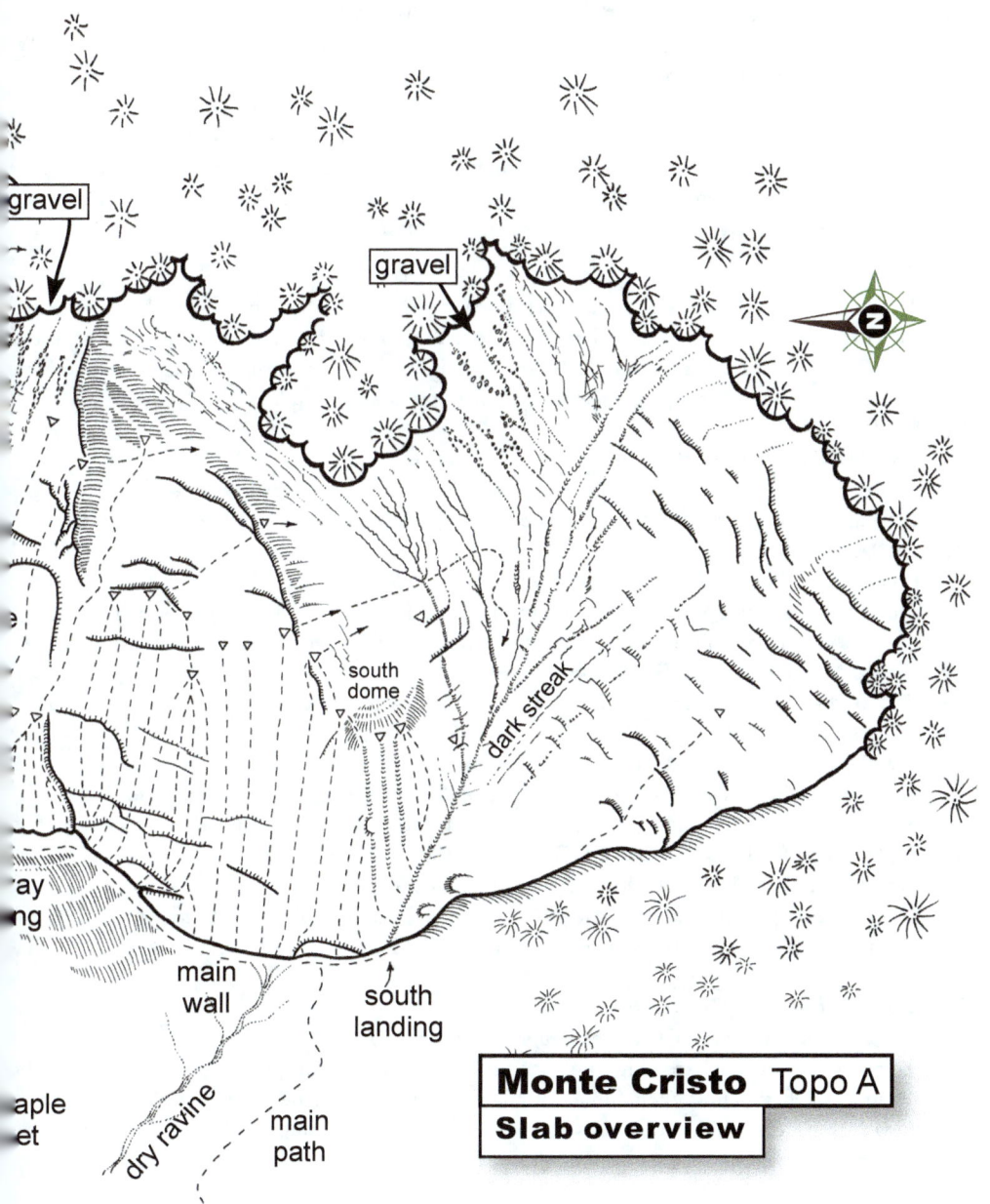

Monte Cristo Topo A
Slab overview

surfaces below various glaciers.

Several basic geographical observations for the MCS site are: elevation at the lowest point (3rd lobe) 3518'; elevation at the highest point (upper northeast end) 3818'; vertical height of slab: 300'; length (south to north): 815'; width at angle (top to bottom): about 510'.

The GPS (via GE [*see Introduction*]) geographical quadrangle coordinates are: UTM 10T 603653 5086444.

MC SLAB BETA

Beta is described from right (South End) to left (North End).

Dark Water Streak   4th class, descent groove, length: 250'

The standard 4th class descent route. This is a dark water stained runnel at the south end of the slab. This water stained groove can be quite slick in early or late season, and after rainstorms. At those times it may be unnegotiable or tricky to descend. A series of three 100' long assistance or emergency rappel (ER) stations exist on the immediate left side of this dark stained water streak, just in case you get caught up topside in a rain shower, or if you are uncomfortable with steep 4th class down smearing descents. To the far right of the Dark Water Streak is a basic **Beginner's Route** on a very low angle slab (5.0-*ish*) that has one 100' lead.

SOUTH DOME

To the left of the Dark Water Streak is a subtle yet broadly rounded dome shaped rock formation with three subtle and slightly darkened water streak grooves trending down its west aspect. The following routes ascend this rounded dome formation. A 70-meter rope is recommended for these routes, but a 60-meter rope is feasible in a pinch if you tie an end knot.

1. **My DNA 5.4**
   Pro: 9 QD's, Length: 110' (70-meter rope recommended)'
   A fun variation next to the dark water streak. Start up the initial part of Outback BBQ, then angle up right at the third bolt to climb up a set of giant steps (6 more bolts) to a belay station.

2. **Outback BBQ 5.4**
   Pro: 8 QD's, Length: 105' (70-meter rope recommended)
   This route is the first primary route left of the Dark Streak. It is a low angle smear run that steepens on its upper portion as it ascends a set of large rounded steps.

   Three Narrow Water Streak Grooves
   Each of the next three routes cruise up a set of three narrow water streak grooves all in a row.

3. **Tor the Hairy One 5.5 ★★**
   Pro: 9 QD's, Length: 105' (70-meter rope recommended)
   This is the right thin water groove. Initially ascend a low angle slab that steepens for its upper portion, generally utilizing the right edge of the groove. Mostly rounded sloping edges.

4. **Blind Deaf Old Goat (aka BDOG) 5.5 ★★**
   Pro: 9 QD's, Length: 105' (70-meter rope recommended)
   This is the center thin water groove. From a big fat natural bowl smear up low angle terrain passing a minor crux on the steeper upper portion. Mostly rounded sloping edges, but with good characteristics and quality.

5. **Count of Monte Cristo 5.6 ★★**
   Pro: 8 QD's, Length: 110' (70-meter rope recommended)
   A good quality climb ascending the leftmost of three water grooves. From a big fat natural scoop step left to a bolt, then climb directly up on low angle smears. A large round natural bowl at mid-height is the transition point where the low angle smears end and the high angle dancing smears (crux) begin on rounded slopers.

6. **MC Direct 5.7**
Pro: 10 QD's, Length: 135'
A brief tricky direct start initial crux move using steeply sloped rounded pockets and smears. A high step puts you onto a round stance, then dash up easier terrain following a string of bolts. This direct start route merges at the large round natural bowl at mid-height into the Count of Monte Cristo.

MAIN WALL OF SOUTH DOME
From the little nook northward is a 40' wide, near vertical sweep of slab that offers a good string of powerful direct starts to all the long routes on the headwall.

Little Nook
A slightly overhung section of rock creates a minor 15' wide nook with a narrow gravel landing. The left side has a sloped step start (Uluru), and the overhung bulge to the right is the route Iceberg In A Sauna. The main climber's path from the parking spot to the crag lands here, too.

7. **Iceberg in a Sauna 5.8** ★
Pro: 11 QD's, Length: 145'
Surmount up out of the little nook over a slightly hung odd crux bulge, then dance up a low angle slab. The route merges rightward into Monte Cristo at mid-height.

8. **Uluru 5.6** ★ ★ ★
Pro: 14 QD's, Length: 145'
A superb climb. Though it has no specific crux move, the climb is a long series of sloping smears lacking prominent jugs. Begin at the left side of the overhung nook by stepping up a sloped step (bolt), reach over the lip to a jug, then from the second bolt continue straight up, past another minor rounded step, then up a long long flat face with thin techy sloped smears (160' to first belay). **Pitch 2:** Climb up (5.0) another 30' to another belay station then walk off south to the 4th class Dark Streak descent water runnel to descend.

9. **Silence the Serenity 5.10a [5.6]** ★ ★ ★
Specs: 5.10a (crux start), max 5.6 on upper ¾ route
Pro: 17 QD's, Length: 200'
Immediately left of the small nook a few feet is a very steep slab. The start dances up thin crux (5.10a) smears past a rounded bulge before easing at the 3rd bolt. The remainder of the route is a great little fun run traveling directly up the wall. Climbs various prominent ramps, scoops, small dishes, a brief thin smear-fest, then as the terrain eases it travels up easy 5.0 terrain to a belay anchor. Walk southward to the Dark Streak to descend.

10. **Sunday's Best 5.11a [5.6]** ★ ★
Specs: 5.11a (crux start) and max 5.6 upper ¾ route
Pro: 16 QD's, Length 200'
A thin tricky crux start smear problem that eases to a sloped ramp. Continue past a series of four closely spaced bolts, then cruise on high angle terrain using smears and rounded pockets. The terrain eases as you reach the upper belay anchor at a rounded low angle crest. Though a mid-belay exists on this particular route it is far

Bob Murphy leading *Uluru*

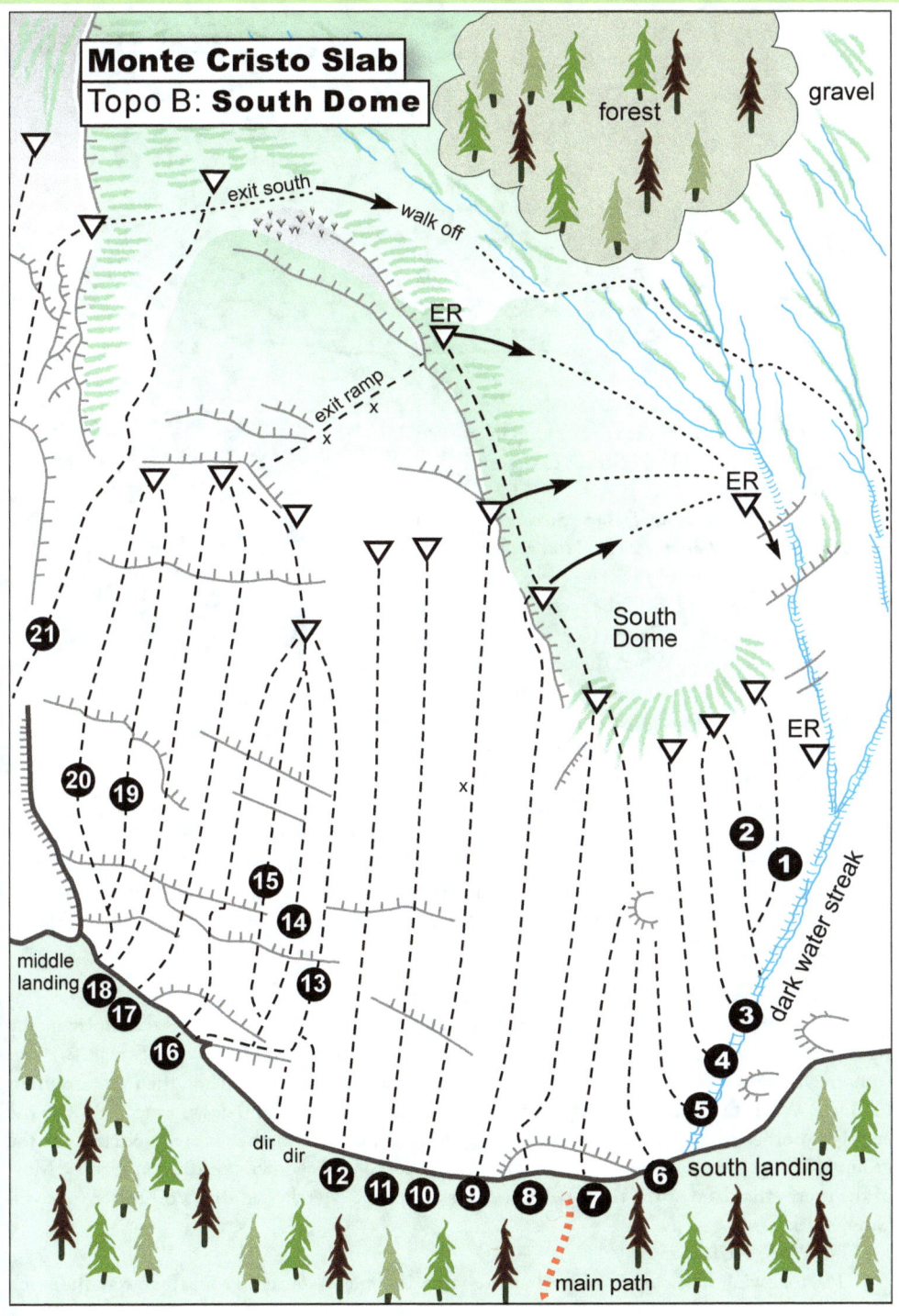

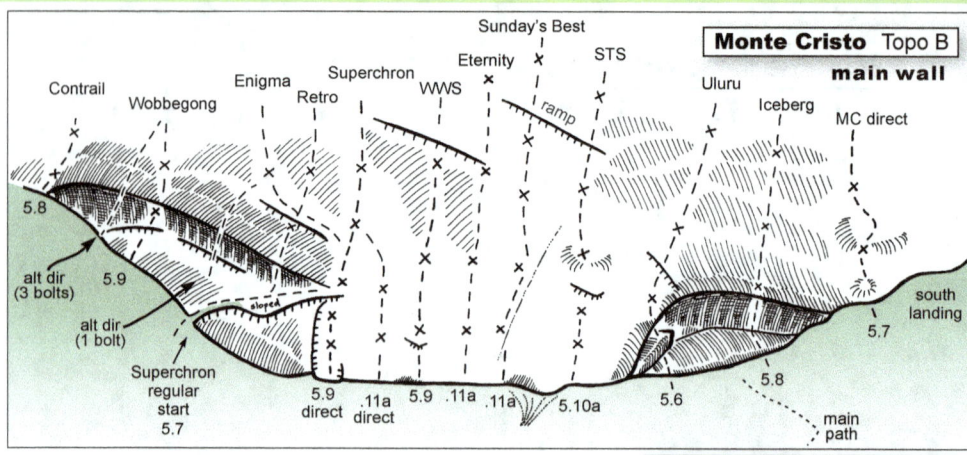

more enjoyable to do the entire climb in one very long lead. Walk south to the Dark Streak to descend.

11. Eternity 5.11a [5.8] ★
Specs: 5.11a (crux start), max 5.8 on upper ¾ route
Pro: 17 QD's, Length: 210' (70m rope required)

Power up a technical thin face (crux). As the terrain eases, dash up a short ways till the face steepens again. Continue up a long run of moderate (5.7-ish) smears, small scoops, and face climbing. When the terrain eases, dash up to an independent belay station. Belay here, then climb rightward to another belay anchor on a rounded crest, then walk off south to the Dark Streak water runnel.

12. Walk on the Wild Side 5.9 ★★★
Pro: 17 QD's, Length 210' (70m rope required)
A fun initial steep crux start using an incut crimp, then the angle eases briefly. When it steepens again continue up a long steep portion (5.7-ish) using smears and edges. The upper part of the route eases and ends at an independent belay station (at same level as Eternity belay). Belay here, then climb rightward to another belay anchor on a rounded crest, then walk off south to the Dark Streak water runnel.

TRIPLE BELAY STATION LEDGE SYSTEM

Several options for topping out from the broad triple belay ledge system. **1.**) Exit horizontally right (2 bolts, 5.0, 30') to another belay station, then walk south down Dark Water Streak. **2.**) Or... from the leftmost belay, ascend 50' uphill (5.0 terrain) to another belay anchor, then walk south to the Dark Water Streak. **3.**) Or...rappel from the leftmost belay station, down exactly 95' (tie the ends) to another rappel station (next to the Midway Landing belays), then rappel from there to the ground (95'). See introduction notes for why its best not to rappel down the 200' long routes. Most of the routes that land at the triple belay stations are a rope stretcher, in that a 60-meter rope will barely work.

Multiple Route Belay
The following four routes all land at the same 190' belay station. From this belay the route

continues briefly upward to the Triple Belay Station ledge system.

13. Superchron 5.7 ★★★
Pro: 13 QD's standard sloped ramp start, Length: 190'
A very good route. **Pitch 1:** Begin by traversing rightward out a sloped ramp for 15' to a narrow stance (bolt), then make a delicate crux smear move and dash up easier slab smears till the wall steepens, then ascend a series of steep wavy undulations. As the terrain eases on the last part of the lead expect healthy runout on 5.0-*ish* terrain till you reach a multi-route belay station. **Pitch 2:** From this belay continue up leftward on low angle 5.0-*ish* terrain (1 bolt) till you reach a flat broad ledge system with three belay stations.
Superchron Direct Start #1: Minor 2-bolt 5.9 direct start exists for this climb which powers up a brief round nose of rock merging into the standard route at a small stance. You will need 2 extra QD's for this variation.
Superchron Direct Start #2: A minor 2-bolt 5.11a direct start exists for this same route. Initial technical crux moves that quickly morphs left into the standard route at the small stance. You will need 2 extra QD's for this variation.

14. Retro Cognition 5.7 ★★★
Pro: 11 QD's, Length: 190'
A superb route! Begin at a sloped ramp (same as Superchron). Surmount a vertical crux step (thin flake crimp), then smear up easy slab. The route steepens again as it travels up various sloped edges and holds. As the route eases to a lower angle, it surmounts one last short step, then eases to 5.0-*ish* terrain (spaced out bolts) ending at a multi-route belay station. **Pitch 2:** continue up left (1 bolt) on easy 5.0-*ish* terrain 30' to another belay anchor. This is the triple belay anchor ledge system.

15. Enigma 5.9 ★
Pro: 11 QD's, Length: 190'
The starting point is the same as the previous route. After the initial flake move, smear left, then up easy slab smear terrain to a near vertical face. Climb this near vertical face and at the upper lip (5.9 crux) slide sideways to the right (odd moves). Once past that continue up easier terrain till you dance up a long smooth slab (5.8). A final 3' high rounded lip is surmounted, then continue up easier runout sections till you reach a belay station at 190' (multi-route belay station). **Pitch 2:** continue up left (1 bolt) till you reach the triple belay anchors on a broad ledge system.

16. Wobbegong 5.9 ★★★
Pro: 13 QD's: Length: 190'
One of the classic routes at the crag with variety and techy movement. Commence the journey by surmounting an initial vertical 5' tall step (5.6), then dash up a long low angle slab to a steep near vertical cliff face. Ascend a crux section of technical movement using various rounded crimps, slopers and thin rounded finger pockets. Move right under a big lip, and surmount this at a big fat rounded pocket (crux). Then smear up a long flat steep face (5.8) till this eases to lower angle terrain. Dash up rightward slightly on healthy runout easy terrain to a multi-route belay station. **Pitch 2:** continue up left (1 bolt) till you reach the triple belay anchors on a broad ledge system.

Family day at *MCS South Dome*

17. **Contrail Conspiracy 5.8** ★★★
Pro: 14 QD's, Length: 202'
A superb classic route with plenty of unique variety, certainly one of the best routes here. Start at an initial steep move (or skip the first bolt) then dash up an easy low angle slab till the cliff steepens to near vertical. Ascend steep delicate movement (crux section) passing a brief lip landing on a stance. Then up a long steep smooth smear slab (crux) which eases quickly when you get past the next minor rounded lip. Continue to dash up considerable low angle slab terrain till you reach the triple belay station on a broad flat ledge system.

18. **Indian Summer 5.8** ★★
Pro: 11 QD's, Length: 202' (a stretch for 60m)
Cruise up a low angle slab, surmount a step, then ascend a tall crux section utilizing various sloped edges. At about 100' the terrain eases to low 5th class ending at the triple belay station ledge system.

19. **Sky's the Limit 5.10b**
Pro: 11 QD's, Length: 202' (a stretch for 60m)
This climb is located where the base trail levels off just below a prominent ravine system. Two climbs utilize the same initial crux bolt at a short lip bulge. Dash up low angle terrain, surmount a minor lip bulge, and dash up more low angle terrain to the rightmost set of bolts on a vertical section of rock. Surmount this dicey vertical crux lip, then ascend a fun steep slab section to a second dicey vertical foot smear lip crux. The slab terrain eases for many meters eventually landing at the triple belay station on a broad flat ledge system.

20. **Griddle Cakes 5.7** ★
Pro: 11 QD's, Length: 202' (a stretch for 60m)
Same starting point as the previous route. Commence up low angle terrain, surmount a minor lip bulge, and dash up more low angle terrain to the leftmost set of bolts on a vertical section of rock. Surmount the vertical crux, then continue up a fun run slab to a second easier rock step. The slab terrain eases for many meters eventually landing at the triple belay station on a broad flat ledge system.

Center Ravine Rappel
A prominent 100' tall deeply cut stepped ravine (rated 5.3) slices the central portion of this wall. To the right of it lay the steep main wall of the south dome. To the left of this ravine is an initial nose-shaped prow, then a long swath of friendly easy low angle slab climbs all situated at the flat sunny Middle Landing.

It is fairly common to rappel from the left belay anchor on the triple belay station ledge system, down 100' to another specifically setup rappel station on a terrace (next to the five other belays that serve the Middle Landing lower routes). From there, rappel again down the ravine 100' to the ground. Beware of climber's below. The rightmost rappel is designed to send you conveniently down the ravine system. Use the rightmost specific rappel whenever the other popular belays to the left are being used.

MIDDLE LANDING (AKA PLAY PALACE)

This wide flat terraced area offers qualitative variety, plenty of 90'-100' leads at a low angle slab with ratings ranging from 5.3 to 5.8 difficulty with some long second pitch leads. This section has some fine thrills that fit a virtual novice lead or top-rope repertoire. Even the old guys enjoy these climbs. There are five belay stations at the 90' mark to allow convenient top-roping for beginner level climbers.

21. **Cosmic Journey 5.3** ★★
Pro/length: P1 6 QD's (100' 5.3), P2 9 QD's (140' 5.3)
A prominent quality prow route. **Pitch 1:** Commence up an obvious steep prow using various

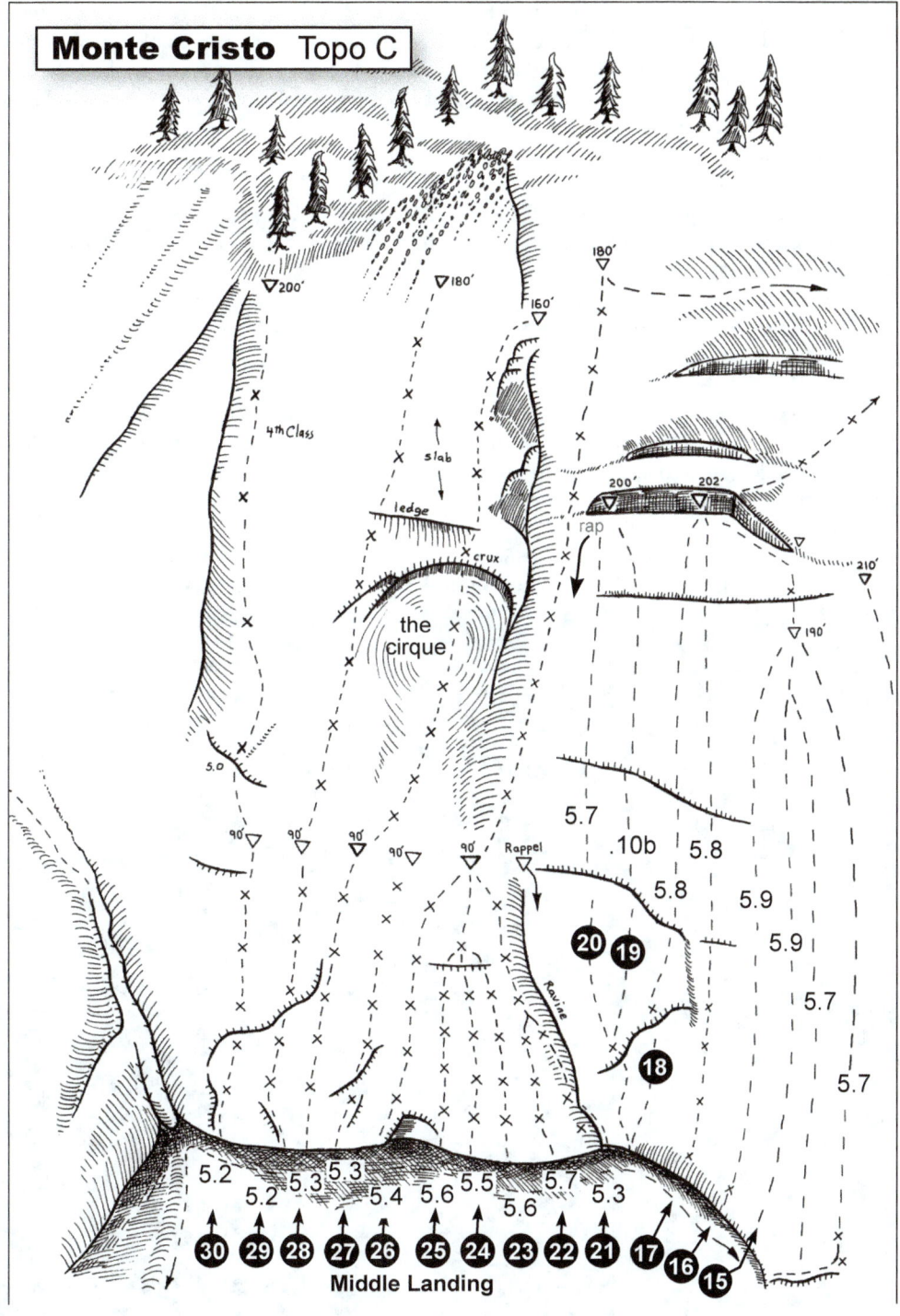

steps and edges. The prow rounds off to an easier angle for the last 25' to the belay station. **Pitch 2:** Let the fun continue by climbing directly above the belay on a subtle rounded buttress (20' runouts) for 180' (passing by the famous triple belay station on your right). The last 40' crosses easy 4th class terrain. From the last belay anchor, walk south and descend the Dark Streak water runnel.

22. Inukshuk 5.7
Pro: 7 QD's , Length: 95'
The opening move is the crux, then some minor smears up near vertical terrain till it merges onto the prow. Finish dancing up the arête to the belay station (same as the previous route).

23. Global Warming 5.6
Pro: 6 QD's, 95'
A nice moderately steep slab route that eases onto flat terrain near the belay station.

24. Raging Sea 5.5 ★
Pro: 6 QD's, Length: 95'
Climb steep steps on a slab passing a crux section (easier on the right side of crux bolt). The fifth bolt is shared with the route to the left. After passing that bolt you land on a wide low angle ledge system (bolt). Continue 30' more to a belay station used by the previous route.

25. Hammerhead Shark 5.6 ★★
Pro: 6 QD's, Length: 90'
A great climb. Start on a steep section of face, smear past a brief crux section, continue up moderate angled slopers till it merges at the fifth bolt, then lands on a wide ledge system (bolt).

MC Slab
Map 2: Midway Landing

Continue 30' more to a belay station used by the previous route.

26. Bronze Whale 5.4 ★★★
Pro: 5 QD's, Length: 90'
A superb easy climb. Start at a slight vertical nook using smears on the left. Continue up a long series of sloped smears till the route eases onto the wide ledge system (bolt). Continue 30' more to a belay station used by the previous route.

27. Black Raven 5.3 ★★
Pro: 6 QD's, Length: 90'
Start up a minor left facing corner on a very low angle slab, then up a series of steep giant steps. When it eases onto a fat wide ledge system, continue up easier slab (bolt) terrain to a belay station.

28. Crooked Finger 5.3 (P2 5.7) ★
Pro/length: P1 5 QD's (90'), P2 9 QD's (160')
A fun run for beginner climbers on the first pitch. The unique second pitch ascends up into a broad rounded scooped out vertical sided rock cirque, but that lead is best for a climber who can deal with an odd crux lip bulge mantle.
Pitch 1: Begin up a very low angle slab, power through a brief steeper section (crux), then up easier low angle terrain to a belay station. **Pitch 2:** Continue up slightly right (bolts) aiming into the center of the rock cirque. When you reach the center bulge in the cirque, surmount the stout lip (5.7 crux) and move up to a flat landing. Continue up a nice low angle clean slab and when the terrain becomes a series of steps angle right to a belay station. Walk off south to the Dark Streak descent runnel.

29. Broken Hand 5.2 (P2 5.1) ★
Pro/length: P1 5 QD's (90'), P2 9 QD's (180')
A fun basic climb reasonable for virtual beginners. **Pitch 1:** Climb up a short very low angle slab until it steepens (crux), moving up slightly right, then continue directly up to a belay station at 90'. **Pitch 2:** Continue up from the belay on a low angle slab until you reach the left edge of the broad scooped out rock cirque. Continue up past its left edge to a brief flat landing, then dance up a nice smooth slab till the terrain eases near a belay station just below the forest.
Note: Scattered gravel lay just above this upper belay station so its best not to climb up beyond this anchor station, but to either exit directly right south onto the rounded crest, and continue south to the Dark Streak Streak runnel to descend.

30. Tour de France 5.2 (P2 5.0)
Pro/length: P1 5 QD's (90'), P2 4 QD's (200')
A good beginner climb for the first pitch. The second pitch involves 25' runout sections. **Pitch 1:** Dance up the initial low angle slab to a minor vertical step (crux), then continue up more low angle slab to a belay station. **Pitch 2:** Continue up over a minor small step, and up easier terrain with well spaced 40' runout bolts on 4th class terrain. The final belay station exists just below a prominent single tree on a small black flat ledge. The upper portion of this climb follows a subtle slightly rounded rock knoll.
Note: There are several brief clusters of rock debris scattered along the cliff top (see diagram) just below the forest. Avoid disturbing both clusters of debris if possible. If there are other persons climbing at the Middle Landing it might help to communicate to each other in advance.

FOUR ROCK LOBES

Looking to the north from the end of the Middle Landing you will see four rock prominence's or rounded rock lobes. This entire remaining northern end of MCS abruptly drops downhill for about 200'. Each rock lobe has a steeper aspect at the lower end of each lobe. Its these steeper aspects that yield a small selection of worthy rock climbs. From the Middle Landing zone walk the forested ridge crest path down hill to reach the next climbable sections. The lobes are described from south to north; the first lobe, the second, a third and then a fourth rock lobe.

FIRST ROCK LOBE

To access the climbs located at the base of the First Rock Lobe descend the trail about 100' then cut in along the base of the lobe. The last three climbs are tucked in a small rock ravine on the left steeper side of the rock lobe. This slab has numerous basic fun routes great for beginner's. Described from right to left:

31. Conscious Haze 5.5 ★★
Pro: 6 QD's, Length: 90'
A quality low angle friction slab ending with a series of large edges in a right-facing corner groove.

32. American Eagle 5.4
Pro: 7 QD's, Length: 90'
A low angle friction slab to a ledge, then delicate smears followed by easier terrain.

33. September Morn 5.3 ★
Pro: 7 QD's, Length: 90'
A series of thin smear moves up into a left-facing corner, then step up right onto easier terrain.

34. Raven's of Odin 5.4 ★★
Pro: 8 QD's, Length: 90'
A nice brief string of thin techy smears on a flat smooth section of the face.

35. Don't Tread On Me 5.2
Pro: 9 QD's, Length: 90'
A fun string of smears and sloped edges, then a steep rounded bulge crux section, which quickly eases as you near the anchor.

Bob M. leading *Seasonal Anxiety*

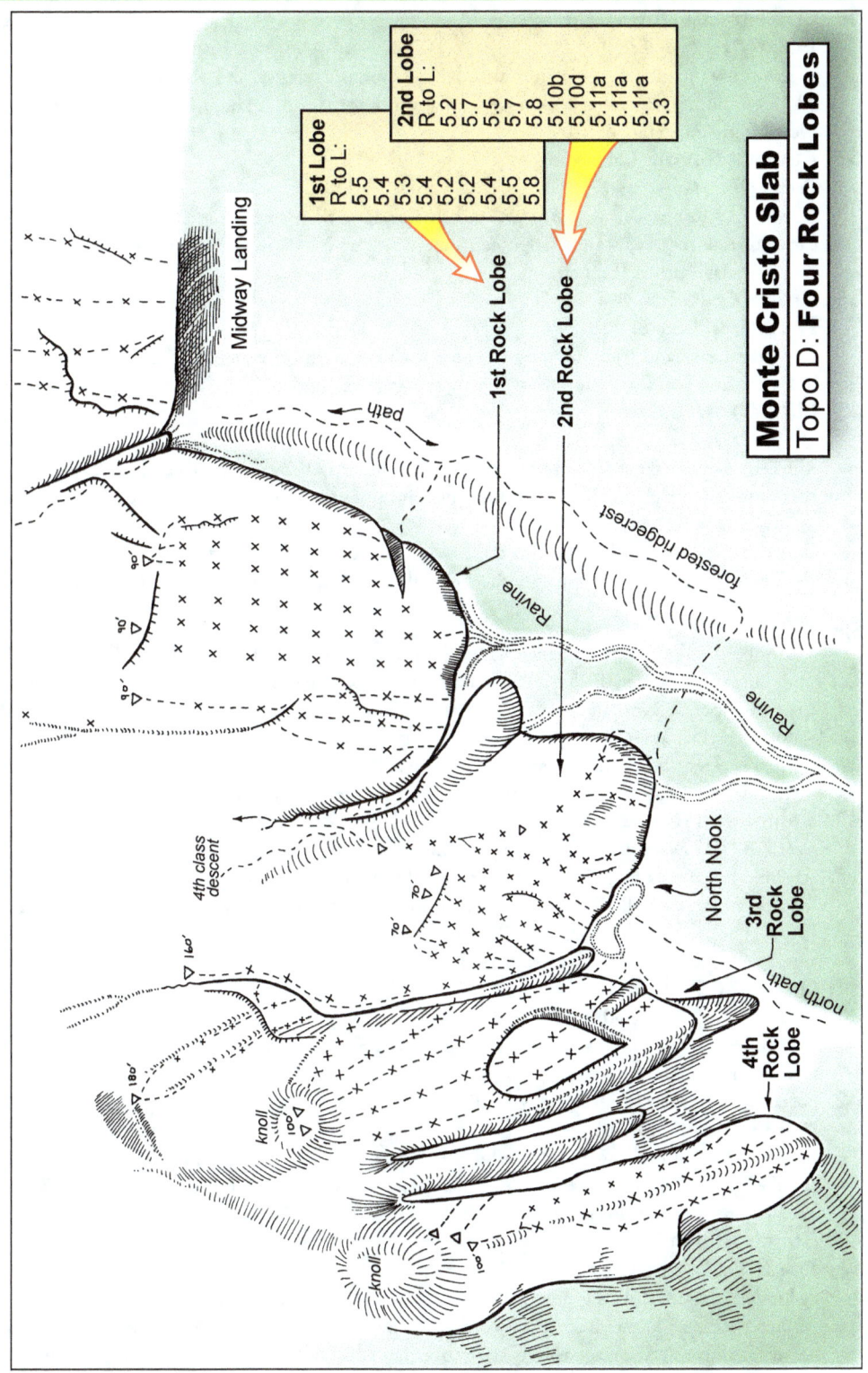

36. **Live Free or Die 5.2** ★
    Pro: 9 QD's, Length: 90'
    A few moves up a slab, a big step, then a brief smooth section, and a series of nice rounded edges on a minor rounded rock nose formation that eases near the belay anchor. Title is the New Hampshire state motto.

37. **Raven's Revolt 5.4**
    Pro: 5 QD's, Length: 90'
    Climb up a minor slab with smears and small edges, then surmount a 4' tall lip, and cruise easier terrain to a flat stance. Then continue up a narrow dark water stained groove another 25' to a belay station. Rappel.

38. **Crows Feet 5.5** ★
    Pro: 5 QD's, Length: 90'
    Ascend smears and friction along a minor rock rib, then up easier terrain to a flat landing. Then continue up a narrow dark water stained groove another 25' to a belay station. Rappel.

39. **Little Crow 5.8**
    Pro: 4 QD's, Length: 90'
    The crux is a briefly entertaining three pocket smear challenge. After the crux it merges into the route to the right at the flat landing and continues up a steep slab to the belay.

    4TH Class Runnel Descent
    Between the First Rock Lobe and the Second Rock Lobe a low angled 4th class rock groove provides an optional down scramble method to walk down off from certain nearby rock climbs.

SECOND ROCK LOBE

This lobe is the next prominence which juts down slope another 100' lower than the First Lobe and lands in an alder thicket. At the base of the lobes steeper aspect is a nice sandy alcove called the Hotspot or North Nook. A fascinating string of high quality power climbs exist here. Walk a forested ridge crest downhill to the base of this lobe and over to the Hotspot landing. This landing area is often sunny and warm, beneficial on cold October days, but a bit extreme if you are there on a sultry hot day in July. The routes are described from right to left for this lobe.

40. **Beginner's Route 5.2** ★
    Pro: 7-8 QD's (max per lead), Length: about 90' to each belay (multi-pitch)
    A viable beginner's first time lead route. Well bolted, and provides a grand tour of the wall for a beginner. Literally starts at the lowest point at the crag, and ends at the top. For **Pitch 1** (5QD's) 5.3, for **Pitch 2** (5 QD's) 5.0, etc. A very brief 12' long 5.5 direct start is feasible via a smear move to reach the standard 5.2 start.

41. **Quasar 5.7** ★
    Pro: 5 QD's, Length: 90'
    Two prominent small pockets on a steep flat face offer a brief technical climb. The route joins into the first pitch of Beginner's Route.

42. **Redneck Knuckle Draggers 5.5**
    Pro: 5 QD's, Length: 90'
    Waltz up a very low angle left trending groove, then dance up rightward on various shaped small edges and sloped pockets, dance through a thin crux smear move, then join into Beginner's Route at its first belay.

43. **Bullah Bullah 5.7** ★
    Pro: 10 QD's, Length: 100'
    A long slab route utilizing one obvious initial large rounded pocket at the start. Get to the pocket, then move up right to a stance, then up left to a sloped stance and make a skinny crux sequence move. A few more thin easier moves lands you at a nice step. Then continue directly

up the face using a variety of smears and sloped stances till it merges with the 3rd bolt on P2 of the Beginner's Route. Bullah Bullah is Australian the aboriginal name for Butterfly.

44. Silk Road 5.8 ★★
Pro: 4 QD's, Length: 60'
Superb route. Smear past several scoops, then smear holdless terrain using slight nuances, then at the final crux make a tricky move up right (or up left) to merge into either next route.

45. Autumn Gold 5.10b ★★★
Pro: 4 QD's, Length: 60'
This is a superb quality friction smear climb with some sequential techy movement. Commence up into a minor left-facing sickle shaped corner. At the top end of the corner the holds disappear, and the technical smear kicks in (crux) on high angled terrain. Dance your way through the tight moves until you reach easier terrain ending at a belay station.

46. Seasonal Anxiety 5.10d ★★★
Pro: 5 QD's, Length: 60'
The ultra classic gem at the north end of the MCS. High angle friction smears, lacking holds, sustained, mentally energetic, with fascinating yet committing sequential movement.

47. Autumn Joy 5.11a ★★
Pro: 4 QD's, Length: 60'
Another uniquely difficult high angle smear climb. Smear up a brief subtle corner 10', then commit to several very sequential moves. Exit the locked in crux moves carefully.

48. Manic Madness 5.11a ★
Pro: 4 QD's, Length: 60'
A shorter smear climb that begins a few yards up the great white dihedral.

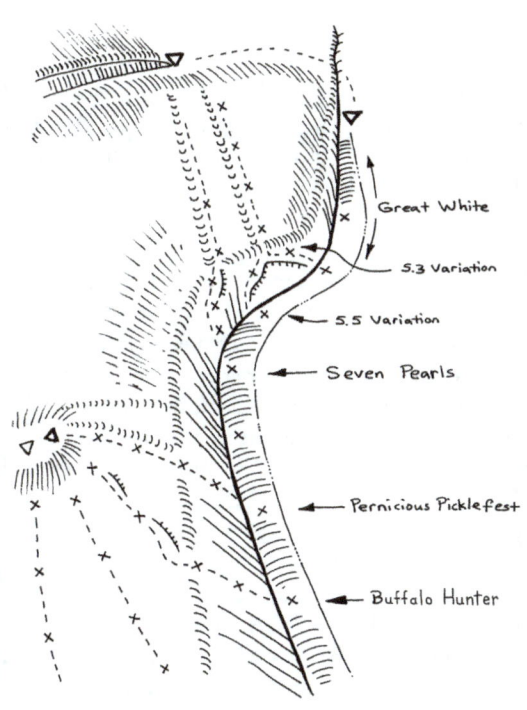

A busy day on *Seasonal Anxiety*

49. Altered State 5.11a
Pro: 3 QD's, Length: 60'
A brief technical smear-fest on steep terrain.

50. Great White Book 5.3 ★★★
Pro: 8-9 QD's, Length: 160'
A very prominent, light toned, deep cut corner ramp system that launches upward from a sandy landing zone. Ascend the dihedral passing a minor crumbly section at mid-height. When the left wall of the dihedral meets a steep cove, it angles up right and becomes a nice light colored fat clean ramp system. To descend: **1.**) climb up leftward to another belay station 30' and walk off around the 3rd lobe in the forest; or... **2.**) rappel (single rope) down to one of several anchors near the top of Autumn Joy.

Chuck on Contrail Conspiracy

THIRD ROCK LOBE
The third lobe is a large rounded buttress immediately north of the deeply cut great white dihedral system. The sunny south aspect of this lobe offers steep techy starts that land on a rounded upper slab. A surprisingly extensive string of superb climbs exist on this lobe (some being way up in the main dihedral). The following routes are described from LEFT to RIGHT (lowest to highest) going up the dihedral as if you are facing this lobe while standing at the sandy landing zone.

51. Forest Fright 5.7 ★
Pro: 7 QD's, Length: 100'
Start on the far left next to a large tree trunk. Step up onto a brief steep face (crux) with sloped holds. You quickly land on a narrow flat ledge facing a big circular donut-shaped amphitheater. Smear up the low angled face to a vertical rock step, surmount the 4' tall step onto a flat landing. Then smear up easier low angled slab to a belay station.

52. Squatch's Travesty 5.8 ★★★
Pro: 7 QD's, Length 100'
An entertaining climb. Ascend a briefly steep face next to a minor rock column. You will land on a narrow flat ledge facing a big circular donut-shaped amphitheater. Smear up the right portion of the slab, angling rightward. Surmount a minor vertical 4' step onto a flat landing. Smear up a holdless long dark water stained groove to a belay station.

53. Barramundi in a Billabong 5.9 ★★★
Pro: 8 QD's (9 QD's if doing the direct), Length: 100'
An ultra quality gem. The great dihedral is initially divided into two grooves at the base in the North Nook. This route has 2 starts (the left direct start is 5.9-*ish* while the right start is a tad easier). *Option 1:* The direct variation start climbs a vertical flat face then merges into the regular route at the 4th bolt. *Option 2:* Climb up the left groove past a brief odd move. Just before a bush step up left onto a steep vertical face, and make a high step exit left onto a stance. Two rounded bulges create two crux friction smear sections. After these bulges proceed up a long dark stained subtle water runnel on a steep holdless friction slab. The route ends on a broad rounded clean rock knoll with several belay stations.

54. Buffalo Hunter 5.10c
Pro: 7 QD's, Length: 100'
Not your casual affair, certainly bizarre, but if you like this kind of stuff, get 'er done. Climb up the dihedral about 30', then step left to the vertical face (bolt). A vertical face has a minor left leaning rail 1" wide. Use a vertical outer fin of a column, layback up, grab an incut (and clip the chain 'biner). Then, a delicate smear kissing moving to stand fully up (use a locking

Monte Cristo Slab ✦ ROCK CLIMBING   99

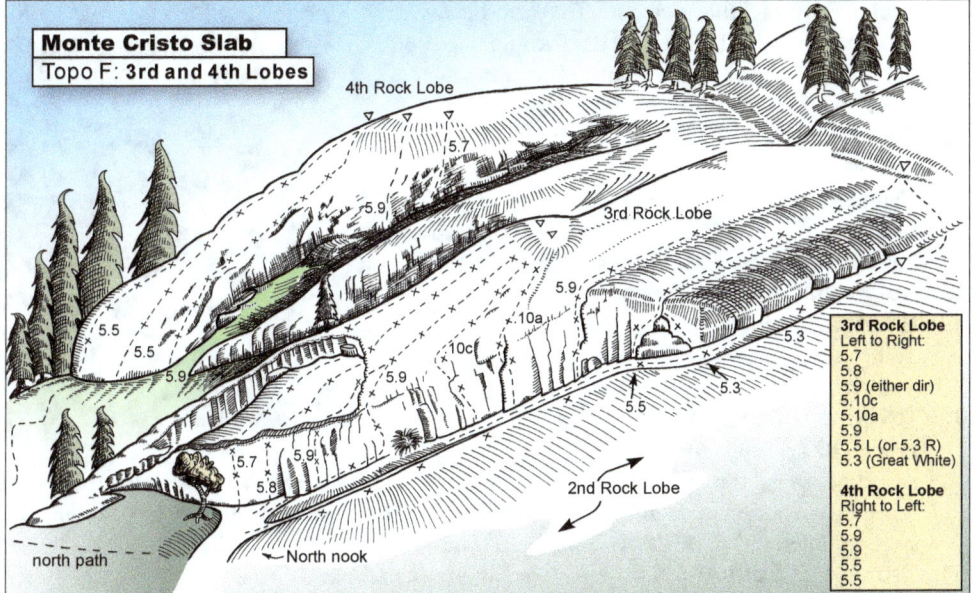

carabiner here). Move left, make the technical crux exit move up onto a steeply sloped stance. Gingerly ascend a series of steeply sloped steps to the belay station on the rounded rock knoll. *Note:* use a locking carabiner on the crux bolt hanger (not on the chain), and don't blow the clip (or you might kiss the slab).

55. Pernicious Picklefest 5.10a
Pro: 8 QD's, Length: 100'
Another odd climb. Dash up the easy dihedral about 40', then step left to the vertical face (bolt). You will be standing below a vertical dark corner system. Layback up to catch an incut, muscle onto a tight stance in the corner, then exit up right to catch an incut wedged block (quite hollow). Another very steep cruxy move to a stance, then more steep, sloped terrain that keeps you focused all the way to the rounded rock knoll belay station. Rappel. (Note: pull downward, not outward on the hollow block).

56. Seven Pearls 5.9 ★
Pro: 11 QD's, Length: 180'
An intriguing climb situated at the dark vertical headwall about ⅔ way up the dihedral. Dash up the dihedral to the ⅔ point, then layback up the incut angled ledges (crux) till the angle rounds off into a long low angle water channel. Dash up this runnel (bolts) to a shared belay station. Rappel with two ropes, or just walk off to the northwest, or to the south (see diagram). *Note:* Be sure to have available 5 QD's for the brief vertical section and beyond, using about six QD's for the lower dihedral. Shares belay with next route.

57. Bookmark 5.5 [L] 5.3 [R]
Pro: 9 QD's, Length: 180'
This route jumps up left out of the dihedral at about ⅔ way up the great white dihedral. Two ways to start this variation (5.5 Left & 5.3 Right) at the crux steep section; both merge after a few moves, then continue up a low angle water runnel (bolts). Rappel over to Great White Book belay, then rappel again. Or walk off to the northwest.

FOURTH ROCK LOBE
This is the final large rounded rock buttress at the far north end of MCS. There are several

entertaining climbs on this rock lobe. To reach this fourth lobe, you need to walk along the North Path for about 50' then cut uphill to the base of this lobe. The routes are described right to left.

58. Slim Pickins 5.7 ★

Pro: 3 QD's, Length: 35'

Unique route. Can be climbed on either the left or right side of the bolts. Just steep enough to keep you feeling on the dicey edge all the way.

59. Norwegian Queen 5.9 ★★

Pro: 4 QD's, Length: 35'

Techy movement with gently sloped holds yet uniquely beautiful in its own special way.

60. Toveline's Travesty 5.9

Pro: 8 QD's, Length: 90'

An odd diagonal traverse climb where most of the holds are steeply sloped to yield a tenuous experience. Start on the right side of lobe. Climb a right trending string of bolts (skipping the last bolt if desired) to a belay station. Rap or walk off.

61. Crowds of Solitude 5.5 ★★

Pro: 5 QD's, Length: 90'

This is the commonly climbed route on the fourth lobe. It starts near the toe of the buttress but on the sunnier aspect, and climbs fairly steep, sloped smears and edges, gradually easing to a long rounded low angle ridge ending at a belay station. Rappel or walk off.

62. Lonely Climax 5.5

Pro: 7 QD's, Length: 90'

The uttermost northern leftmost climb and a variation with a fair amount of moss on it. This starts at the utter lower leftmost portion of the buttress toe. It merges with the previous route on the final 30' of terrain (near the second to last bolt) to the belay station. Rappel or walk off.

OH8

Beta written by Kay Kucera and Paul Cousar

OH8 is a small but conveniently situated road side crag along old highway 8 on the northeast side of Rowland Lake located at the extreme west end of the Catherine Creek syncline. Though easy to drive right past the fractured cliff, upon closer inspection you will find an interesting little treasure of rock climbs scattered along this fairly lengthy flood basalt rock formation. The crag faces west making maximum use of the afternoon sunshine suitable for a fast workout in the early Spring and Fall seasons. The basalt is a slightly grainy textured surface to which rock shoes readily stick, but the routes are deceptive; what appears easy and lower angled is actually surprisingly steep and difficult.

Accessibility and Awareness: Virtually all the rock climbs require some trad gear. Don't climb here if you don't have various cams, stoppers or hex's. The rock is a bit chossy so a helmet is advisable. Avoid walking along the rimtop as this will damage various ecological plants. The Barretts Penstemon is an endemic cliff-dwelling wildflower of colorful purple clustered blooms that makes its home here. Removing cliff dwelling plants and moving talus is prohibited. Most fixed belay anchors are not accessible from above so you must be a competent lead climber to use this place. Owners should keep their dogs leashed or leave them at home. Expect ticks, rattlesnakes, wasps, friable rock and plenty of poison oak along the cliff base. If you are susceptible to poison oak it is best to avoid this site. The rock climbs are listed from right to left as you are walking uphill.

1. **Blind Ambition 5.10b** ★★★
   Pro: 6 QD's, two ½" cams, one each 2" cam, ½" nut
   Thin cracks lead to a pumpy vertical face.

2. **Buckwheat 5.10c** ★
   Pro: 9 QD's
   Same crack start. Two bolts to ledge (runout) then left up smooth face. Finish left over roof.

3. **Just a Freakin' Rock Climber 5.11a** ★★
   Pro: 7 QD's and one each 1", 1½" cam
   Two roofs, one low and one high with a crack.

4. **Ron Love Verly 5.10a** ★
   Pro: 6 QD's
   Technical move in corner, easier climbing above. Has a 5.12b 2-bolt extension.

5. **Hostile Old Hikers 5.9+**
   Pro: 3 QD's, and two each 1", 2", 2 ½", 3 ½" cams
   Follows beautiful hand crack in corner onto ledge; finish up slabby ramp to crack in corner.

6. **Rattlesnake 5.9** ★★★
   Pro: 6 QD's, two 1", one each 1 ½", 3", & 4" cams
   Wide crack start, hard past first bolt then easier above.

7. **Sasquatch 5.11c** ★★★
   Pro: 8 QD's, and one each ½", 1", 1 ½" cams
   Technical, long, and pumpy. Lots of fun!

8. **Tidewater 5.9** ★★
   Pro: 8 QD's, and one each ½", 1" cam
   Cruise past small roof to ledge, then up and right.

9. **Wind Dummy 5.9** ★★
   Pro: 8 QD's and one 1" cam
   Start at Tidewater but climb straight up off ledge.

Dave leading *Carl's Route 5.11b*

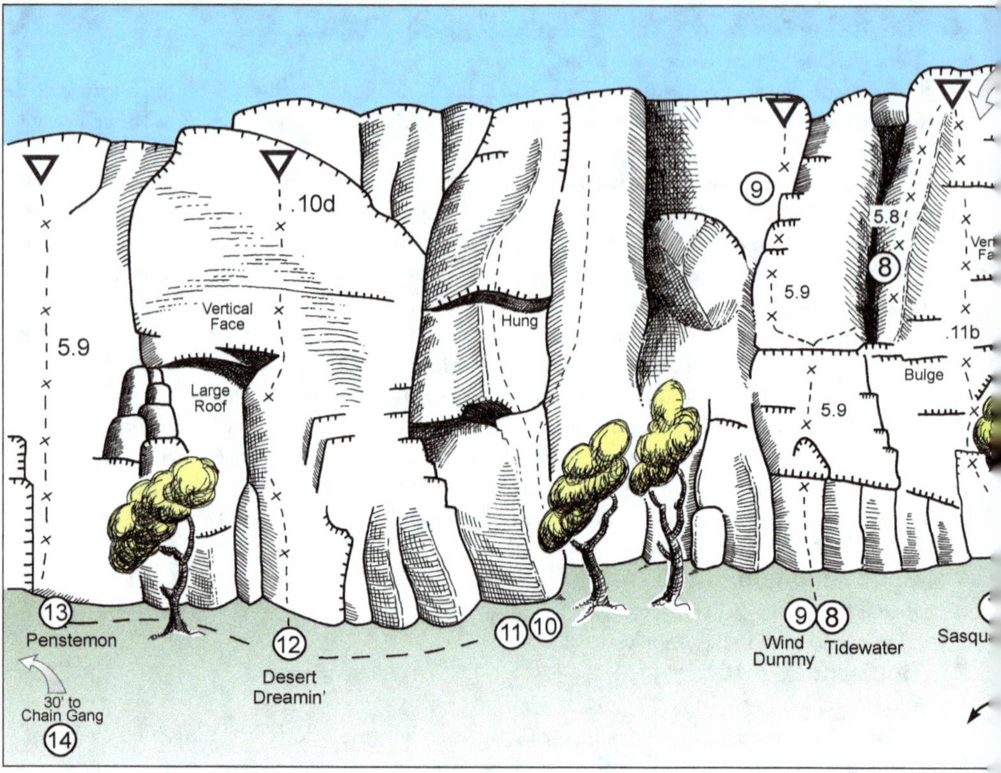
5.9
.10d
Vertical Face
Large Roof
Hung
9
5.9
5.8
8
.11b
Bulge
5.9
13
Penstemon
12
Desert Dreamin'
11
10
9
8
Wind Dummy
Tidewater
30' to Chain Gang
14

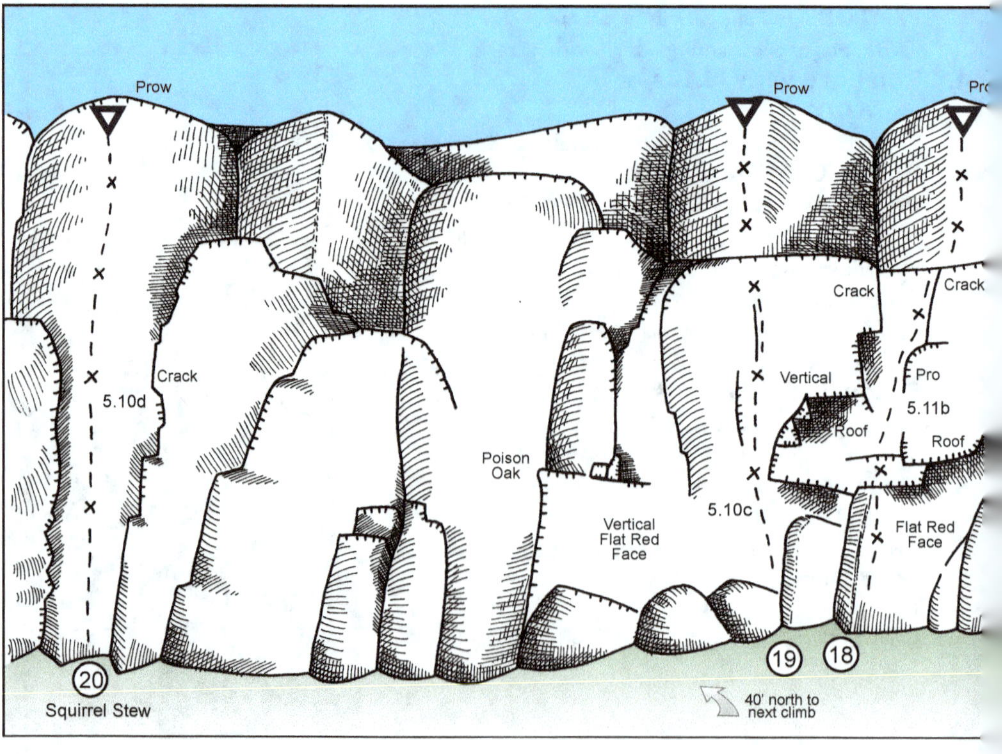
Prow
Crack
5.10d
Poison Oak
Vertical Flat Red Face
Prow
Crack
Vertical
Roof
5.10c
Crack
Pro
5.11b
Roof
Flat Red Face
20
Squirrel Stew
19
18
40' north to next climb

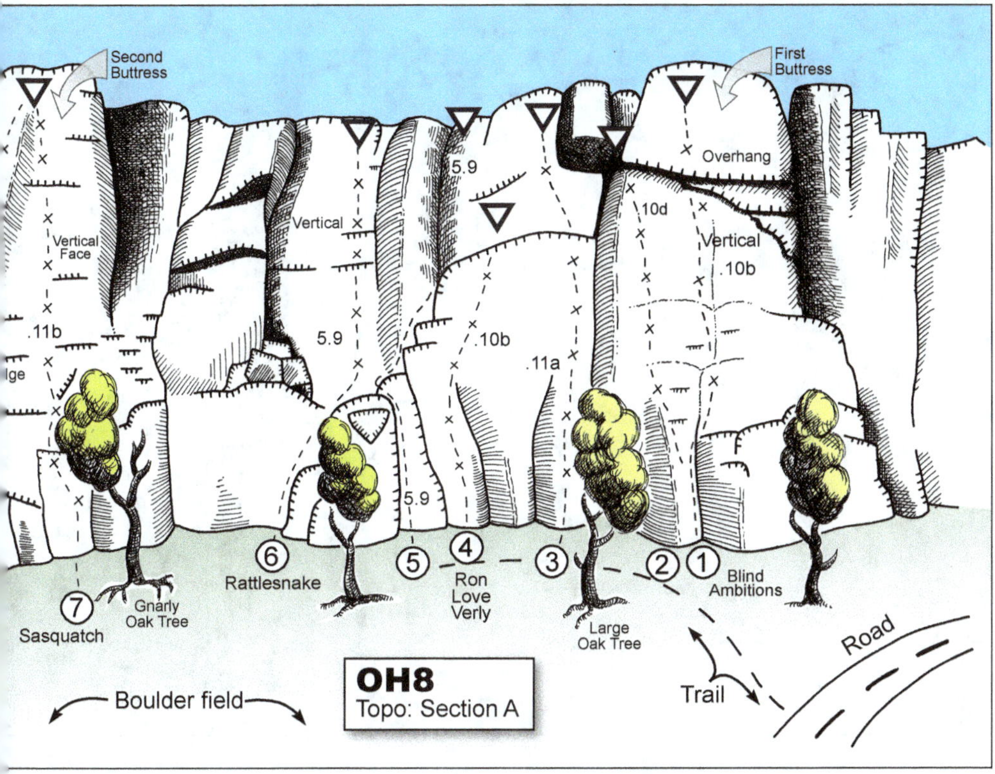

OH8 Crag ✦ ROCK CLIMBING 103

OH8 Topo: Section A

Second Buttress — First Buttress — Overhang — Vertical Face — .11b — Vertical — 5.9 — 5.9 — .10b — .11a — 10d — Vertical .10b — 5.9

(7) Sasquatch — Gnarly Oak Tree — (6) Rattlesnake — (5) — (4) Ron Love Verly — (3) — (2) — (1) Blind Ambitions — Large Oak Tree — Trail — Road — Boulder field

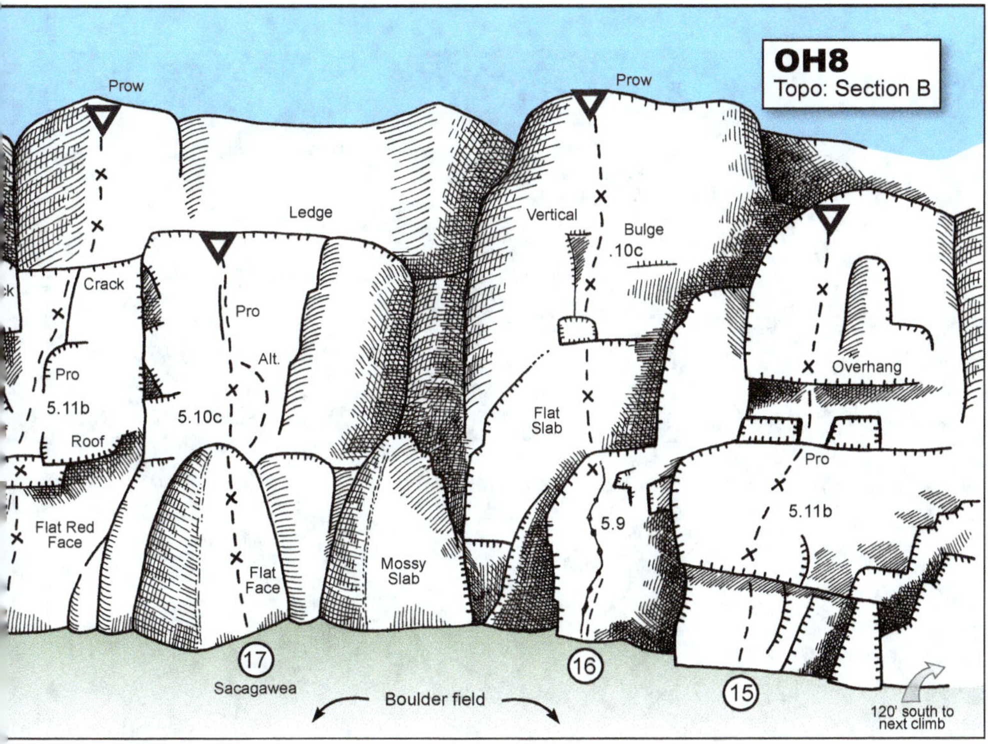

OH8 Topo: Section B

Prow — Prow — Ledge — Vertical — Bulge .10c — Crack — Pro — Alt. — Overhang — Pro — 5.11b — Roof — 5.10c — Flat Slab — Pro — Flat Red Face — Flat Face — Mossy Slab — 5.9 — 5.11b

(17) Sacagawea — (16) — (15) — Boulder field — 120' south to next climb

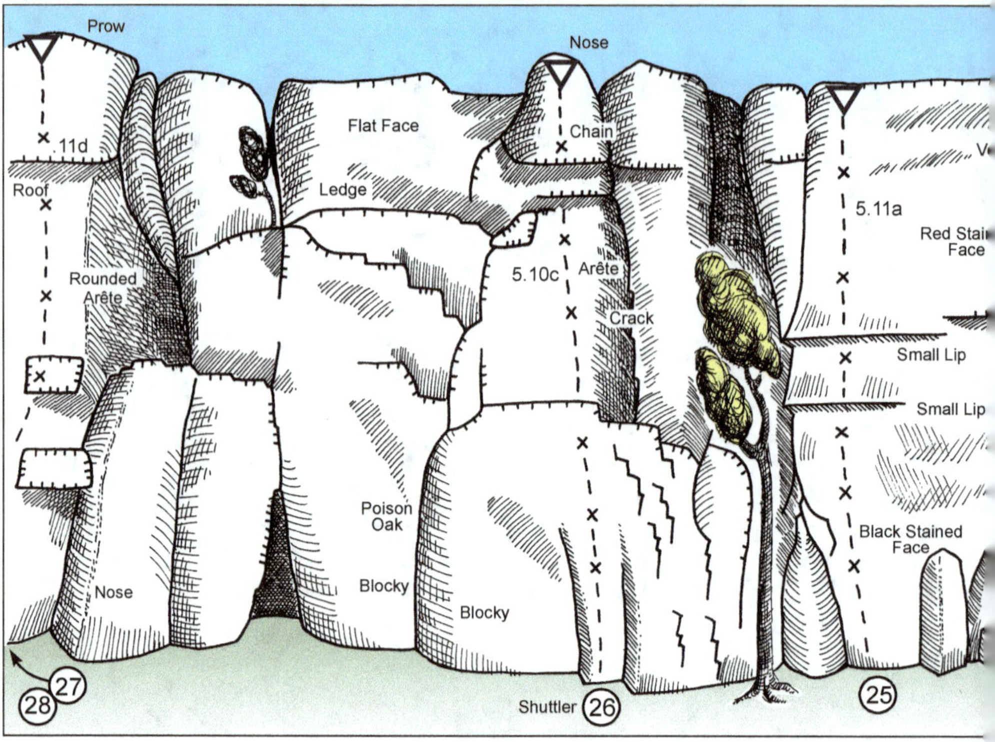

104 COLUMBIA GORGE ✦ OH8 Crag

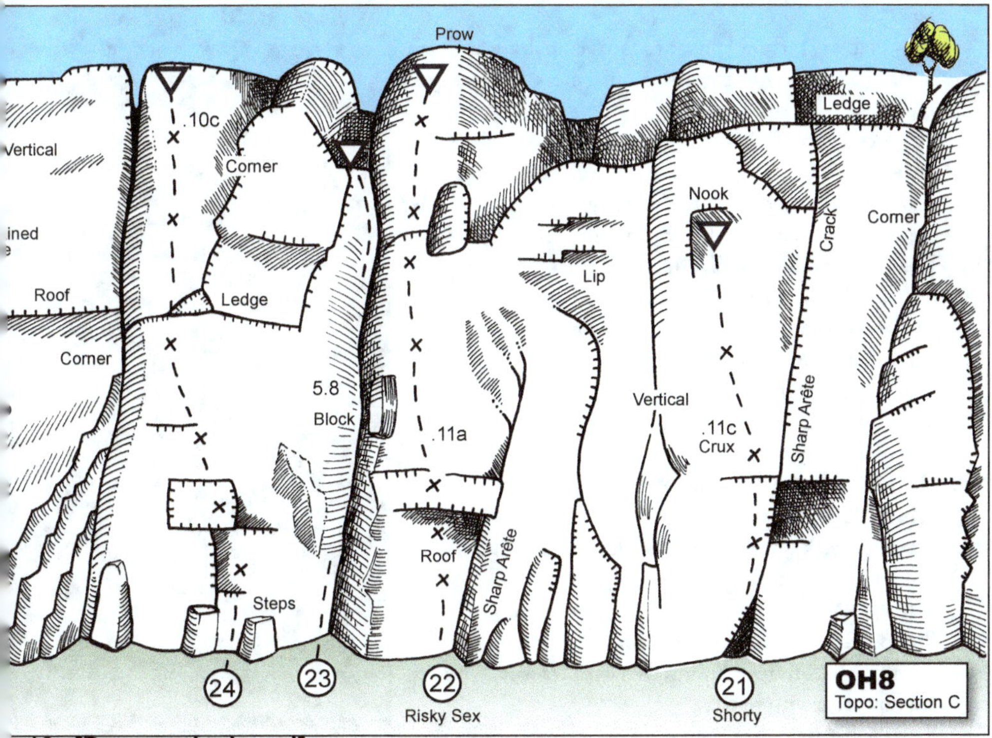

10. **[Decommissioned]**
11. **OCD 5.11d**

    Pro: 4 QD's, and one each ¾", 2", 3" cams

    Climb blocks and cracks, then left up bulging arête.

12. **Desert Dreaming 5.10d**
    ★★★

    Pro: 4 QD's, one ¾", and two 1"

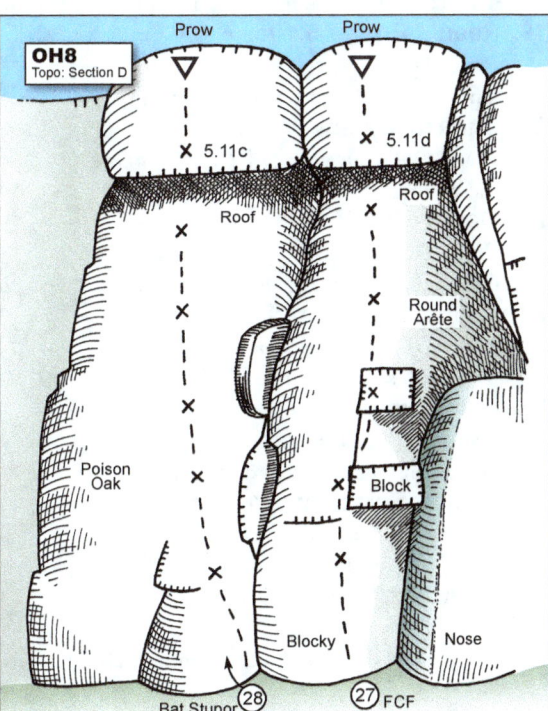

cams

Gray slab at start morphs into faux sandstone at finish. Easier (5.9+) if you traverse right before the last bolt, and then up to the anchor.

13. **Penstemon 5.9+** ★★

Pro: 5 QD's

Start on gray face, do a tricky mantle, then climb past the penstemon at mid-height to more red rock.

14. **The Chain Gang 5.10c** ★

Pro: 4 QD's, one each 1", 2", 3" cams

Chain on second bolt at roof; super fun.

15. **Carl's Route 5.11b** ★★

Pro: 5 QD's and cams to 1"

Start up the left half of a flat gold face, then surmount steep bulge above.

16. **Molly's Route 5.10b** ★★

Pro: 4 QD's and gear to 1"

Start up crack on front face to a ledge, then up a slab to a bulging crux face.

17. **Sacagawea's Route 5.10b** ★

Pro: 3 QD's, one each 2", 3" cams

Start on smooth protruding face with fractures. Avoiding flowers, romp to top.

18. **Paul's Route 5.11b**

Pro: 4 QD's, one each 1", 1 ½" cams

Thin crack to bulge, finish high on prominent prow.

19. **Reed's Route 5.10c** ★★★

Pro: 6 QD's

Unusual movement on angular terrain.

20. **Squirrel's Stew 5.10c** ★★

Pro: 4 QD's, one each ¾", 1", 1½" cams

Increasingly difficult to bulgy prow.

21. **Get It, Shorty 5.11a** ★★

Pro: 3 QD's

Crux at each bolt, excellent movement; tiny test-piece.

22. **Risky Sex 5.11a** ★★★

Pro: 7 QD's, one ½" cam or nut

Two bolts to roof; crux is the final bulge.

23. **Butt Shiner 5.8**

Pro: lots of cams, some small nuts

Discontinuous cracks in dirty corner.

24. **Itchy & Scratchy 5.10c** ★★

Pro: 6 QD's, one ¾" cam

Wander up and left to bolted arête finish.

25. **Open Space Plan 5.11a** ★

Pro: 6 QD's

Initial moves on black rock, pumpfest above in red.

26. The Shuttler   5.10b
★★★

Pro: 6 QD's
Broken columns to smooth face; wild arête finish.

27. Forest Circus Fiasco 5.11d ★

Pro: 6 QD's
Thoughtful moves below, footless mantle to gain right hand roof.

28. Bat Stupor 5.11c ★

Pro: 6 QD's
Easy climbing past questionable blocks, crimpy crux guards anchor above the left hand roof.

29. Spring Breezes 5.10d ★

Pro: QD's
About 50' left of Bat Stupor. Initial bulge with crimps, then eases to 5.6 climbing.

30. The Gap 5.11d

Pro: 3 QD's
Short face, surmount large steep faceted block to anchor.

31. Columbina 5.10a

Pro: QD's
About 10' left of The Gap is this short face line.

32. End of the Line 5.9

Pro: QD's (optional gear to 1")
Very short climb just left of Columbina; last route at crag.

HORSETHIEF BUTTE

The popular Horsethief Butte offers an ideal respite from the liberal amounts of western Oregon rain where you can often find sunny weather crag climbing by the Columbia River.

For rock climbers it offers a tremendous variety of short boulder problems within a series of corridors in the inner portion of the butte. This site offers an effective means to practice and enhance the basic concepts of rock climbing and rappeling. The natural open atmosphere of the inner butte offers easy communication from instructor to climber.

Brief History of the Area:

The Butte is a prominent feature within the Columbia Hills State Park and is a popular site for climbing as well as hiking. The nearby lake was formed when The Dalles Dam was built.

For centuries local American Indians lived near the Butte. The ease of access to the river also provided excellent opportunity for them to catch some of the seasonal migration of salmon for food and for barter. Celilo Falls was the heart of a long established trading region that sustained a thriving community of native Indians from the Wisham, Cloud and Lishkam tribes. The Lewis and Clark expedition camped at a village during their journey west in 1805-1806. Salmon caught near the Celilo Falls provided an important source for trade and barter with other indigenous native tribes of the region. Excellent remnants of native Indian petroglyphs such as *'she who watches'* provide visitors with archeological insight of ancient tribal customs.

Visitor considerations and state park regulations:

- Horsethief Butte has several areas signed as 'no climbing' for cultural resource protection. Columbia Hills State Park has archeological sites including Horsethief Butte which are protected by State and Federal laws. Disturbance and/or removal of any artifact, pictograph, or petroglyph is prohibited.

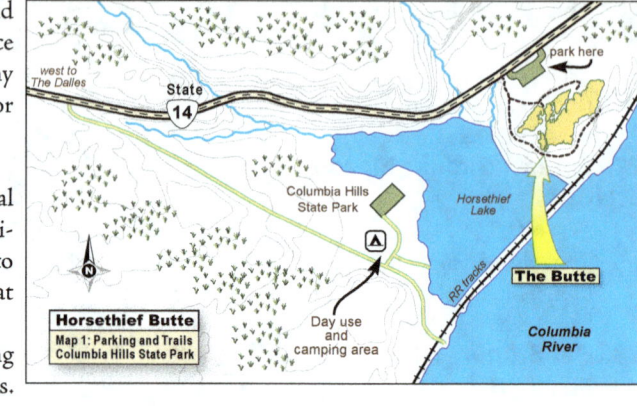

Horsethief Butte
Map 1: Parking and Trails
Columbia Hills State Park

- Expect windy conditions.
- Beware of the occasional rattlesnake. Frequent visitor foot traffic tends to keep most rattlesnakes at a distance.
- Poison Oak grows along the base of several walls. This thick short shrub has seasonal glossy leaves which grow in groups of three per branch and have small white berries.
- Ticks are common in the Spring and Fall seasons. Ticks are quite small so be certain to inspect frequently for ticks if you visit here. There is a plethora of bouldering problems far beyond what this section could possibly convey, but this in-depth treatise strives to detail the greater portion of the well traveled climbs found at the Butte.

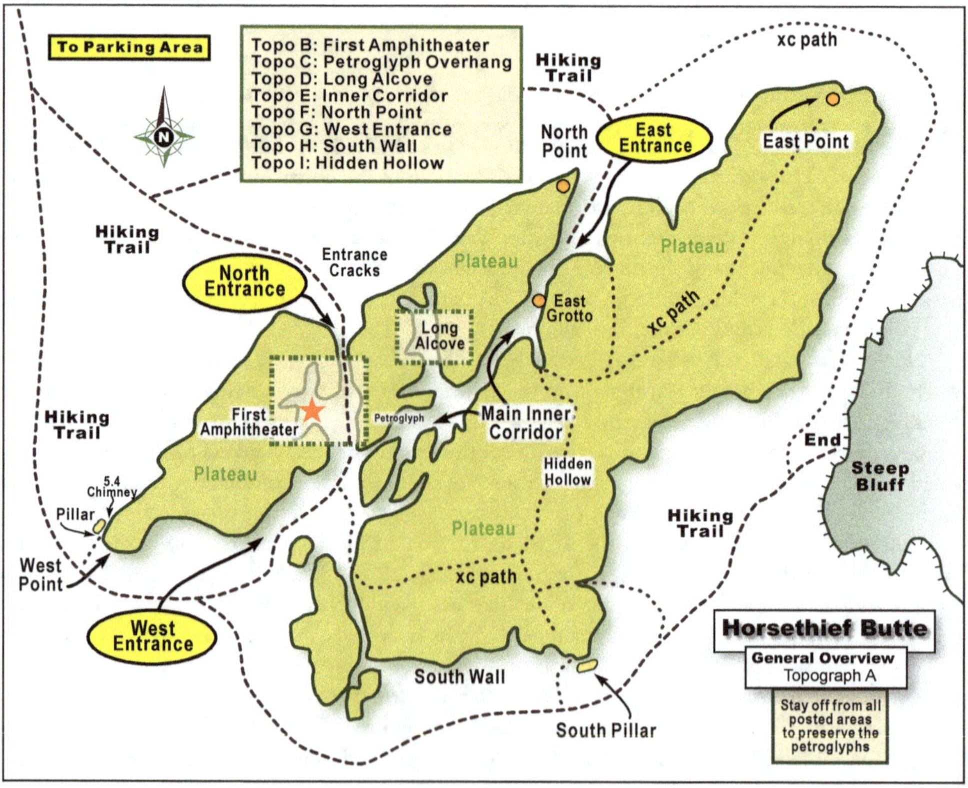

Most of the beta within this particular section includes dual grades, the standard YDS grade (5.9, etc) as if you are going to lead (or top-rope) the climb, and the bouldering V-scale grade, as if you are going to treat the route as a solo bouldering event. A few routes are generally only viable as top-roped lines, while a few very short problems are typically only bouldered. Horsethief Butte is ideal and often utilized for both types (climbing or bouldering) of recreation activity.

Directions:

Directions from Oregon: From exit #87 at The Dalles drive north across the Columbia River bridge on U.S. 197 for 3½ miles, then east on Washington State 14 for 2¾ miles to Columbia Hills State Park. The Butte is located east of the lake at Mile Post 85. Hike on the path south to the butte and enter either via the west side trail or at the 'Entrance Cracks' gap in the wall. Camping (closed from Nov. thru March) is available at the developed facility on the west side of the 90-acre Horsethief lake. Climb safely and enjoy your visit!

ENTRANCE CRACKS

1. **OW & Hand Crack 5.9 (VB)** ★★
   Left of the left prow are several climbs in the shaded portion of the bluff. Both begin up the same crack using edges and steps. From the midway stance, embark up *left* in a wide offwidth crack using a small hidden edge in the offwidth which leads to better edges at the top. The *right* jam crack is closer to the arête. Ascend the lower crack to the midway stance, then embark up right into a jam crack which forces you to use the arête more than the crack. There are several more thin optional climbs just to the left of these two climbs that are fairly difficult.

2. **Jam Crack 5.9 (VB)** ★★
   Great hand and fist jam climb. Start initially in the Left Entrance Crack and punch out left to a short vertical jam crack.

3. **Left Entrance Crack 5.10+ (V1)** ★★★
   This is the left major corner system. Ascend the steep tricky corner by smearing delicately on smooth sloped holds using the thin crack where possible. No such thing as a free lunch.

4. **Arête 5.12**
   Between the two Entrance Crack routes is a technical minor arête top-rope.

5. **Right Entrance Crack 5.10- (V0)** ★★★
   This is the right most (and best) of two classic corner systems known as the Entrance Cracks. Involves long reaches, technical smears, and powerful layback moves using a jam crack. On the right face of this entrance crack is another minor seam that branches up right at about 5.9.

THE PASSAGEWAY

These two under-age minors are together on the east wall of the Passageway just as it opens into the First Amphitheater.

6. **Face 5.10- (V0)**
   A short smooth face ending on a ledge.

7. **Arête 5.10+ (V1)**
   Another short problem.

The next two routes are on the west wall of The Passageway.

8. **Corner 5.8 (VB)** ★
   Layback up the pillar and then stem the corner.

9. **Corner 5.7 (VB)** ★
   Climb up a crack in a corner with a long reach to finish.

FIRST AMPHITHEATER

The following string begins on the west side of the Passageway and curls around the initial buttress counter-clockwise into the First Main Amphitheater. Two nooks (north tree nook and west nook) provide a great series of problems.

Wide Buttress

Tymun bouldering at *Tree Nook*

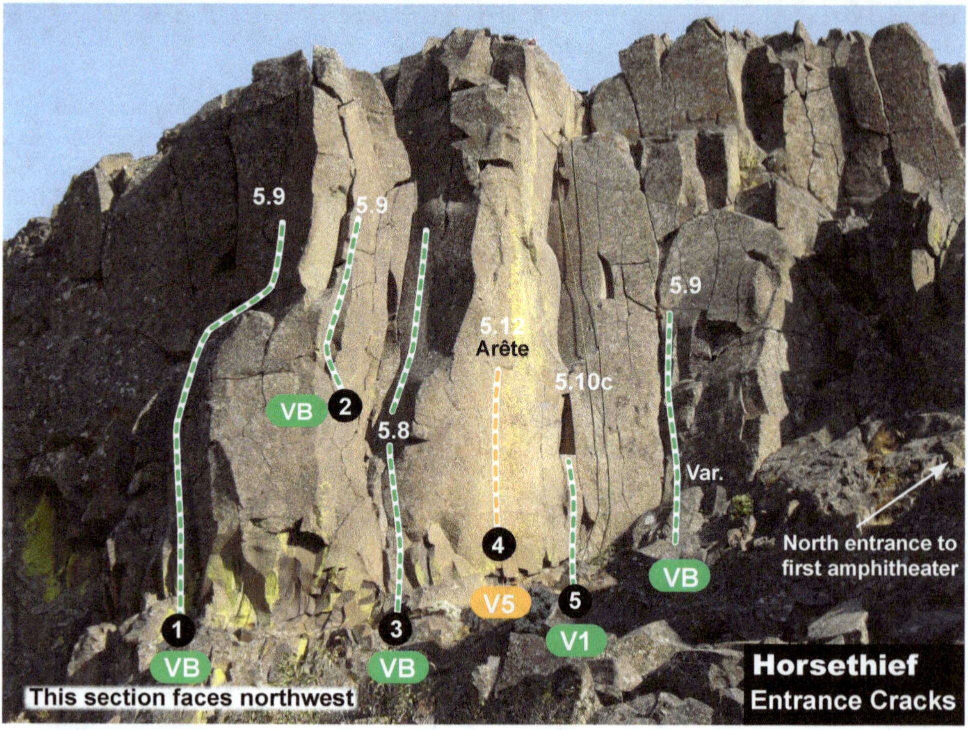

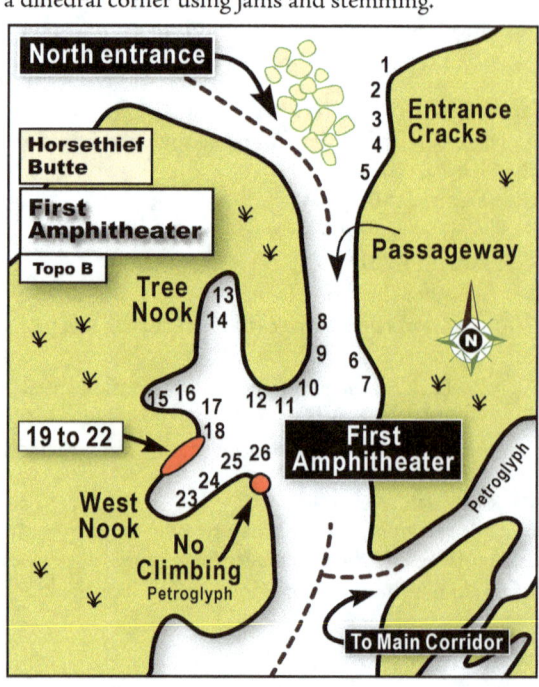

10. Groove 5.10- (V0)
Right side of the buttress.

11. Smooth Dihedral 5.7 (VB)
In the middle of the buttress climb up a dihedral corner using jams and stemming.

12. Discontinuous Cracks 5.10- (V0)
Broken cracks on left most side of buttress.

Tree Nook

A tiny nook with a small tree tucked in the corner.

13. Face 5.9 (VB) ★
Deep in the Tree Nook on the left side before the small tree is a tall face. Climb up the well-featured and cracked patina face to a tricky finish.

14. Crack-Prow 5.10+ (V1)
In the same Tree Nook left of the tall face is a crack/prow. You can jam or bear hug this.

Half Nook

15. Thin Crack 5.10+ (V1)
A stubby. Use the right diagonal crack on a smooth slab.

16. Green Slab VB
This is the outermost nose of a low angle slab.
17. Prow 5.10+ (V1)
Climb the left side of the prow to a mantle.
18. Overhang 5.10c (V1)
Start on a left trending seam. Climb up to a jug and mantle.

West Nook - routes on the right

West Nook offers a great punchy thin traverse all the way to Half Nook.

19. Flake 5.8 (VB)
A great warm up flake climb.
20. Crack Seam 5.10+ (V1) ★★★
This classic line (and the next one) are the central feature of the West Nook. They offer complexity, steepness, and quality great for bouldering or for a top-rope.
21. Corner 5.11- / 5.12 (V2-4) ★★★
A stellar V2 thin crack corner that is much harder than it looks. Using rules staying in the crack will make it V3. Traversing in from the far left then up the central corner crack is V4.
22. Face 5.13- (V7)
Climb the thin face left of the corner using just the small holds on the face.

West Nook - Left routes

23. Low Angle Face VB
This is on the south side of the West Nook. Climb up on jug holds.
24. Face 5.10- (V0)
Climb up through the missing block.
25. Crack System 5.11- (V2)
Start on the jug and climb up the shallow crack to a flake.
26. Arête (CLOSED)
This is the outer buttress with posted off-limits signs informing visitors of the aboriginal petroglyph graffiti.

INNER CORRIDOR

From the First Main Amphitheater walk through a small opening in the cliff scarp (The Narrows). This quickly opens up into the Main Inner Corridor or Grotto. On your immediate left is the Petroglyph Over-

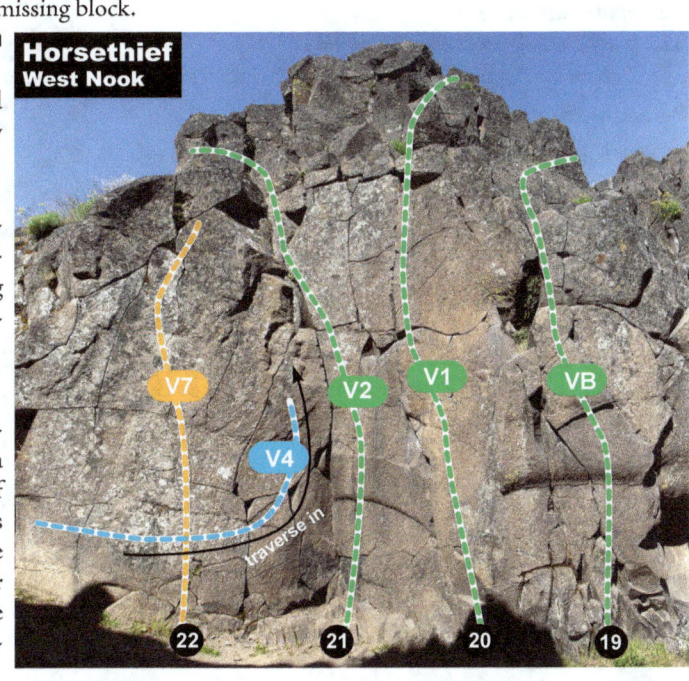

Horsethief West Nook

hang and just beyond (also on the left) is the Sunny Patina. A smidge beyond on the left is the Long Alcove. If you continue walking directly east all the way through this Main Inner Corridor you will pass the Long Wall and exit out the East Entrance to the North Point.

THE NARROWS & PETROGLYPH OVERHANG

The first problems are located on the right (south) wall in The Narrows just as you are entering the Main Corridor across from the petroglyph 'off-limits' sign.

27. Thin Crack 5.10+ (V1)
Jam the crack in the corner.
28. Steep Face 5.10- (V0)
Climb up on fractured jugs.
29. Bulging Prow 5.11- (V2)
A minor prow.
30. Tall Face 5.11+ (V3) ★
A very committing tall boulder problem.
31. Tall Arête 5.12- (V4) ★★
A difficult line with tenuous pinches and smears on the lower half of a tall arête. Lock into each sequence, hold the balance, then slap for the rounded sloper.

Traverse Challenge
32. Narrows Traverse 5.11+ (V3)
Traverse from before #27 passing the tall arête #31.

Petroglyph Overhang (CLOSED)

This is an overhanging inner scoop on the north side of the inner corridor at the narrows. There are posted off-limits signs informing visitors of the aboriginal petroglyphs.

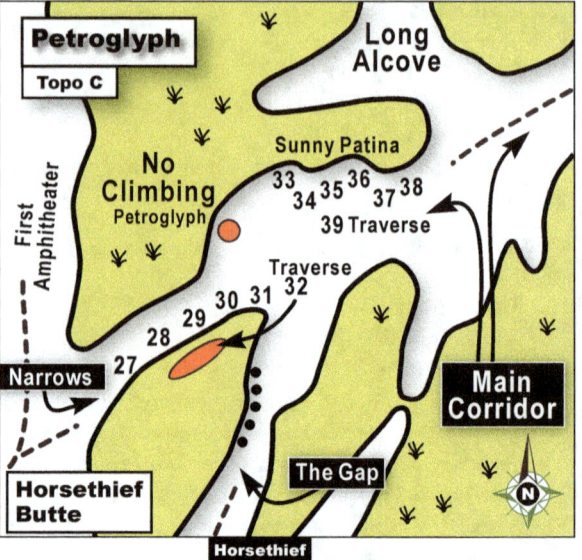

SUNNY PATINA (TOPO C)

After you admire the off-limits petroglyphs wander a few yards east to a great little sunny kink where this fine selection of favorites can be found. Definitely fire up the triangular shaped pocket climb called Arrow Point. In the distant past this line had a small block wedged in the triangle pocket with two ¼" bolts and a slice of metal holding it in place. Now days we all just enjoy the nature of the line without all that old hardware.

33. Arête VB
Short and juggy and a little loose on top.
34. Face 5.10+ (V1) ★
A bump problem over a slight hang on a nose. A bit loose at top.
35. Arrowhead 5.11- (V2) ★★★
Certainly one of the best line face climbs at the Butte. Start left of the corner and balance up using the triangular arrow-like feature with your left hand. Power through a series of wild

Horsethief Butte ✦ ROCK CLIMBING 113

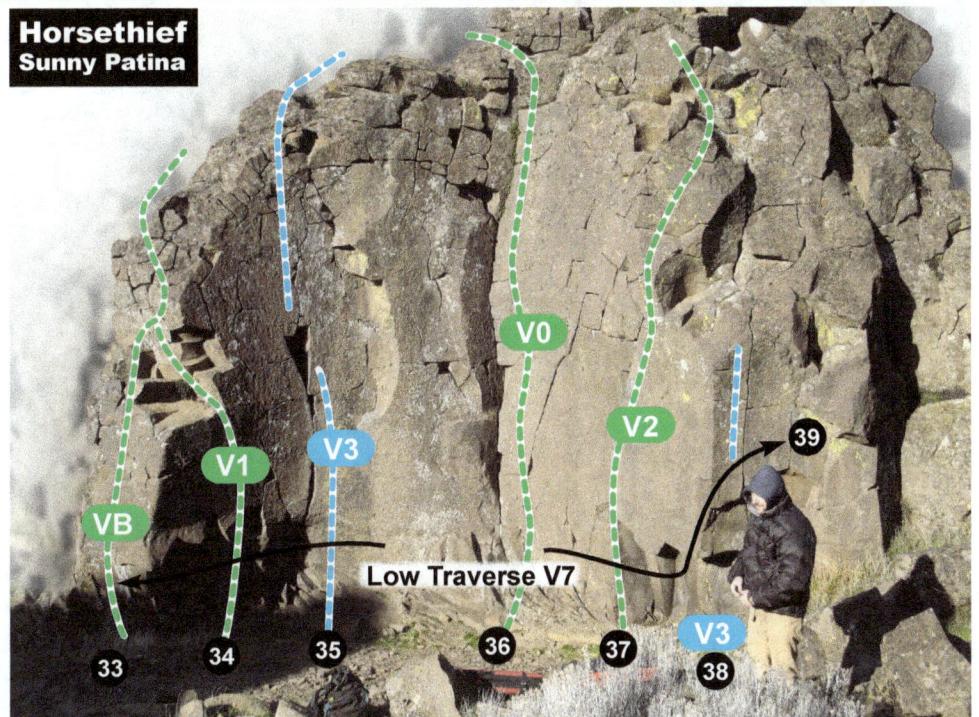

face crimper moves past the triangle, and to slightly loose jug holds at the top. Eliminates are possible also.

36. Cool Corner 5.10- (V0) ★★★
A classic stemming problem in the corner.

37. Thin Crack 5.10+/5.11- (V1-V2) ★
Two thin cracks power up away from the corner. Using both thin cracks work up rightward and trick your way carefully onto the slopers above. Eliminates possible.

38. Arête 5.11+ (V3)
Sit start at hidden undercling and ends with a mantle finish.
The **Triangle of Pain V5** rules on this same arête: sit start to jug undercling, left crimp, triangle crimp in middle of face, left arête, mono-pocket right of the arête, and top to a mantle.

Traverse Challenge

39. Low Traverse 5.13- (V7)
Start on #33 and traverse right staying low to finish on top block 6' right of route #38. It is about V4 if you start and end high, and V7 if you start and end low.

THE LONG ALCOVE (TOPO D)

Walking east along the Main Inner Corridor (or Grotto) past the Petroglyph Overhang you will find a Long Alcove running left (north). This long alcove splits into two directions; the longer portion continuing north while the Veranda cuts back hard west to a very popular cul-de-sac.

Veranda

The Veranda is a stellar slice on the immediate left in the Long Alcove. This north facing and very flat smooth face has become one of the most popular spots to power up. The tick-list of problems here and the quality of the rock (smooth and slippery) combine to provide a string of favorites that will keep you jumping. The first problem starts on the very nose while the remainder is on the flat, steep, north-facing shaded aspect.

40. Outer Buttress 5.10+ (V1) ★
Crimps and stemming lead to jugs and a nice finish. Variations (V2-V3) exist.

41. Arête to Corner 5.10+ (V1) ★
Smear up ramp using a seam, palm the minor arête onto a tiny perch, then finish up a small inside corner.

42. Thin Crack 5.11- (V2) ★★★
Classic boulder problem, and polished from plenty of use. One of the most well-known Horsethief problems.

43. Thin Face 5.11+ (V3) ★★★
Start on the lowest holds 5′ up for V3. A Horsethief test-piece.

44. Face 5.11+ (V3) ★
Avoid the good jug on the right or it will be easier still.

45. Face 5.10- (V0)
Right most very short problem. The finishing block seems kind of sketchy.

Traverse Challenge

46. Long Traverse 5.13- (V7)
Start on Arête (#41) and traverse low for the full length of wall, ending on the top of down climb rocks after Face (#45) and ends at the bush.

Horsethief
Veranda

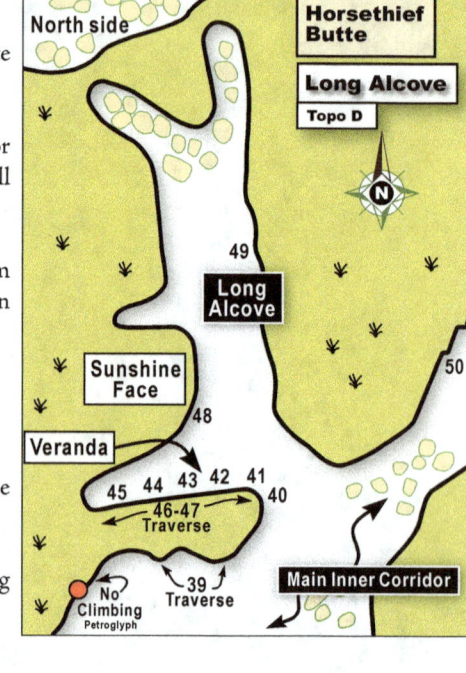

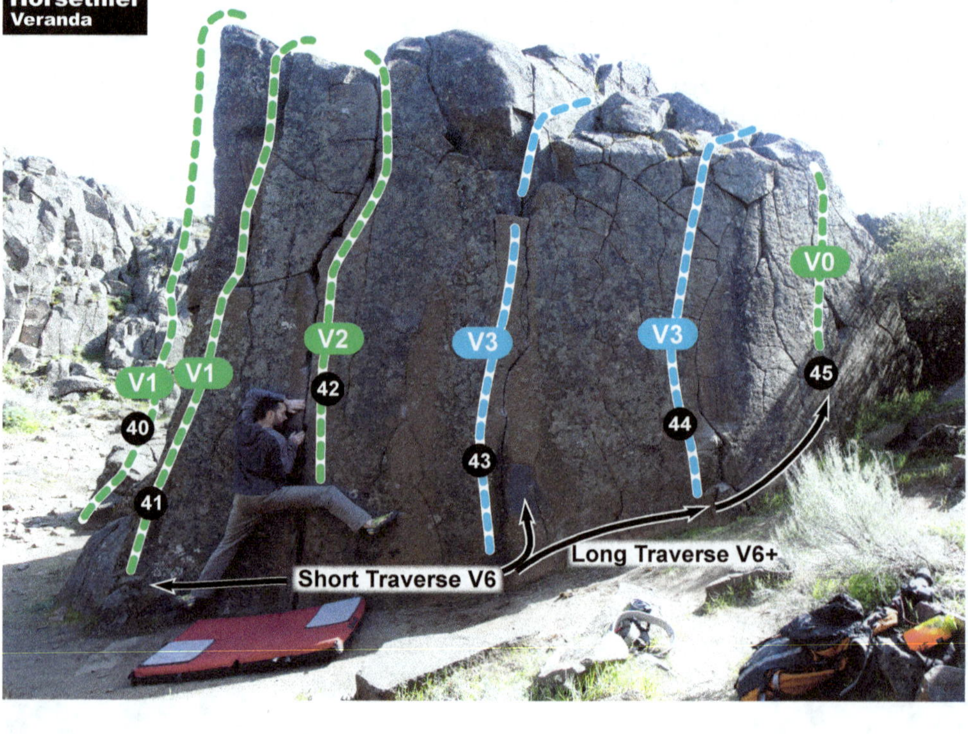

47. Short Traverse 5.12+ (V6)
Start on Thin Crack (#41) and traverse right to Face (#43) and finish up to the top on that route.

Sunshine Face on left side of Long Alcove

In the Long Alcove is this sunny slice of rock which faces southeast and offers several top-rope problems of moderate difficulty on a nice wide and tall section of wall.

48. Main Face 5.6 to 5.9 (VB) ★

Plenty of variables on a steep face quite suitable for top-rope climbing. Even has a few V2-V4 eliminate problems if it catches your eye just right.

East Face of Long Alcove

Walk deeper into this Long Alcove until you are surrounded by poison oak bushes. On your left (west) side of the long alcove is a viable narrow minor arête with a thin left crack and edge-like features. On the right (east) side of the long alcove several fine long lead or top-rope climbs are available with plenty of variations, so do not feel limited to the only over-aged hillbilly listed below.

49. Crack Corner 5.7 (VB) ★

The obvious tall crack and corner climb (multiple exits) on east wall of the Long Alcove.

EAST HALF OF INNER CORRIDOR

Walk further east along the Main Corridor beyond the Long Alcove. The Classic Arête is located on the sunny north side at a kink, while the ever popular Long Wall is on the shaded south side of the Corridor. At the far east end of the Main Corridor you will see the East Grotto Face, while beyond is the East Exit/entrance that quickly leads over to the North Point.

The Classic Arête

The next three problems are on a stellar sunny steep flat face with a prominent crisp short arête. Working the arête is one of the finest problems at the Butte. I never knew that V1 could be so fun till I tried this one. Nice sandy landing.

50. Dull Prow 5.10+ (V1)

A minor round prow as a left exit.

51. Sharp Arête 5.10+ (V1) ★★★

Use the sharp arête and gingerly slide up left into the inside corner, and then dance up on intricate small edges to the large incut hold at the top. Classic Horsethief boulder problem.

52. Seam Only 5.11+ (V3) ★★

Avoid arête on the left at this grade. Involves a long lock-off to a mono-pocket, and then to a jug hold (wobbles but still there).

THE LONG WALL (TOPO E)

The Long Wall is one of the most popular sections of wall at the Butte for top-rope climbing. This portion of wall faces north and on hot days stays shaded while offering a plethora of fine problems, including one of the best traverses at the Butte.

Many of the rock climbs along the Long Wall offer numerous variables, so rather than attempting to solve every idiosyncratic nuance, just get the rope out and set up a top-rope and have at it.

53. Face to Mantle 5.11- (V2)

Immediately south of the Long Alcove on the shaded Long Wall. Down climb off right immediately after the mantle.

54. Thin Crack 5.8 (VB) ★

The striking thin crack with good pure jamming, but is short lived.

55. Green Slab 5.6 - 5.9 (VB)
A long green slab with many variations; some are harder while some are easier.

56. Short Overhang 5.11-/5.11+ (V2-3)
Start sitting and end on ledge…or stand and make it V1 fun.

57. Corner to Ledge 5.7 (VB) ★
Climb the shallow inside corner to an awkward move getting on the big flat ledge, then waltz up the right face to top out.

58. Face to Groove 5.8 (VB) ★★
Great line! Climb the steep face on good holds to finish up a lower angled groove.

59. Steep Face 5.10- (V0) ★★★
Super classic line. Start at the thin crack and climb up an awkward face past missing blocks.

60. Face to Groove 5.7 (VB) ★★
Climb up the enjoyable well-feature face that has lots of cracks and holds until it eases in difficulty in the groove to the top. Beware of a loose thin flake up high.

61. Face 5.8 (VB) ★
Steep face with sequential holds.

62. Thin Block 5.7 (VB) ★
Grab the thin block and climb up to a big edge and finish on the lower angle rock.

63. Groove 5.5 (VB)
A moderate groove on good rock at the far left end of Long Wall prior to the uphill scramble.

Traverse Challenge

64. Long Wall Traverse 5.11+/5.12- (V3-V4) ★★★
A totally stellar boulder traverse can be done along the Long Wall in either direction. Start just west of Corner to Ledge #57 and continue to Groove #63. Likely V6 if staying low for the entire traverse.

East Grotto Face

A good location for top-rope climbing. The rounded slab formation is less than vertical and has many cracks and seams crisscrossing the face at angles.

65. Face 5.7 to 5.10- (VB-V0) ★
Nice blocky climbing on a wide rounded face with a corner in the middle of the wall.

NORTH POINT (TOPO F)

The following routes are quite tall and are on the North Point which is a sharp prow of rock facing out over the East Entrance. Most climbers reach this locale by walking through the entire inner main corridor. A large boulder field is located at this East Entrance.

66. Old Bolt 5.10 (V0-V1)
Cruises up a smooth vertical face (several old ¼" bolts studs) past an upside down triangle roof feature on a flat patina face. Once you power past the triangle into the thin jam crack to a stance, continue up easy steps in a corner to the top. Somewhat loose at the top. About 30' left of this line is a nice short VB (5.9) jug haul boulder problem on a flat face.

67. North Point Crack 5.10b (V0) ★
Climb a steep crack to a stance, and then climb a smear move into a corner system immediately left of the arête.

68. North Point Arête 5.11c ★
Start at the North Crack and launch up right (2 bolts) on a smooth face, and then power out (3 bolts) the severely overhung arête to the top.

WEST ENTRANCE (TOPO G)
There are several options near the West Entrance that are good for learning technique.

69. West Chimney 5.4 (VB)
The West Chimney is found at the very tip of the West Point, and is a nice chimney smack between the main wall and a large obvious isolated pillar. Stem the chimney to the top of the pillar, and then launch up the nice series of steps and ledges to the tip of West Point. Once you top out on the tip you can easily descend southward down a boulder field slope. Or you can continue up another short steep step onto the main upper plateau and walk east to descend

into the First Amphitheater.

70. Tall Corner 5.6 (VB)
A fairly well-used corner climb is available to your immediate south as you are hiking up the slope of the West Entrance.

SOUTH WALL (TOPO H)

To reach the South Wall river face hike past the Western Entrance south eastward around the Butte until you can see an obvious isolated pillar separate from the main massif. Scramble up a boulder slope to the base of the west-facing slot formed by this isolated pillar. These two climbs are on the main wall just to the left of the slot.

To set up a top-rope anchor walk east past the pillar to a steep ravine that accesses the top of this bluff. Or walk south across the plateau from the Main Inner Corridor to the top of the formation above the isolated Pillar.

71. Corner and Roof 5.10a (V0)
A good long climb and best done as a top-rope. Climb a steep corner and power out the overhang directly to the top.

72. Face and Prow 5.9 (VB)
Begin by powering up left using the prow and nearby features and continue to the top.

HIDDEN HOLLOW (TOPO I, J, K)

A quality string of short problems on a rock plateau south of the inner corridor. To reach it, ascend up a big stepped slot from the Inner Corridor at the Long Wall that land on a scenic plateau, then drop down into another low grassy dell.

North side - Hidden Hollow:

The beta details for the north side problems, L to R

(West to East).

VBss High Nose
Begin on low horizontal, then power up over high nose

V0ss Crack
Climb crack

VBss OW Arête
Climb the face with right hand on the arête. The arête has a deep offwidth crack behind it.

V4ss Outer Point
Climb outer point.

V6ss Flat Face
A slightly overhung tall flat-face with a sharp outer edge on the lower left. Sit start on crimps with left initially low on outer edge. Crimps mid-face, yet has better exits holds up high.

V4ss Face
Thin face problem immediately to the right of the previous line.

V3ss Low Bulge
At east end of Hidden Hollow. Sit start a short low bulging overhang using just the round arête.

V2ss Crack/Face
A short crack corner that is overhung. Climb mostly the deep V-shaped crack corner.

V0ss Shorty
Shorty round bulge with crimps.

South side - Hidden Hollow:

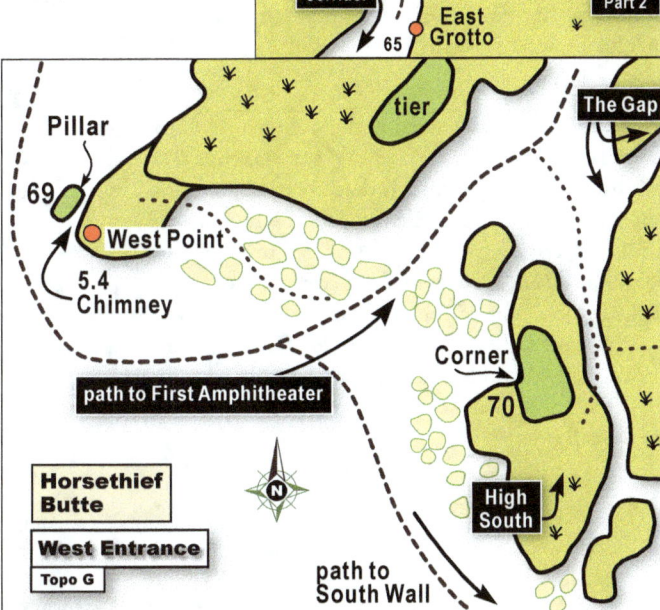

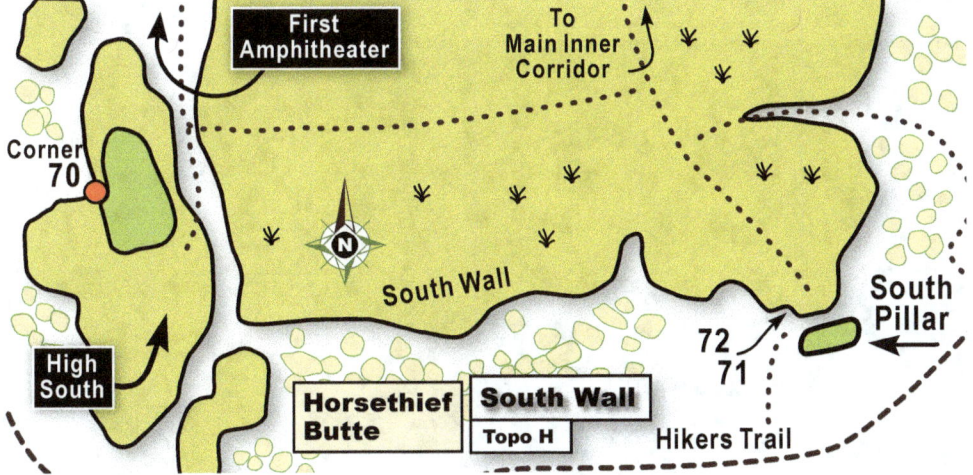

The beta details for the south side problems, L to R (East to West).
V1 Outer Arête
Climb the left-leaning arête of wide flat face. Left hand is on arête, right on crimps.
V0 Face
Numerous thin cracks and edges crisscross at angles on a nice wide flat face.
V0ss Jugs
Jugs on a short face.

A gap of about 30' to next problems.
VBss Jugs
Jugs on a short flat face.
V2ss Crimps
Short low sit start using crimps and left prow, but marginal smears for feet.

HH PLUS

This is an extension of the Hidden Hollow (Part 1 & Part 2). This "plus more" zone extends as a northward deep long trough that eventually dumps out onto the north slope talus field. Here you will find a select string of unique boulder problems to spark the quest. A series of short crimp lines and/or juggy highball power lines beckon (see topo).

The HH+ Part 1 first deep low grassy zone has a brief pack of VB-V0 problems (one is V-hard).

The HH+ Part 2 yields about 3-4 problems, some a bit on the tall side.

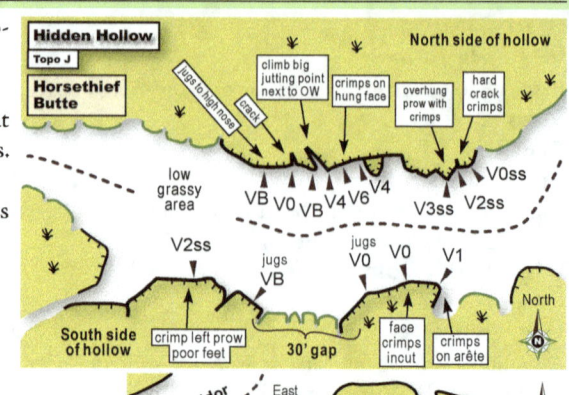

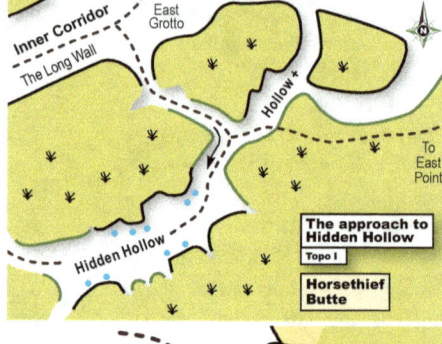

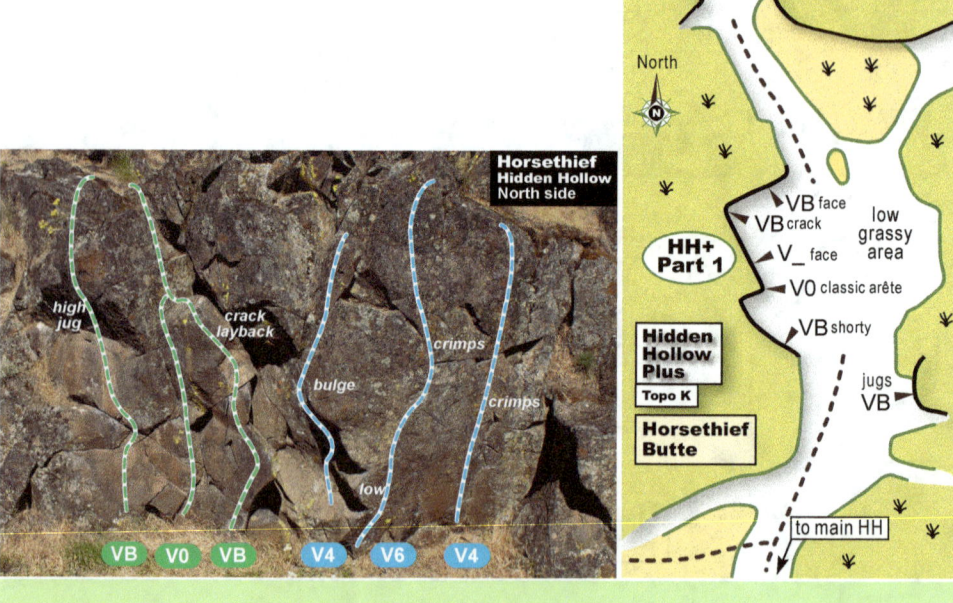

Alternate Cragging Options

Though few of these crags will be on your primary list, the following select crags do have appeal. Some are popular for all the odd reasons (ultra convenience like Salmon River Slab), some are much less popular, and some are superb quality crags but lightly utilized (like Hunchback). Yet all are viable crags to have on your future 'go to' list for a day of rock climbing.

MOSQUITO BUTTE CRAG

With a name like 'mosquito' it must be good. This site offers a small but fine selection of climbing opportunities from 5.6 to 5.11, and adequately fits a general theme suitable to most climbers: quick access, a nearby camping area, and a nice lake for swimming. An idyllic weekend retreat.

Mosquito Butte Crag (aka Trillium Crag) is situated on a lightly forested rounded rock knoll. The crag is an eroded short steep little bluff composed of grainy textured Tertiary andesite from an old lava flow. Climbing routes offer steep knobby holds or small edges for crimping.

This secluded west-facing bluff is situated in the High Cascades and offers a climbing season ranging through the entire summer from mid-May to October. The primary nuisance you can expect is the pesky mosquito during early summer. The bluff is about 40' tall but yields a fine selection of short rock climbs from 5.6 to 5.11. Not every single climb is described in detail here (some other fairly clean climbs exist in the general area). This small bluff has been utilized as a rock climbing site for well over 25 years. A short rock wall on the east side of this rounded butte also may yield 6-8 additional potential rock climbs, but has only seen minimally use to date. Enjoy the scenic nature of this site; do not litter, and maintain the quality of this site for future generations. This crag is best for small teams but not suitable for large groups.

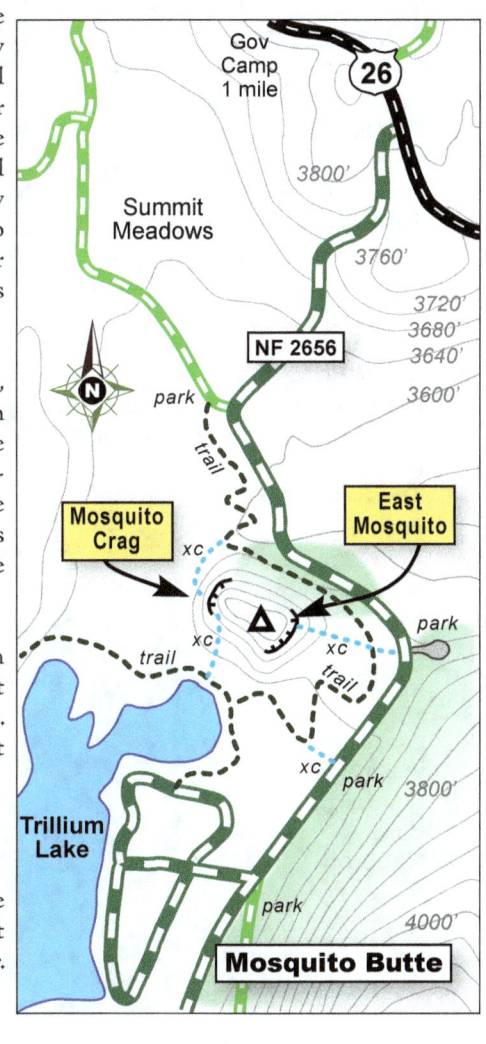

Directions:

Drive east from Government Camp on U.S. 26, and turn south on NF 2656. Park near the Trillium Lake Campground and walk to the north end of the campground, then follow a well-maintained round-the-lake trail. Near the northeast edge of the lake angle up toward a small bluff but angle around to its lower west side to access this small crag. Alternate approaches exist.

1. **Classic Arête 5.10c** ★★★
   A superb arête climb. Power start under an overhanging nose of rock. Reach around left then continue up using pockets and the arête. Ends on pumpy sloped holds near the top. Exit left along the rim to the anchor.
2. **Cool Crimps 5.10b/c**
   Quality face climb with a load of fun crimps.
3. **Pockets 5.8** ★★★
   Great route with sloping pockets (crux) at the start on a steep face, then ends by using the left edge near top just before you reach the anchor.

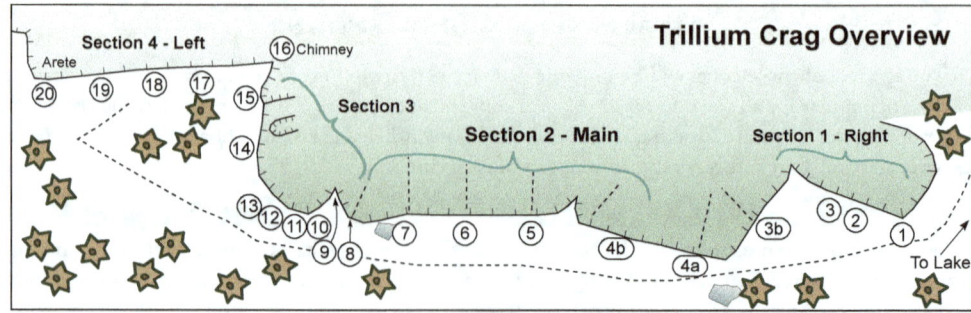

Trillium Crag Overview

3b. **Mosquito 5.7** ★
On left flat aspect is a vertical short six bolt route (crux is first moves).

4a. **Easy Slab 5.3**
Big pockets and holds. Four bolts.

4b. **Short Arête 5.3**
Very short arête. Three bolts.

5. **Fun Slab 5.7** ★★★
The standard popular route and a good introduction to the crag.

6. **Fun Run 5.7** ★★
Vertical (and slight bulge) for the first portion of the climb.

7. **Two Small Lips 5.7** ★★
Two variations on the lower part of this climb. Both are nearly identical in difficulty but most people enjoy the right variation. Fun climb.

8. **Minor Prow 5.8**
Located on the right face of a deep wide corner system. Starts up a steep slightly hung section but quickly eases.

9. **The Ravine 5.6**
Pro to 3"
Wide corner system (a bit mossy). Pro can be found on left side and in small cracks.

10. **Classic Tall Prow 5.8** ★★★
A roman nose rock feature that is an enjoyable surprisingly steep face climb.

11. **Nubbins 5.10b/c** ★★★
Great climb that starts up a slight bulge then dances up plentiful

small chickenhead nubbins on a very steep face to the anchor.

12. Crimper 5.10d
★★★

Power up the initial jugs then crimp the remainder of the overhung moves in a timely fashion, then gingerly exit up right onto small knobs on the final slab.

13. Crack 5.11a
Balance up an odd steep crack in a slight overhang till it eases some.

14. Rock Horn 5.11a
Ascends a vertical face busting over a lip onto a steep prow on a tall rock horn (TR).

15. Steep Face 5.11c/d
A very steep face climb that ascends up the wall immediately right of a vertical off-width corner.

16. Fat Crack 5.9
Pro to 4"
Obvious gutter ball mossy off-width corner system that is slightly hung near the top.

17. Right Crack 5.9
Pro to 3"
A overly mossy thin crack next to the chimney corner system. The right most thin crack.

18. Center Crack 5.9 ★★★
Pro to 3"
This is the area classic and a must for every hunter who enjoys climbing a steep face using a variable sized thin crack on a flat face. The middle crack.

19. Left Crack 5.8 ★★
Pro to 2½"
Long left crack system that angles up to a belay near a large tree. Several bolts keep the last part of the climb reasonable.

20. Cool Left Prow 5.8 PG ★★
Pro to 3" including cams (4" cam if you have it)
A great steep arête face climb on the far left side of this flat wall. Climb over two slight bulges to a stance. Wrap a very long sling around the large fir tree at this stance, otherwise it is a heady unprotected move to the belay anchor.

HUNCHBACK WALL

The Hunchback Wall is an excellent rock climbers haven offering good climbs on a vertical 100' high wall composed of andesite rock. The technical nature of the rock climbing routes tend to make the place primarily suitable for experienced hard core face or crack climbers who are well honed at long, stout, sustained climbing. The site has a plethora of steep rock with flat face sections that often make very powerful leads ranging from 5.10 to 5.13-. The cracks luckily clock in at moderate ranges from 5.9 to 5.11 but are generally long and sustained in nature (and often very wide). The crag is convenient in its near proximity to Portland (1 hour drive) and has paved road access to the parking site.

Hunchback Wall is nestled quietly in a tall wonderfully serene Douglas fir forest locale, sitting amongst tall 180' fir trees, never getting the direct blazing hot sunshine as other crags do. A gentle breeze generally keeps the place comfortable even on hot summer days (we have been there even when its 90°) when other places are simply too muggy. This is a place where the sounds of nature predominate; no highway noise, and no boom box noise; instead you will find a quiet setting designed for those who relish quiet back woods climbing while still seeking high-end technical enduro rock climbs.

Leading Technicalities:
The face routes are very technical and highly demanding of skill. This type of andesite has some fluted vertical features, or a pattern of box-shaped very flared closed seams on a flat face that require entire relearning a new spectrum of technique just to master the seam flares which are so prevalent. The crack climbs tend to be very long, sustained, and usually wide (2" to 12"), and sometimes quite flared. This mix makes for some really entertaining highly skilled climbing with a full range rack of gear. The popular sections to date are generally the left (north) end of the Notre Dame Wall, and the impressive South End Amphitheater overhanging alcove.

A Brief History:
The site was initially explored by Don Gonthier, Craig Murk and friends in the early 90's. Craig and Don referred to the place as the Hunchback secret. Upon arrival during their first exploration of the crag they were impressed with the potential scope of the massive wall. They recruited several buddies, but kept the place in general secrecy. Some additional early partners were Clif and Justin. Don also invited several other folks to the cliff to join the adventure. Some of the friends in this original crew cut the original rough path all the way up to this wall, using a deer trail for minor portions of the approach hike. They climbed a few routes, partly rap cleaned 1-2 other lines, and rappelled down other sections of the bluff. The initial team though parted ways soon thereafter, and the place sat quiet until late 2010 when higher grade level of rock climbers found interest in the place. That crew found

the Hunchback Wall to be a superb crag to fit their expectations of power climbing. More recently another young generation of climbers have begun tackling HW anew.

Route development:
Route development requires patience because the cracks and face options are long and tend to be a bit mossy and dirty in places. Often the route will be much harder than it appears, so if it seems like it might be a 5.10- anticipate it being a 5.10+. The stoutest potential for face routes at Hunchback is probably about 5.13-, and so far even the thinnest sweeps of rock seem to be quite climbable for dedicated power climbers. Fixed gear (bolts) are a common necessity if you plan to develop a new rock climb at Hunchback Wall.

Use the midway terrace with caution if climbers are at the base of the wall. Though the sloped terrace is quite grassy, there is some loose rock material which can jeopardize folks standing at the base of the wall. Most climbs are designed to end below the lip of the main cliff, thus avoiding the mossy, gravelly steep dirt slope of the midway terrace. By placing the anchor on the steep face 10'-15' below the terrace it avoids displacing excessive amounts of dirt and moss and keeps the terrace in a virgin like state. Stay off the upper tier wall entirely; though it may be tall and appear visually appealing,

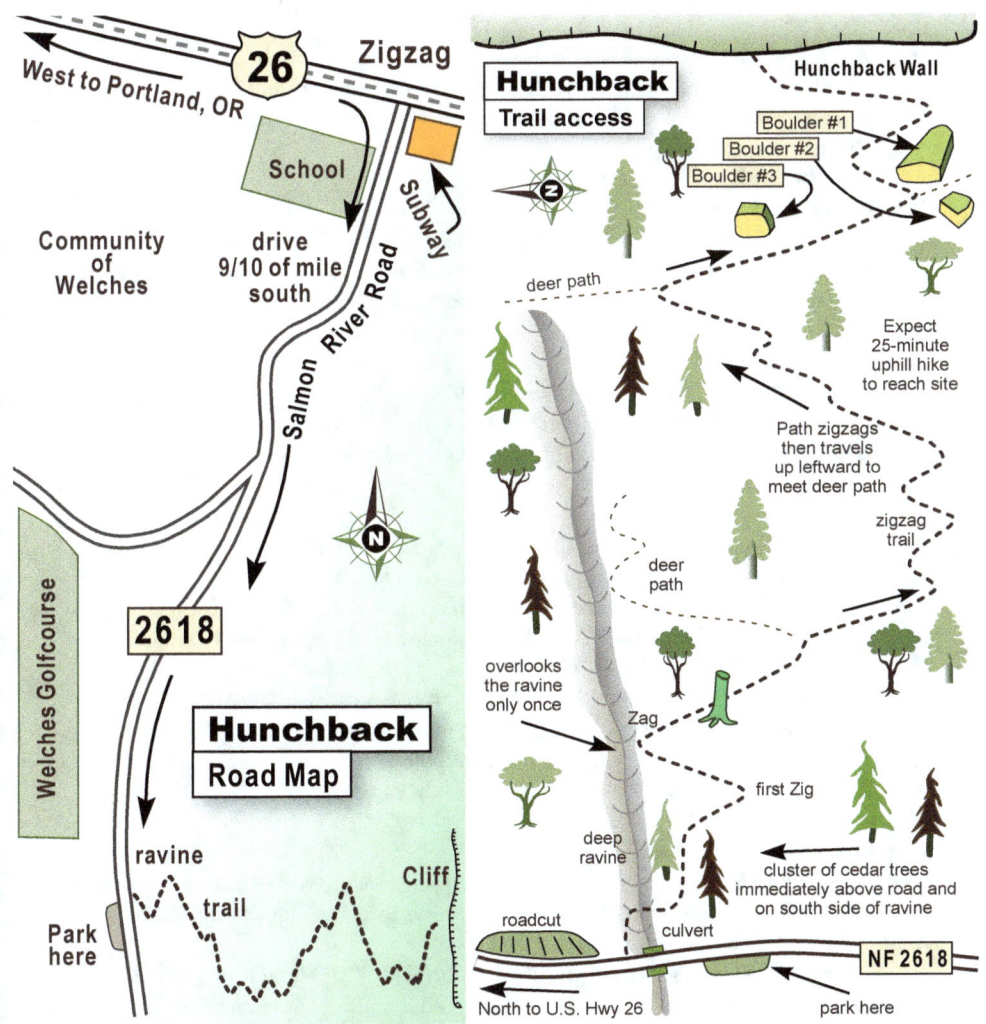

significant loose rock would be a potential hazard to climbers using the main lower wall.

If climbing on the upper tier beware of other climbers who might be at the base of the wall. Those persons hiking up to the midway sloped ledges to set up new projects will need to remain in close contact with their partners below so everyone safely steps back from the locale of your new project (loose rock risk). The vertical upper tier cliff is an impressive steep headwall buttress reaching an additional 100' higher above the lower 100' of main cliff that climbers use, so if you're climbing on the upper tier keep aware of other people down below you at the ground level.

Directions:

Drive east on U.S. 26 from Sandy, Oregon till you reach Welches. Turn south at the Subway store onto Salmon River Road (NF 2618). Continue about 9/10 mile south passing a guardrail on the right and a small rotten roadside bluff on the left, then a deeply cut water ravine exists also on the left. Park immediately on the west side of the road at a minor pullout. Step into the dry waterless ravine for a few yards, then angle up right onto the south slope into a grove of cedar trees. A faint path begins there and zigzags gently uphill, and gradually steepens for the remainder of the hike. The uphill hike is 25-minute approach time to reach the base of the wall so pace your hike well to avoid a sweaty over exuberant experience getting up there.

The crag is split into several sections; the north Notre Dame, and the South Wall.

NOTRE DAME - NORTH SECTION

This very long main wall travels from the Central Ravine northward and gradually fades to lower angle mossy sloped sections of minor bluff at the far north end of the main wall. The beta is described left to right (from north to south).

1. **Critical Conundrum 5.10b/c ★★★**
   Pro: 9 QD's, height 70'
   Climb out an initial crux overhung bulge, up a brief short slab, then up through a vertical second crux (bulge on your left), and up another brief short slab. At a slight overhung lip, power up onto a vertical final face on a minor prow that has incuts and positive holds all the way to the belay. Rap from belay.

2. **Tilting at Windmills 5.9**
   Pro: Nuts (to 1") and Cams (to 2.5"), height 70'
   Climb a prominent crack corner system (5.8) to a small midway stance (also used by next route), then bust out left over the crux bulge into the upper quality crack system.

3. **Metamorphosis 5.11c/d ★**
   Pro: 9 QD's, height 70'
   Start up initial easy small edges over the first bulge (5.8), then power over a second larger (crux 5.11d) overhung bulge. Continue up a rounded low angle prow (5.8) to a small flat stance (recompose your energy here), then power out a brief crux overhang (5.10c) up a vertical prow with incut edges to a high belay. Rappel. Note: 5-bolts on lower; 4-bolts on upper section.

4. **_____ P1 5.7, P2 5.8 [?]**
   Pro: __", height 40' (P1), height 70' (P1 & P2 total)
   Right angled crack system starting at the foot of a notable buttress. **P1:** Climb the crack to a very large midway ledge (belay). **P2:** Climb a short steep deep corner to another ledge belay. Rappel. Note: Route 4b is an alternate start leading up into the same double cracks [5.9?].

5. **Mothership Supercell 5.11a/b ★★**
   Pro: 4 QD's, height 40'
   Step into first bolt from the right, then climb overhung face up past a giant gas pocket. Top half is delicate left handed side pulls, then easier exit moves to a large sloped ledge (belay).

6. **Meister Brau 5.6 ★**
   Pro: gear to 3.5" (or clip bolts), height 35' (P1), height 70' (P2 total from ground)
   Climb a short fun fat offwidth crack to a very big ledge and belay. Continue up the fat offwidth

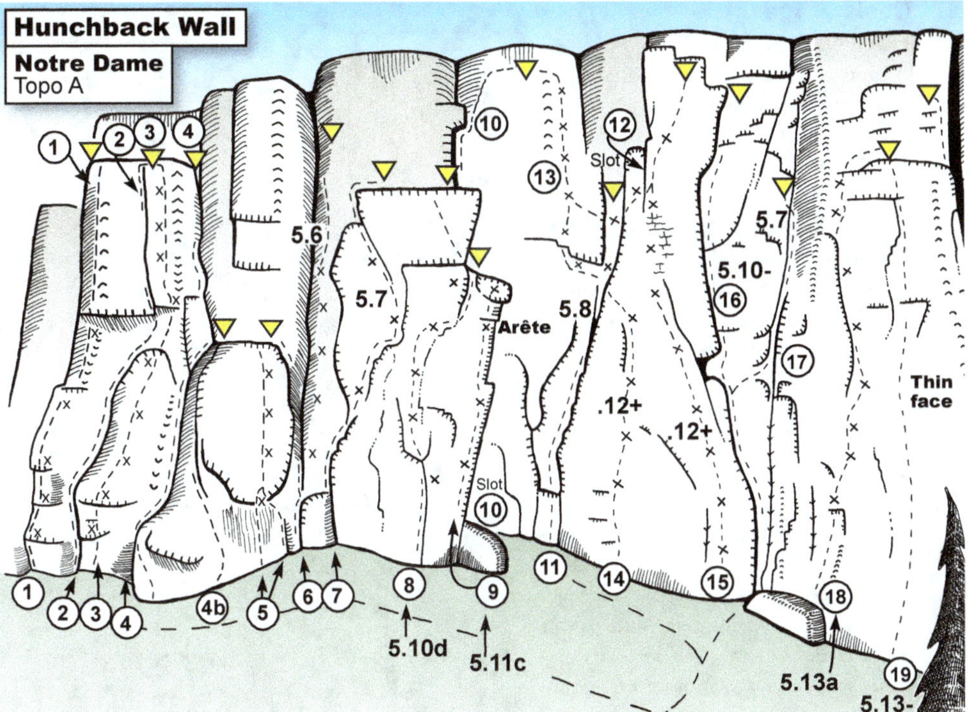

Hunchback Wall

Notre Dame
Topo A

corner system to another higher belay. Rappel.

7. Mirage 5.7 ★★
Pro: gear to 2"
Climb initial step, then (bolt) tricky right trending tiny ramp to stance (bolt), then up left via a thin face and crack to big ledge and belay. Rappel.

Hunchback Map 1: Notre Dame

8. **Oasis 5.10d** ★★
   Pro: 5 QD's height 45'
   A thin techical face climb that stays sustained all the way to the ending on a small perched ledge. A quality route in a forested oasis. Shares same belay anchor with the next route.

9. **The Tallest Pygmy 5.11c** ★★★
   Pro: 4 QD's, height 45'
   The prominent and stellar overhung wild arête ending on a small perched ledge. Shares the same belay anchor with the previous route.

10. **Lord Frollo 5.10a**
    Pro: .5" to 5" cams and nuts, height 65' (upper belay)
    Deep corner (5.9) crack offwidth system immediately behind the wild overhung arête. Climb up till it exits left at midway point to a belay. *The full length lead deal option*: continue up and power out a crumbly roof (5.10a) then up a short small crack to another higher belay.

11. **Axe with a Passion 5.8** ★★
    Pro to 3" including cams, height: 65'
    Start up onto a small stance, then climb up right on a thin jam crack passing a crux. At the first roof (bolts) the crack widens to a chimney. Finish up the chimney (bolts) to the belay anchor. Note: AWAP.

12. **Abby Normal 5.9** ★
    Pro: same gear as the Axe plus 3 more QD's, height 70'
    This extension launches off from the last bolt on AWAP and steps right out onto the vertical face and finishes to the anchor for the 5.12c.

13. **Peloton 5.11b/c**
    Pro: gear same as Axe (plus QD's)
    Climb AWAP, then at midway bust left (at 2nd AWAP bolt it's 5.11) and climb past a small lip up a vertical face. Note: If you move left at the 3rd AWAP bolt it's 5.10+.

14. **The Magician 5.12+** ★★
    Pro: 6 QD's, height 65'
    A fasinating technical route with very thin crimps. This face route merges left onto the AWAP crack at mid height.

15. **Magic 5.12+** ★★
    Pro: 9 QD's, height 75'
    Prominent flat buttress formation near belay anchor. A powerful superb face route that begins on a broad face immediately left of S&E and launches up a flared crack on the vertical upper buttress face. Thin technical holds for a 15' long crux section before easing slightly to better holds

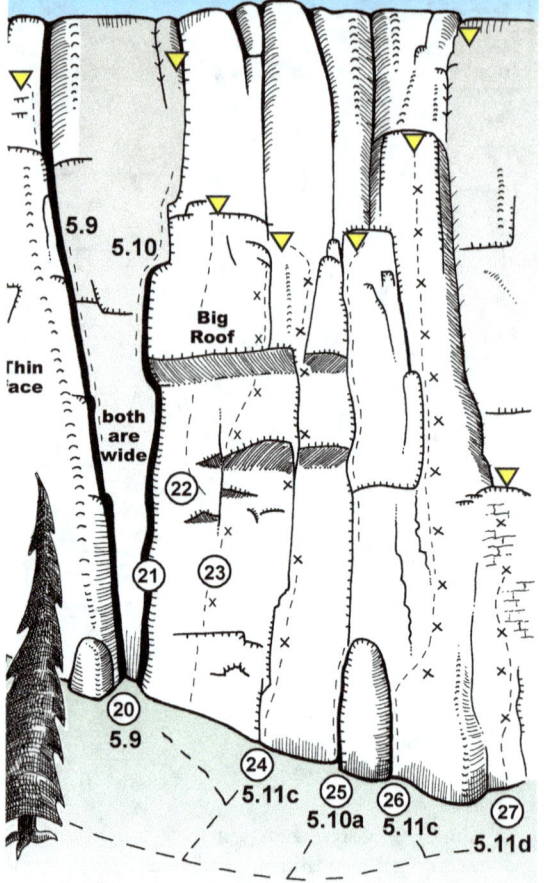

above a series of small lips. Continue up the final moderate terrain to the anchor.

16. Slanted and Enchanted 5.10b ★★
Gear to 4" including cams (optional to 5"), (Singles up to .5 inch, triples 1 and 2 inch, otherwise doubles), height 65'

Climb up the leftward angling crack to a good rest stance. Power over a steep crux flared slot, and continue up past several more small lips to an anchor. Crux is wide, but the upper portions are nice hand jams to a technical face finish.

17. Esmeralda 5.7 ★★
Gear to 2" mostly nuts and TCU's, height 55'

A nice fun corner crack system that starts at the same as SE. March about 20' up SE, then bust off right into the crack and climb this to an anchor. Takes excellent bomber gear placements. A first class route for sure.

18. Quasimodo 5.12d ★★★
Pro: 8 QD's, height 60'

A burly techy thin face climb that starts with a stunning 4.5' long reach off a flake. Then very tricky balancy movement, followed by a snappy final crux at the lip where it is quite deceptive to line up for the final sequence.

19. _____ 5.13-

Pro: __ QD's

Another superb quality technically stout face route, one of the hardest routes at HBW.

20. **Gypsy Dance 5.9** ★

Pro: .5" to 6" cams, Nuts to 1", height 90'

Nice long offwidth jam crack that angles up leftward on steep terrain. Good pro and mostly moderate 5.7 climbing except for a short crux section at the upper last part.

21. **Archdeacon 5.10c**

Pro: .5" to 7" cams, Nuts to 1", height 90'

Ascends a very wide vertical corner system. Eases at mid-height, then steepens again in a deep easy slot corner on the upper portion of the route. Rappel from a high belay.

22. _____ 5.12+ [?]

Potential over the left part of the large roof (well...maybe).

23. _____ 5.13 [?]

Pro: 6 QD's, height 60'

A superb technical power crimps face climb that goes through two large roofs.

24. **Hangin' with the Hunch' 5.11b/c** ★★

Pro: 7 QD's, height 60'

On the immediate right side of the double roof is a thin seem. A tough climb with powerful moves passing two roofs. The last portion eases but has a tricky exit to the anchor.

25. **Murky Waters 5.10a** ★★★

Pro: gear to 4" (includes cams), height 60' (P1)

One of the original routes established by the crew way back in the 1990s. A fine long technical and occasionally flared crack system with a belay at the mid-point on the cliff scarp. Rappel. The P2 section to cliff top is quite dirty (though it's been led to Zeno's belay).

26. Zeno's Paradox 5.11c ★★
Pro: 11 QD's, height 75'
A stellar technical climb. Start up the right side of a small pillar, then step onto the face and finesse through a very techy crux section till it eases at a flared crack. Prance up the flared crack using mostly nice edges and round features to a small perch below a minor lip (the Murky Waters route anchor immediately to the left). Step right (crux) onto a vertical face and send a double arete face that offers unique box-shaped flared seams for hand and foot holds.

27. Persistence Is Futile 5.11d ★
Pro: 5 QD's, height 40'
A short 40' very oddly techy climb on very flared box-shaped surface textured rock. Layback, then smear, layback then smear. Considered to be a unique challenge.

28. Plaid's Pantry 5.10b/c
Pro .5" to 6" cams, Nuts to 1", height 80'
A long crack with a prominent large ledge about 35' up, then continues up a long wide slot crack system to a belay near the top of the cliff. A midway belay and upper belay exist.

29. **Phoebus 5.10- / .11a** ★★
Pro: .5" to 6" cams, Nuts to 2", height 80'
Mixed gear/bolt free route. Climb initial part of the previous crack route to the ledge, then embark up right (bolts/gear) on a long face section with occasional gear placements.

30. **Achilles 5.9** ★★
Pro: .5" to 6" cams, Nuts to 1", length 60'
A steep cool jam crack that punches over a small lip, and continues up a steep crack section on a high rounded rock pedestal ending at a belay anchor at 60'. Wide pro at top. Rappel.

31. **Djali 5.10b/c** ★★
Pro: .5" to 4", Nuts to 1", length 60'
A excellent quality vertical jam crack ending at same belay as the previous route. An alternate direct boulder move face start is 5.11-.

32. **Ho' Lotta Shakin' 5.11a** ★★★
Pro: to 3.5" for main crack, then 4 QD's to finish, length 80'
Climb a superb right facing corner crack system that to the roof, then bust out right at the roof up past a stout crux at the first bolt, then continue up tricky face climbing (bolts) to the belay station. Rappel.

33. **Notre Dame 5.12b** ★
Pro: 9 QD's, length 80'
A powerful crimps face climb immediately to the right of the previous jam crack.

34. **_____ 5.9 (P1 & P2)**
Pro: .5"to 6" cams (plus doubles large sizes), Nuts to 1", slings for blocks, length 100'
Climb a wide mossy corner that lands on a midway ledge (belay), then embarks up a second even wider chimney system to the top. Belay/rap using the Plaid's belay.

35. **_____ 5.11+ [?]**
Pro: 4 QD's, minor gear to .5", length 40'
Climb a short crack (use gear here), then move up right onto a face (bolts) as it ascends a slight overhung crimp featured scoop. Rappel from belay.

NOTRE DAME - SOUTH SECTION

36. **Three Martini Lunch 5.10d** ★
Pro: 3 QD's, length 35'
A minor 35' long short arête that lands on a large belay ledge. This route gives quick access to several upper routes above the ledge.

37. **Cathedral 5.10d** ★★
Pro: 4 QD's (+ minor 2" gear), length 50'
A quality route starting with a series of enjoyable face moves. The power crux climbing eases for a short bit at the short crack, then gets energetic for a final punchy ending near the belay.

38. **_____ 5.__ [?]**
Pro:
Short vertical jam crack that abruptly exits right and lands on a large belay ledge. An alternate second pitch will eventually embark up left onto a tall prominent face prow.

39. **Victor 5.8** ★★
Pro: 2" to 6" cams, Nuts to 1", length 40'
This is the left deep flared groove (with aid bolts). The route ends on a large ledge with a belay station.

40. **Hugo 5.10c/d**
Pro: 1" to 6" cams, Nuts to 1", length 40'
This is the right fat offwidth crack, of the two side-by-side flared offwidth cracks.

Hunchback Wall ✦ ROCK CLIMBING 133

41. Laverne 5.10b/c ★★

Pro: 4 QD's , length 40'

Power crimping on the flat vertical left aspect of a prominent tall rock outcrop formation with a large ledge. Rappel from belay.

42. _____ 5.__

Pro to ___, length 40'

Crack interspersed with minor steps and ledges. On right aspect of the same tall outcrop.

CENTRAL RAVINE

The Central Ravine gains access to several minor short lead routes scattered along the inner aspects of the ravine system.

SOUTH WALL

From the Central Ravine southward is the grand South Wall, a very vertical formation with potential for single and multi-pitch lead routes, easy and stout.

SOUTH AMPHITHEATER

At the far south end of the South Wall you will find a superb major amphitheater for the grand finalé. Some routes in this giant alcove lean in your face 5°-15°, leaving a very naturally clean wall of hard core face, crack and incipient seam routes, perfect for a string of classic hardman climbs.

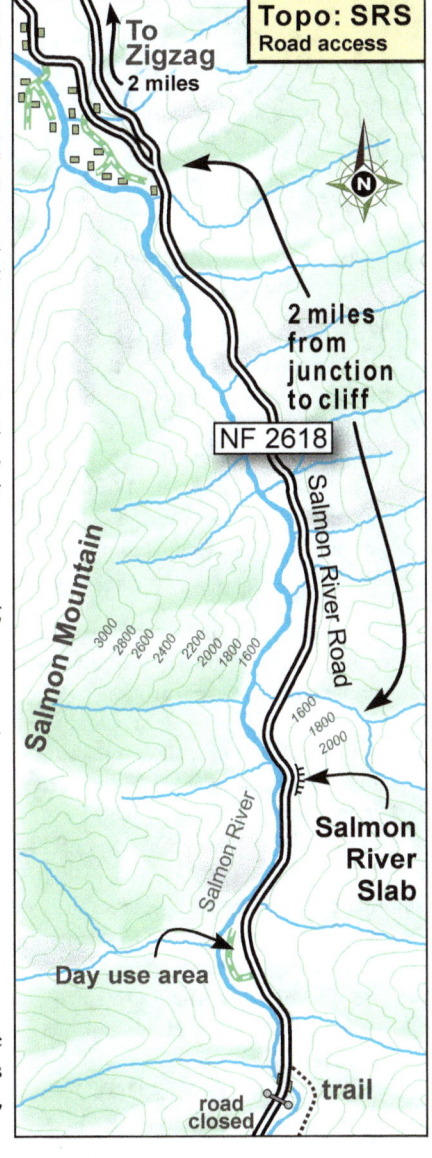

Topo: SRS Road access

2 miles from junction to cliff

NF 2618

Salmon River Slab

1. Hunch Sack 5.10d / 5.11a ★★★

Pro: 10-11 QD's

Superb climb on the left side of the stunning narrow fin arête. A low crux around the 4th bolt and a high crux on the last 2 bolts. Harder if you stay left, easier if you embrace the exposure and hang over the arête.

2. _____

Pro:

An unfinished project. The right side and overhung aspect of the fin arête.

3. _____

Pro:

A deep crack corner on left face of the amphitheater.

4. _____

Pro:

A crack on the center face of the amphitheater.

5. _____ 5.12- [?]

Pro:

An impressive extreme looking seam on face.

6. Mellow Drama 5.10c ★

Gear to 2", has 7 bolts

Start up an easy wide crack ramp to where the headwall steepens following discontinuous cracks and ledges. Follow the thin steep crack to the top,

avoid the overhang on the top by going to the right through the narrow chimney to the rap anchors. A 60-meter rope will just barely get you back to the ground.

UPPER SOUTHERN TIER

This is a brief upper tier section above the South End Amphitheater, thus it offers second pitch leading options above certain amphitheater routes, if you are so inclined.

7. Jon Pussman 5.9
Pro: 3 QD's, height 30'
This is located above the **Hunch Sack** route. From that belay embark up right for some exciting exposure stepping out over the abyss and onto the short face above the massive roof. Ends at a belay on a ledge. Rappel to previous belay, then to the ground.

SALMON RIVER SLAB

Salmon River Slab is a steep slice of exposed rock face located at a small road side pullout just a few short miles south of the tiny community of Zigzag. The rock climbs here provide a comprehensive cluster of well-bolted sport routes on a smooth flakey rock.

The rock bluff faces west and is shaded during the morning hours. The best time to visit here to climb is from May to October (on a sunny day!) so you can take advantage of the great Salmon River swimming hole just a few steps across the road from the rock climbs.

Directions:
Drive east from Sandy, Oregon on US Highway 26 to the tiny community of Zigzag. Turn south onto the Salmon River Road (FS road 2618) and continue due south on this for 4 miles. The popular summer time swimming hole is on the west side of the road, while the tiny bluff is located on the left (east side) of the road at a small dirt pullout.

1. Climbing Theme 5.6
45' (13m) in length, 5 QD's
A basic minor rock climb, but it crosses several brief sections of hollow or slightly loose rock.

2. Brown Rice 5.9
50' (15m) in length, 8 QD's
Considered to be one of the better climbs here. The crux is at the small overhung lip a few

moves below the belay anchor.

3. **Camel Back   5.9**
   50' (15m) in length, 8 QD's
   A popular climb and an interesting lead on the long central part of the slab.

4. **Cave Man   5.7**
   50' (15m) in length, 7 QD's
   Pull past a steep short bulge section for the initial opening moves, then cruise up a moderately easy steep slab using numerous edges to the belay anchor at the top of the cliff.

5. **Salmon   5.5**
   45' (13m) in length, 6 QD's
   Start on the right side of the cliff. Power up an initial steep section while angling up leftward to easier ground. Route has numerous edges with some minor dirty sections to contend with.

South of the main cliff about 200' are several very short low angle slab routes.

The left shorty slab route: Spawning Sockeye 5.4, length 30', 3 QD's.
The right shorty slab route: Moist Minow 5.3, length 30', 4 QD's.

WANKERS COLUMNS

This quality 50' tall basalt bluff is situated on a prominent south facing syncline immediately west of Rowland Lake. This syncline (aka Syncline Wall) overlooking the Columbia River is a scenic region to visit whether you are rock climbing, biking or hiking.

Wankers offers distinctively steep columnar crack climbing opportunities good for Fall, Winter, or Spring climbing, especially when the west side of the state is too rainy. The columns have a southwesterly facing orientation which takes advantage of the sunshine on wintery days.

Fixed anchors exist along the rimtop above most of the popular climbs making it well suited for setting up a quick top-rope although some routes are leadable. The easiest climb is a stout 5.7 so the site may not be conducive to beginner climbing. The routes are seldom lead, although the classic 5.7 Hanz Crack on the far left is definitely worth the blast either as a top-rope or lead.

Certain rock climbs start easy and then steepen to roughly 80°. In some cases, the routes start surprisingly easy on the lower half only to end ridiculously thin on the upper half. The basalt bluff has a right leaning two-directional tilt with slightly weathered cracks.

Flora & Pests:
Ticks are active in the Spring season. Anticipate rattlesnakes during the warm season. If you are susceptible to getting the itch from poison oak it's best to avoid climbing here. Consider bringing a ground cloth to protect your rope.

Directions:
Drive east from Bingen, Washington on State 14 for three miles. Convenient roadside parking is available at the old Highway 8 turnoff next to Rowland Lake, or at a popular mountain biking trail next to Locke Lake alongside Courtney Road. The approach will take about 20 minutes. Follow the narrow hiker/biking trail uphill as it follows alongside a small stream. When the trail crosses the stream, a prominent rock bluff is located directly uphill on the east slope of the stream.

SOUTH END
Near a lone oak tree are some future potential options on the columnar formations facing SSW but certain portions are a bit detached.

RATTLER AREA
Common zone to begin climbing as it's where the rough climbers path first meets the cliff.

1. **____   5.12- [?]**
   Three very closely spaced narrow columns yield one difficult route. Hard TR on steep thin narrow columns. Starts just north of an oak tree.

Wankers Columns

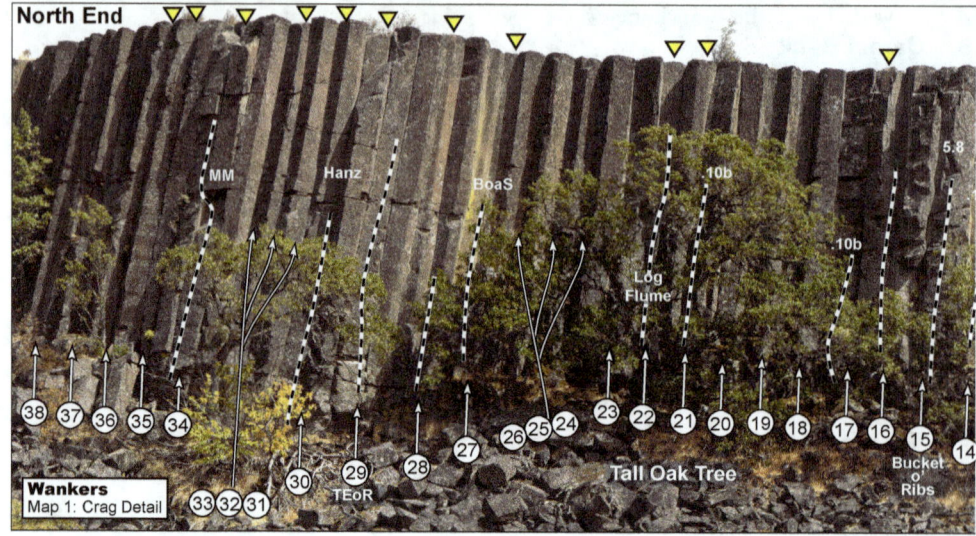

2. **Buried Treasure 5.9**
   Tall box corner chimney system.
3. **Seven Eleven TR 5.11+**
   A thin jam crack that starts easy but closes tight on the upper part of the route increasing the difficulty the higher you go.
4. **_____ 5.__ [?]**
   Potential corner system.
5. **_____ 5.12- [?]**
   The infamous detached column chimney is gone. Now its a powerful thin seam cruising up an orange colored face of a slight boxed corner. Top-rope.
6. **Rattler 5.11+ [?]**
   Climb the initial corner system (of the above route), then move fully into a vertical left seam about 12' up the route.
7. **Measure of Pleasure 5.8 ★★★**
   Located on the outside of the buttress immediately left of the detached chimney column. Clamber up past a stubby tree at the start, and cruise up a long steep crack corner. This long consistent hand jam crack is a stellar little climb.
8. **Wendell's Big Mistake TR 5.10+**
   Near the middle of the crag, about 15' left of Measure of Pleasure.
9. **_____ 5.9+ (?)**
   A tall boxed corner system.
10. **Nuggets 5.7**

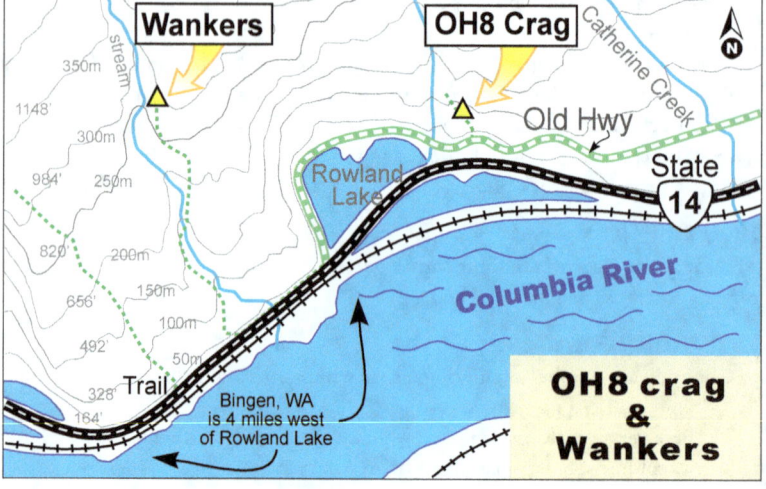

★

Climb a low angle slab and edges, then at mid-height, step left and continue up an obvious crack to top up. Use Sluice Box belay.

11. Sluice Box 5.9 ★★
Climb low angle steps, and when the crack steepens stay in the crack corner. Tight opposition stemming smears to finish the upper crux part.

12. _____ 5.10 c/d
Lower slabby climbing to upper tricky balancy face climbing. If you can't figure out the upper part don't be surprised.

13. _____ 5.11b
A thin seam in a slight corner.

14. _____ 5.11b ★
Stay in the thin seam in a tight corner the entire way using an occasional left jug.

15. Bucket o' Ribs 5.8
A dirty rib with jug holds and edges on the outside of a column. Avoid the crack on left.

TALL OAK TREE AREA

This section has a large oak tree at the base of the wall next to the popular Log Flume route.

16. _____ 5.8 ★★
Quality crack corner system (2-bolts). Gear to 3").

17. _____ 5.10b
Starts up a steep slightly mossy face, then punch past a tiny lip midway up the route.

18. _____ 5.__ [?]
19. _____ 5.__ [?]
20. _____ 5.__ [?]
21. _____ 5.10b
Climb a corner system immediately right of

Log Flume (which ends at same belay anchor).

22. Log Flume 5.10a ★★
Start in a steep double corner behind the large oak tree. At the mid-point small edges launch into a series of tight oppositions stemming smears to finish the upper crux part.

NORTH END
23. _____   5.11-
The upper half is a thin clean corner-*ish* seam.
24. _____   5.__
25. _____   5.__
26. _____   5.__
27. **Birds on a Shelf 5.10+ (TR)**
A wide stem box corner above a mossy shelf.
28. ___   5.11+
A very thin crack with a slight right lean to it.
29. **Thin Edge of Reality 5.11+** ★★
A top-rope that uses a combination of two
tight seams on a steep face. Merges into Hanz crack for the last move.
30. **Hanz Crack 5.7** ★★★
A stellar jam crack worth leading or top-rope.
31. _____   5.11
Immediately left of Hanz Crack are three thin cracks on a steep face. This is the right and shortest corner seam.
32. **Ptero 5.11** ★
Middle thin corner seam.
33. **Latent Genes 5.11+** ★
The leftmost of three thin seam crack corner.
34. **Mouse in a Microwave 5.10a**
Climb easy crack to a stance capped by a small lip. Surmount lip and climb a jam crack to top.
35. _____   5.11- (?) ★
Long thin tips crack corner with quality climbing.
36. _____   5.__ (?)
37. _____   5.__ (?)
38. _____   5.__ (?)

World of Bouldering

BOULDERING INTRO

Bouldering opportunities in Northwest Oregon and Southwest Washington

Encapsulated within this section you will find a brief study on the subject of bouldering around NW Oregon and SW Washington. The world of regional outdoor bouldering, centered around Portland, Oregon has been a rapidly changing game, bringing new opportunities for the quest seeking, nuance-driven boulderer who is determined to tap the latest cool problems found in the sport of bouldering. This section provides a power-packed analysis of numerous new and well established bouldering sites that are sure to spike your enthusiasm to a new high.

Today's boulderer can easily maintain 12-month continuity fitness levels throughout the year thanks to indoor sports gyms. Indoor sports bouldering gym facilities, first established in Portland in the early 1980's, are today quite numerous and very popular. Today these sports gyms provide quality indoor training and practice environs where dedicated individuals can build their skills base before venturing outdoors to the vast treasure of old and new bouldering sites this micro-region has to offer. This modern trend, mixing gym training sessions with an expansive wealth of new bouldering site options is a far cry from the limited choice of early era bouldering sites like Carver Boulders and BOGB. Indeed, year-round sports gyms have gradually, yet radically increased the appetite for people to step outdoors and explore this fascinating plethora of bouldering opportunities.

Considering the limitations that cold, rainy winter months have on this outdoor activity in western Oregon, it seems a bit odd that the activity has attained considerable increased value. Yet, using each good weather window, and tapping the sunny south-facing (or breezy) aspects of certain sites, you can extend your outdoor bouldering opportunities to virtual year-round sessions. Several mini sites such as Hamilton Boulders and Horsethief Butte offer year-round bouldering.

Portland has not been viewed as a primary bouldering haven in the 90's, nor during the early part of this century. Quality new sites such as Hamilton Boulders, Alpenglow, and the Empire Boulders abound, and this series of close proximity sites offer superb opportunities for today's boulderer who no longer must endure long drives to Sisters Boulders.

Mix a sweet combination of numerous city-based indoor bouldering gyms, numerous well-established (and new) bouldering sites with 3000+ total problems, stack on top of it Northwest Oregon's largest bouldering site (Lost Lake Boulders), toss into the mix about six months of great bouldering weather, and we may possibly have a nice comprehensive micro bouldering region after all (...maybe). So, grab your rock shoes and chalk bag and hit the road, and go visit some of the wealth found at Port-

Preston at *Empire Boulders*

land's best bouldering sites.

This analysis on the activity of bouldering around Northwest Oregon is purely introductory in scope, just one mere edge of the sport, and not a 'complete' discussion of it. Using Lost Lake Boulders as an example: it barely started seeing substantial sending activity in late 2013, yet when it is eventually fully tapped will easily qualify as the biggest bouldering site in this particular micro-region. With all consideration toward all the numerous sites that compose regional bouldering in/near Northwest Oregon, certainly the sport of bouldering has essentially become its own stand-alone sport.

Outdoor recreation based sports in Oregon is increasingly popular, and growing community networks of sport enthusiasts have made shared responsibility stewardship trends integral to their core group message, and have established relational goals in conjunction with local land managers in recent years. Ethical responsibility and an earnest desire to see more openness for climbing or bouldering helps frame citizen communication networks of stewardship based cooperation.

CLIMATE

Northwest Oregon can get downright stifling hot (90°-95°F) in July and part of August, but don't hide because your favorite bouldering site is a boilerplate. Instead go to high altitude stellar bouldering sites that offer ideal 'heat-escape' locales far better than the low elevation bouldering sites. Just look at the string of viable options: Larch Mtn Boulders, north ridge of Silver Star Mtn on Ed's Trail, Three Corner Rock Boulders, Timberline Boulders, Cooper Spur Boulders, including a fine string of lightly forested sites like Bulo Point, Lost Lake Boulders, or even Rock Creek Boulders. Some folks are determined to crank only V-hard, so full sunshine bouldering may be too limiting on the hottest summer days, but for those who relish VB-V3 there is an unlimited plethora of stuff at all the higher altitude sites, with minimal to zero moss, and a general lack of mosquitoes (at breezy sites).

BASIC GEOLOGY

Its a quirk, at least in the eye of a boulderer, that the greatest percentage of large stone clusters found in this region (of high quality and quantity) are composed of andesitic-basaltic rock characteristics. From a geological perspective, this is readily apparent, simply because most of the Pacific Rim volcanoes (from Japan, to the Alaskan archipelago, and from western Canada / western U.S., to the Andes mountain range of South America) actively expelled (in recent history and to this date) voluminous quantities of igneous lava, some of it being old lava flows with andesitic characteristics. Andesite rock, in essence, is water, gas content, bits of sediment, and a healthy dose of silica sprinkled in, all previously subducted by an oceanic plate, conveyor belt fashion down beneath the continental plate. These two plates rub and drag sediment material downward, in a process which heats and melts the rock, pooling into massive molten structures that, being lighter than the surrounding older congealed rock structure, rises slowly to the surface

venting explosively as volcanic mountain peaks.

The results of this conjunctive igneous mix produce lighter colored silica-rich lava rock types (breccias, tuffs, andesites, dacites, and rhyolites) of volcanoclastics found along the entire Pacific Rim volcanic string. After long periods of erosional and chemical weathering processes, the resultant forested landscape revealed exposed clusters of large andesitic boulders (or short vertical escarpments), in surprisingly extensive quantities throughout the northern Oregon Cascade Mountain range.

INHERENT RISKS

Boulderers are like railroad train engineers, wrapped in centric steel-like tendinous muscle, on a sports quest, and sometimes on a sophist quest. The game of bouldering is somewhat like mixing vodka and a race car, so if your not expecting to see a volatile reaction, guess again. Bouldering necessitates logical judgment skills, so consider carefully prior to delving heavily into the outdoor bouldering scene. Beware of the inherent risk of personal injury, especially if you are prodded on with guttural boosts from your bouldering partner. A mixed recipe of this sort sometimes presses beggarly for potentially serious consequences. You might prefer to live without thirteen steel pins holding your ankle together (one of the uglier risks of this sport). When you get high on an 18'-24' tall stone, well above that postage stamp sized crashpad, one mere slip and your 5-day week occupational reality show might end as an internal compression injury, or something far uglier. If your doing a quick send on an 18' hi-ball off the deck, be careful. There is no guarantee that your hands won't peal off first when plowing sideways across an overhung roof. The word 'crash'-pad should provide a clue. Face it, rock climbing is obviously inherently risky, while the bouldering game is a subtle degree beyond that.

BOULDERING GRADE SCALE

Boulder problems use the well-known Verm or V-rating system. This effective grade comparison scale is designed to articulate a relational comparison involving short bursts of energy typical of concise boulder moves. Though it should relate to actual exact lead rock climbing grades it does not quite parallel, due in part to broad variables encountered in protection based roped climbing.

V-scale	YDS scale
VB	5.9 and under
V0	5.10a/b
V1	5.10c/d
V2	5.11a/b
V3	5.11c/d
V4	5.12-
V5	5.12b/c
V6	5.12+

Dave S. on 60° of Desperation

V7	5.13-
V8	5.13b/c
V9	5.13+
V10	5.14a
V11	5.14b
V12	5.14c
V13	5.14d
V14	5.15a
V15	5.15b
V16	5.15c
V17	5.15d

Beta Nuances (Sit Start, Grades)

In this bouldering book the V-scale grading units have meaning (sometimes subtle). VB means anything 5.9 and below. If it's shown as V2 (V4) the left rating is 'standing start' and the parenthesis is a 'sit start' rating. A single grade, like V2ss, is used if sit start is the common way its done, thus 'ss' is Sit Start. If no parenthesis grade follows the first grade then the listed grade is generally assumed to be sent as a standing start (typical for tall boulders).

Broadly listed ratings (such as V5-7 or V6-V9) are merely an approximation, but it's probably within that range. And that type of graded problem may (or may not) be done. If done, it's usually narrowed to one single V-grade (but not always) or at the most two (V4/5) side by side grades.

A question mark '?' after the grade indicates an unknown rating (or possibly not yet seen an ascent). If the grade has a plus '+' symbol it's an open-ended grade assumed to be a minimum of that grade (or stouter); its a mere generic estimate not intended to indicate its final real difficulty. Any V-number may, theoretically, be off a bit. Lastly, some V-numerics on the topo are mere generic approximations, not implicatory of finality. What is not science is science fiction.

INFO SYMBOLS

A selection of boulder problem descriptions may have additional icons representative of other potential challenges found at that particular boulder or problem. The ⚠ symbol indicates our cutting edge of real high-ball problems at 17' (5-meters) and above. Tall problems below that range may still be spicy, but are not indicated in this guide. A jagged edge ⛰ symbol indicates a rocky or hard to protect landing (where extra crashpads and spotters are wise protocol).

It's A Bouldering World

PART 2 Bouldering Opportunities

BOULDERING

This bouldering chapter is compiled of sites in close proximity to Portland, thus providing you a productive method for quick goal planning. This small select core group of bouldering sites can help enhance your fitness continuity goals.

The Larch Mtn Boulders, due to its close proximity to Vancouver-Portland area is a good quality place to expand your bouldering skill set. Larch Boulders is located in the hill country about 30-minutes north of Camas, Washington.

LARCH MTN BOULDERS

High quality granodiorite bouldering on Larch Mountain surpasses all expectations, producing some of the finest bouldering opportunities in our region. Located a mere 23 miles from Portland, this quality site exceeds 100 boulder problems, ranging from VB-V7 (potential to V9+). Many hi-ball problems (12'-35' tall), stellar long rail traverses (4' tall x 25' long), overhangs, and techy vertical crimp lines, something for every degree of bouldering. The site is a combination of boulders and rocky outcrops spread over a large area, and in short time certain sections became quite popular, such as the Wild West Bluff formation. The site may eventually yield a minimum of 150+ boulder problems.

The rock has lightly weathered minimally abrasive surficial features that give it a rich texture from long-term weathering processes of the exposed rock surface. The result is ideal for crimps and smearing friction abilities with minimal moss or lichen.

The rock type reveals peripheral composition variables depending on specific locale, but general samples have black, pink, and opaque phenocrysts (1-2 mm) evenly distributed with dominant quartz crystal (2-3mm) in the matrix. The overall area has slight compositional matrix shifts depending on zone of peripheral surrounding rock (its the utter south end of the granodiorite formation).

Seasons:

A viable 5½ month fair weather window from mid-May to October is best, with optional days outside of that, as well. Situated at the 3,200' level, with frequent beneficial breezes, cool crisp days in late season (sometimes even in December) with enjoyable bouldering on classic stuff in full sunshine with great scenic views. Spacious views of the entire region looking south over Vancouver and Portland, including northern views of Silver Star Mtn., and east to Mt Hood.

Advantages: no poison oak, no ticks, 2-wheel drive vehicle accessible to the lower boulders along the L-1500 road (i.e. the Leavenworth Boulders). Disadvantages: some areas may be used by target shooters (if you do not like the sound of cannon-fire in the distance you might want to boulder elsewhere); if gated its a ½ mile uphill trek past the yellow gate to the upper boulders. The mainline gravel road, though graded regularly, is a bit rough in spots.

Directions:

From I-205 bridge drive east on State 14 highway to Camas, WA. At the signal light junction of 3rd avenue in Camas, drive northeast from Camas on state 500 road (passed Lacamas Lake). Turn right at NE 19th (at Fern Prairie store) and drive east 1 mile, and take a left at the "Y" and drive north uphill on 272nd. This winds north and east for 2 miles to a 3-way stop intersection. Turn north (left) on 292nd and drive one mile. Turn north onto Livingston Road and continue uphill for one mile till you reach L-1000 forest road which is gravel. Drive on L-1000 for 3-4 miles to a 4-way intersection. Turn right (east) uphill on gravel forest road L-1500 for one mile till it turns right and levels off (passing a yellow DNR gate on the left). Drive east along this generally level portion of the gravel road for one mile to an open area passing another common target shooting spot. Both the Leavenworth Boulder and Black Forest Boulder are located uphill above a secondary road, while the Eiger and Matterhorn

144　COLUMBIA GORGE　　　　　　　　　　　　　　　　　Larch Mtn Boulders

Abbott on *Mag Seven*　　　Brian on *Junfrau Prow*

stones are below the road.

To reach the Wild West Bluff formation at the upper knoll, continue east on L-1500 till you reach a saddle between two hills (at two roads with two metal gates). Park here (near the yellow gate) and hike uphill ½ mile to the bluff (or use AWD to get up the steep road). Scramble up the steep rocky slope to either the west side or east side of the butte. Road L-1500 is a bit rough but is 2WD viable.

Note: There are several alternate methods to reach Larch Boulders: via Hockinson (paved entirely to the 4-way interchange), or north from Camas past Fern Prairie store, or up the Washougal River a several miles turning left up onto Bear Prairie.

LEAVENWORTH GROUP

The **Leavenworth Boulder** is one of the premier boulders at Larch Mtn., and its situated at the very first locale (when driving north from Camas) on the peak. Park on a dead-end side road directly below the boulders. Walk uphill one minute (80') to two massive boulders. The Black Forest Stone is the smaller boulder, and Leavenworth Stone is the giant 15' x 30' x 30' behemoth. The flowers are in full bloom in June-July. This is the most convenient bouldering site at Larch Mtn for 2-wheel drive vehicle access. Plenty of powerful overhanging bouldering lines from juggy fun problems to delicate core intensive power crimp-fests. The Leavenworth Stone is considered to be the rare gem at Larch Mtn., of the type and quality found only once at the great bouldering sites. GPS UTM 10t 555669 5061306 Beta is listed left to right.

Leavenworth Boulder

VB Crazy Get Down ★
A short juggy basic problem on west face.

VB (V0) Terminate This ★★★★
Fun warmup problem on a short hung arête.

V1 (V2ss) Super Cool ★★★
Start on the same arête (of previous problem) but on the right side.

V2 (V3ss) Back In The Day ★★★★
Great line with a series of good holds.

V3 (V5ss) Iron Giant ★★★★
The classic center south face line, a 12' tall hi-ball. Start on left pinch, and aim up to a slight groove where better holds near the lip await.

V7 (V8ss) Iron Clad ★★★
Upper body core intensive movement. Start on Iron Giant aim up left, then fall onto the minute rock horn protrusion, then power up to the top near **Back In The Day**.

V8 Octagon ★★
Quality hard core hi-ball line.

V5 (V6ss) Dragon's Tail ★★★
No jugs route. Start on under clings to thin crimps. Tough to see crimps, and the exit is thin and tricky. A 14' tall hi-ball.

V6 (V6ss) Scorpion King ★★★★
Cool techy hi-ball line with a crucial right hand

crimp up high.

VB (V0ss) Embers ★★
On the east face of the block is a series of large steps. Sit extends line by starting low on left.

THE TRAVERSES:

V3 Liquid Metal ★
An uphill rising traverse on the left (west) aspect of the rock formation.

V9 Leavenworth Traverse ★
From 'Terminate This' to the far rightmost route.

Black Forest Boulder

This stone is just below the Leavenworth Boulder and offers more of the same quality problems on high quality rock. Beta is L to R.

VB Get Down
A minor down climb on the west end.

V1ss Soot
Just uphill of the hung west prow.

V1ss Jungfrau ★★★★
The overhung classic arête on the west end.

V3ss The Great Escape ★★
Start on next problem and use the sloped face to two small divot holds to exit.

V0 (V0ss) Climbingruven ★★
Start on small left-facing fins and finish up right on large appearing edges to a not so simple crux exit.

V1 (V3ss) Red Barron ★★
Underclings to good hold and finish same as previous line.

VB (V1ss) Black Forest ★★★
A classic basic line with great holds.

VB Chocolate
Short basic fun run.

THE TRAVERSE:

V4 Black Forest Traverse ★★★
Start on the route #1 and fall into position on the arête, and continue across the south face of the boulder.

EIGER-MATTERHORN GROUP

The Eiger and Matterhorn Boulders are located below the car parking spot at Leavenworth Boulder zone. Use the new bulldozer road grade that cuts down from the west to the cluster. The Eiger is 18' tall on its south aspect, and the Matterhorn has a short flat slightly hung face with a host of powerful problems.

Matterhorn Boulder ⚠

VB Hot Butter
The leftmost face line.

V1 Melting Hot ★
Start at the slight undercling.

V2 Sunburn ★★
Move into it from left, then directly up.

V6 Where's da Shade ★★★
The center thin crimps face.

V3 Summertime ★★

V5 Rising Sun ★★★
Start low on right, and run left along the horizontal seam to far left end.

V0 Hot Tin Roof
This is the rightmost crimps problem.

THE TRAVERSE:

V7 Matterhorn Traverse ★★
Traverse entire face, avoid top lip.

Eiger Boulder ⚠

VB Titanic Ego
The leftmost crack corner.

V1 Whymper's Wonder ★ ⚠
Run the tallest part of the south face.

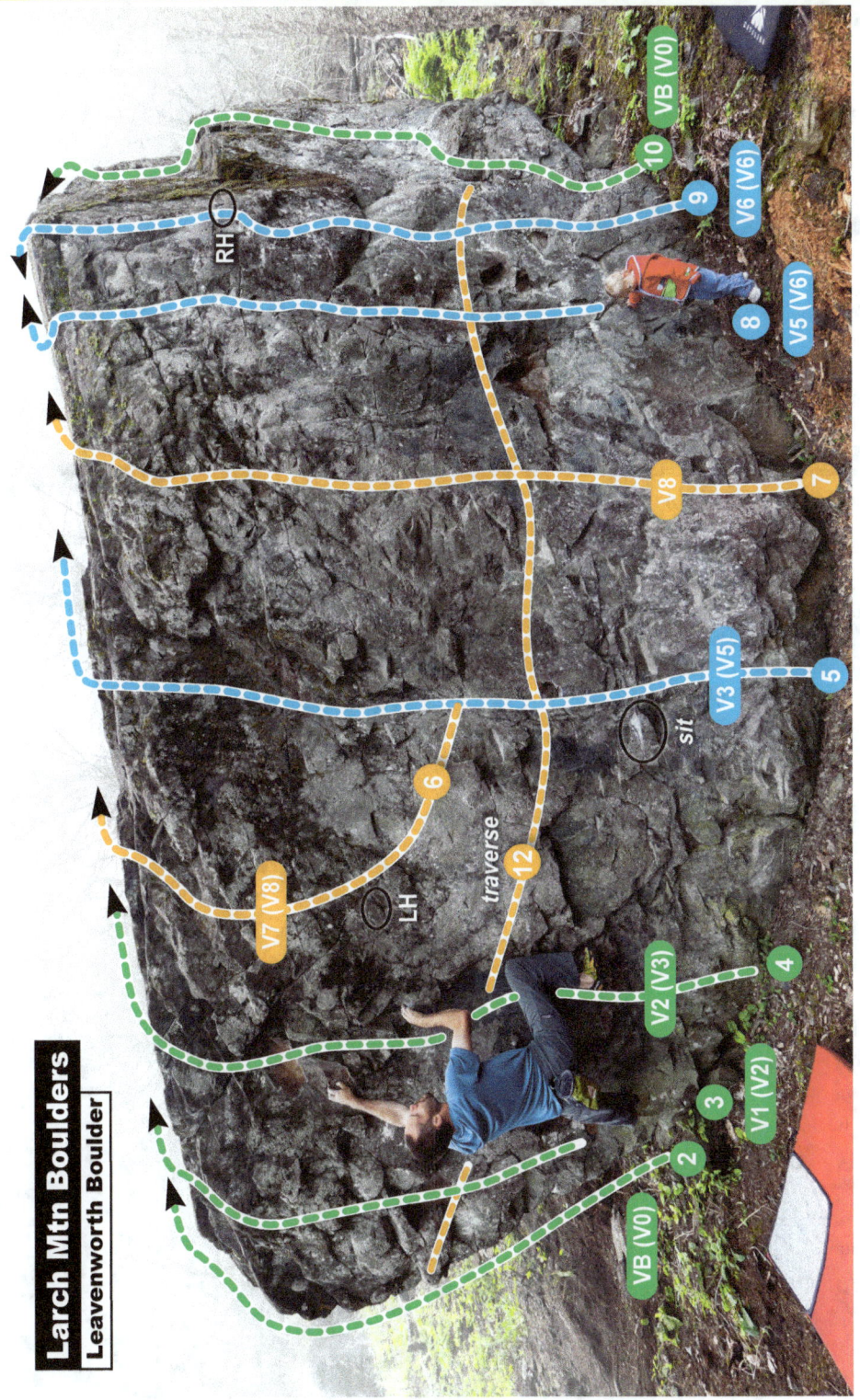

148 COLUMBIA GORGE — Larch Mtn Boulders

V0 Collateral Damage ★ ⚠
Up south face and exit right onto the rib.

VB Rogue Nation
The low angled minor rib.

VB Garbage Talk
The short east face slab.

Charcoal Bluff ⚠

Above the Leavenworth Boulders, a short walk (30 yards) uphill, is a short cliff formation, with a slabby 25' wall about 80' wide viable for either TR options or solo VB/V0 runs. There is a 25' tall hi-ball, 5° overhung flat face with sharp crimp holds (V4?), and several other V3-*ish* problems just down to the right at a landing.

East Bluff

A quality east-facing 15' tall by 30' wide bluff (this bluff is visible from the east Yellow Gate). Below the wall 3-4 large boulders yield some minor bouldering. Walk horizontally to the right in the forest about 70' to reach the Halfway Slab (20' x 30' wide slab with four VB's). About 70' further right is the Great Northern Slab (50' wide x 30' tall, 50° slab).

VB War Zone
Far left crack / left face.

VB House of War
Start off top of small rock pedestal.

V0 Pacific Pearl ★ ★ ★
A vertical thin crack.

V5 Count Down ★ ★ ★ ★
Thin powerful hung face.

V3 Fireworks ★ ★ ★ ★
Techy hung face.

V0 Double Trouble
The double crack slot.

V3 Coup d'etat ★ ★ ★
Hung face (+ 1 variation).

V0 Pearl Hunter ★ ★ ★
The hung seam.

V2 Frosted ★ ★
Rightmost line, but go directly up (using the left top out variation).

V2 Flakes ★ ★
Same start as previous, but move up right immediately onto round nose (variation).

Two boulders just below the east bluff:

VB SOS
The lowest outer point; cruise up rightward.

V2 Loco Citato
Sit start up a series of hung jugs.

On the next stone (the rightmost stone):

VB Locus Minoris
Tall easy outer lower prow.

Great Northern Slab ⚠

V_ _____ *(left face shorty)*

V2 Ad Infinitum ★
Crimps to slopers on face.

V0 Cold Kiss
Short and minor.

VB Slabrageous ★ ★
A fun slab face near the prow (5.4).

VB Lost World ★ ★
Start at the point and cruise face and corner up left (5.4). Or climb straight up to top.

VB Hidden Treasure ★ ★
A tall face immediately right of offwidth.

VB Great Northern Slab
A long angled slab route.

VB The remainder of the slab is basic.

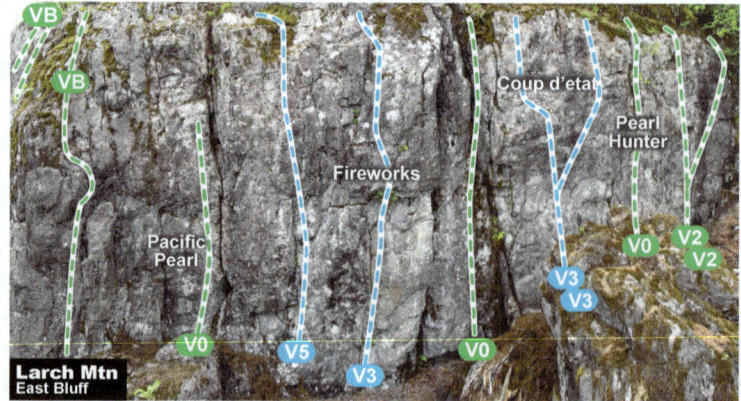

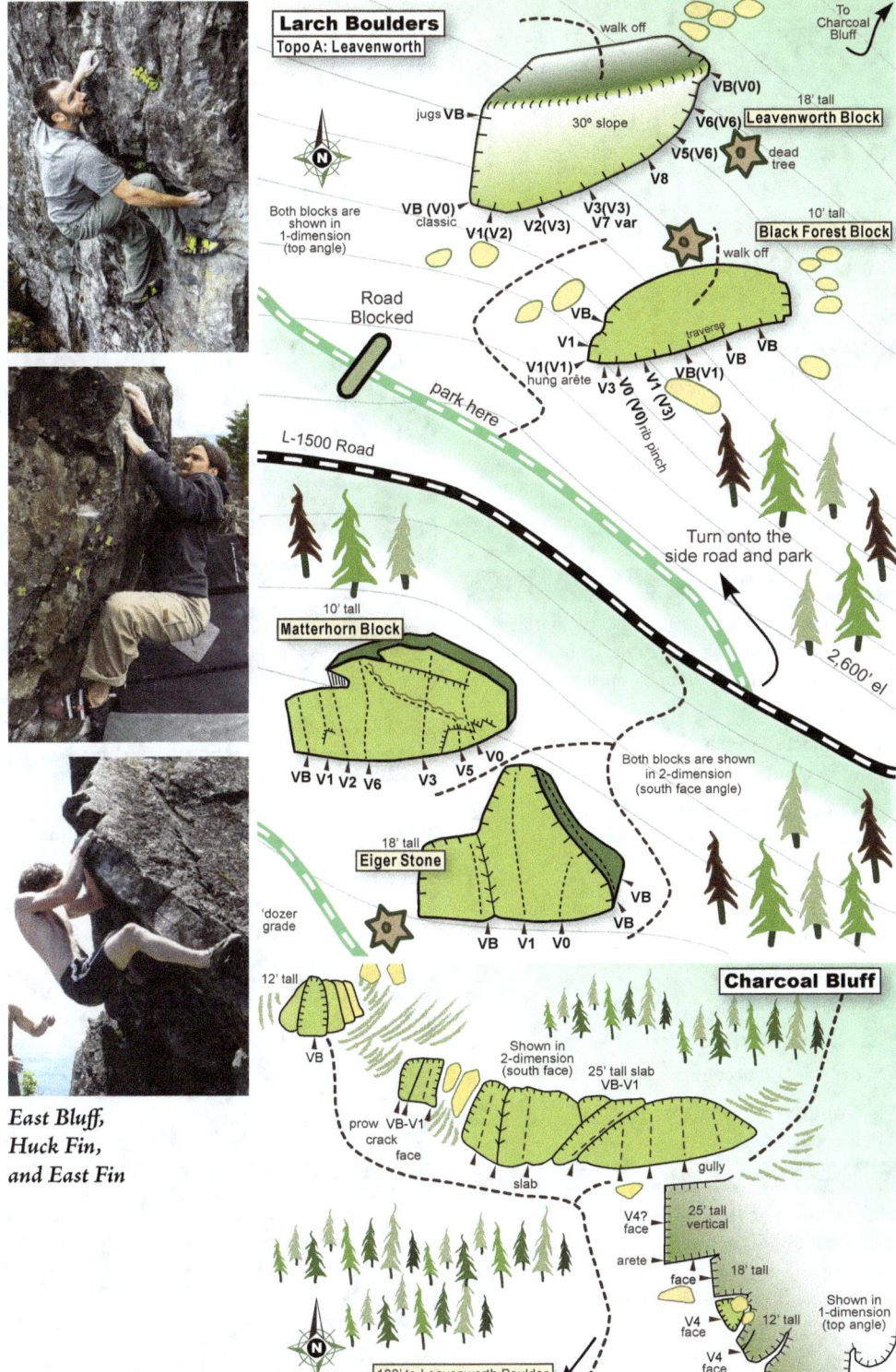

East Bluff, Huck Fin, and East Fin

NORTH SLOPE TALUS

At a flat landing walk east uphill on a narrow rough path to reach K2 stone. Then descend north across a broad talus slope. The site offers a series of five northward sloping talus fields separated by vine maple thickets. A good locale to escape from hot scorching temperatures of summer (even when it's 90°F boilerplate hot).

K2 Boulder

This trail side boulder (and next stone) is part of the initial talus slope visible from the road. There are several additional stones in this vicinity to tap.

V2ss Lucida Sidera ☐
Leftmost stout line starting on low sloper.

V1ss Texas Wronghorn ★ ☐
Sit low, grab a high right side pull, high step.

V2ss Lorem Ipsum ★ ☐
Use the large incut jug hold to start then use crimps to finish.

V2ss Locus Standi ☐
Use the sloped nose.

V2ss Locum Tenens ☐
On the south aspect of the stone.

V3 Traverse ☐
The sit start lip traverse.

Silver Star boulder

One nice line, the **Silver Star** (**V5ss**). This is slightly uphill of the previous boulder (great views of Silver Star Mtn). Start low, bear hug both arêtes, finish direct to top.

Walk down hill northward to the next talus

field to reach the Cornerstone Boulder.

Cornerstone Boulder

A big double faceted block with a roomy crashpad landing zone. The block is about 14' tall with two main aspects and a prominent 130°

Larch Mtn Boulders ✦ OR&B 151

overhanging arête. Beta is left to right:

V1 (V2) Infinite Reality ★★
Leftmost problem on crimps and slopers.

V2 (V4) Cannibals & Crowbars ★★
A tech face with crimps. Catch the pinches on finishing rail, move up left and top out.

V5 Modus Operandi ★★
On the face immediately left of arête.

V1 (V2) Land Down Under ★★★★
Ultra-classic super overhanging arête. Sit start and bump a long reach to a high left hold, then to ample holds on right side.

V1ss Illuminate This ★★★
Bump up 2-3 times to fat holds at seam, up left to arête, finish to top.

V3 Bad to the Bone ★★
Corner and face busting over small roof on right side.

V3 One Bad Jackal
Rightmost variation of the previous problem.

V5 Cornerstone Traverse ★★
Full traverse of both facets of the boulder.

Silver Boulder
Overhung north facing aspect offers some wild stuff. Beta left to right.

V4ss Lone Ranger ★
Sit start over a bulge and up the left prow.

V3ss Hi Ho Silver ★
Punch past the overhang, then seam, aiming up to the right.

V5 Silver Bullet
Standing start to a dicey mantle.

Huckleberry Boulder
This is a stellar 45° super-overhung rock fin. Beta is listed left to right:

V1 Bear Treats
Run the rail on the far left shaded side.

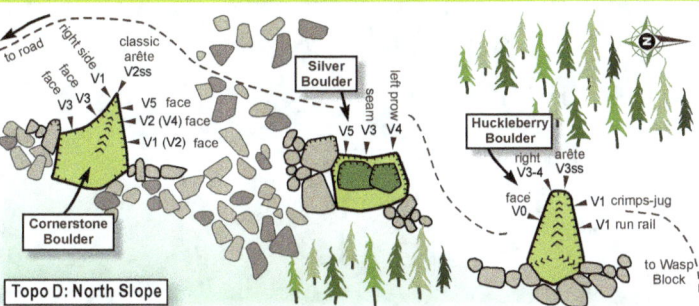
Topo D: North Slope

V1 Tom Sawyer ★★
Crimps to a jug, then a tricky mantle onto that large jug.

V3ss Huckleberry Finn ★★★
Using crimps, angle up onto the left side of the

Larch Mtn North Slope Cornerstone

Larch Mtn North Slope Cornerstone

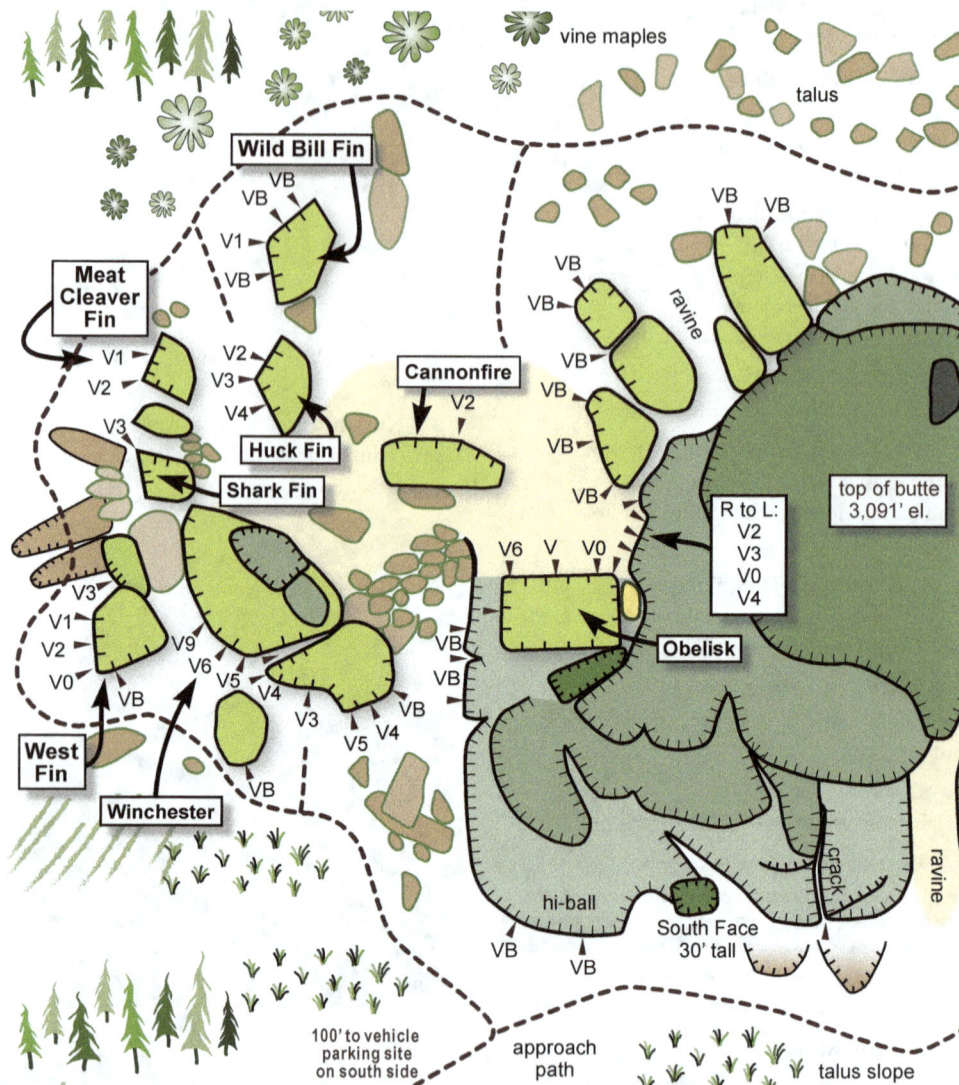

130° overhanging arête. Difficult to top out.

V4ss Doc Holliday ★★★ ☐
Virtually same as previous except bump up to jug high and right, then up and over the very nose of this 130° feature.

V0 Right Face ☐
A minor problem on the right face.

The traverse:

V4 Huckleberry Traverse ★★ ☐
A very stout traverse of the entire face. Start on the right and swing along on the jugs and positive holds below the nose.

WILD WEST BLUFF

This is a steep sided rock butte great for bouldering, on the west and east side of the formation. The west side boulders encompass the four Minor Fins, the mega West Fin, and Bonanza Boulder. Plenty of varied lines and the most common starting place to experience Larch Mtn.

FOUR MINOR FINS

A set of four minor boulders. Most are sit start problems. All are well developed.

Wild Bill Fin

This upper left stone offers four minor prob-

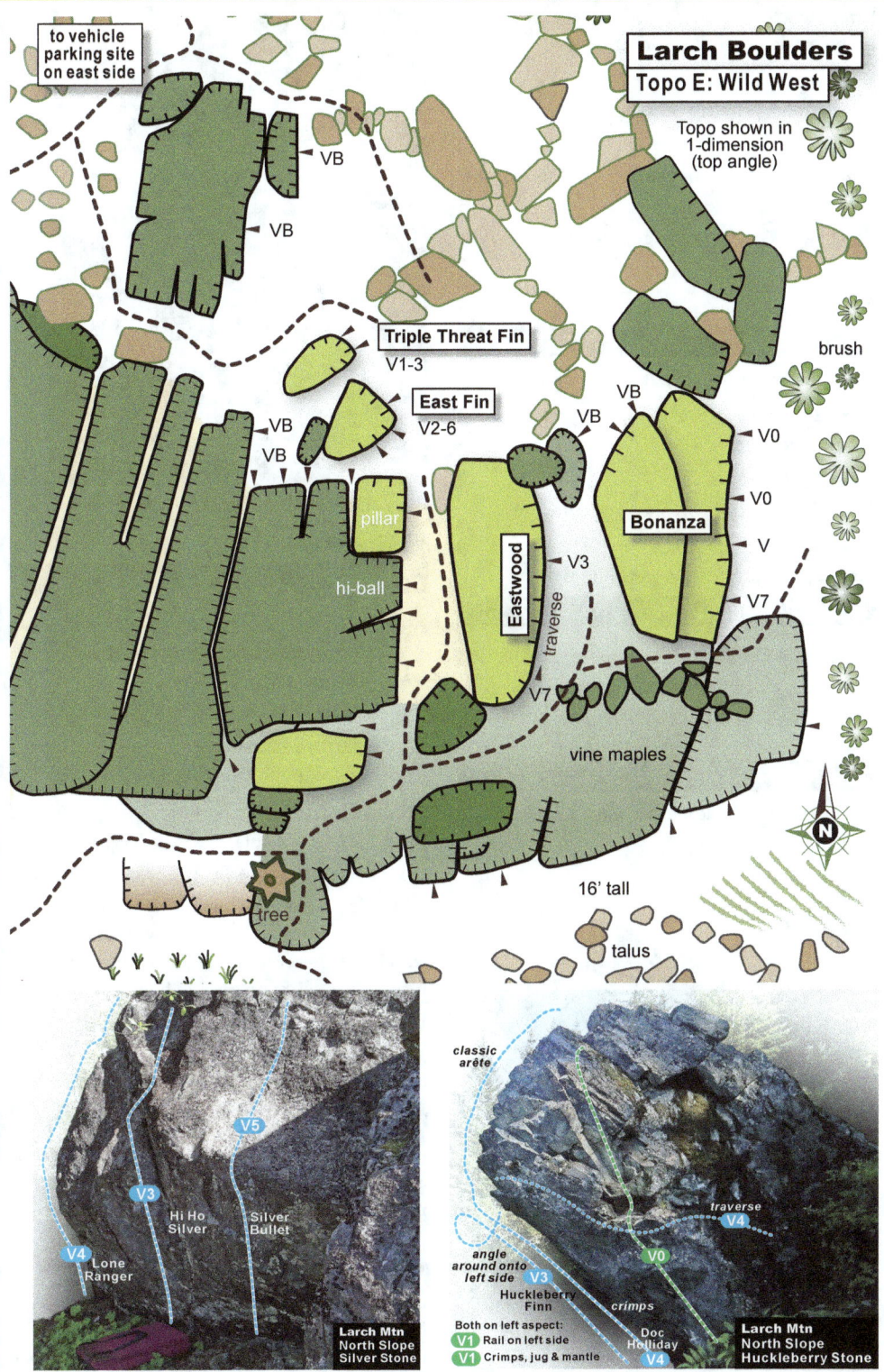

lems. Beta is left to right. Though minor, the problems do seem to attract attention.

VB _____
The leftmost problem on a flat face.

VB _____
The face just left of the hung rib (+ var).

V1ss _____
The hung center problem as a sit start (+ var).

VB _____
The rightmost hung problem.

Huck Fin

Offers three powerful sit start problems.

V2ss Showdown ★
Ascend the left face aspect.

V3ss OK Corral ★
Start on same short rib but go up left.

V4ss Most Wanted ★★
Sit start at short rib and power up right.

Meat Cleaver Fin

V2ss Meat Cleaver ★★
The lower left stone in this group. Sit start, reach, cross to jug, find the lip, top out. The thin cleaver blade is long gone.

Shark Fin

The lower right stone is a squat low overhung

detached block held in place by stacked blocks.

V3 Shark Fin

West Fin

It's the giant 17' tall fin, a very popular fin to warm-up on. Ultra cool virtual hi-ball status.

V3 Wrestling with 'Gators
Bust out from the nook cave on the left.

V1 Gun Runner ★★
The left edge of the monster fin; odd top out.

V2 Smith & Wesson ★★★
Send the face. V3 rules avoiding large right jug.

VB (VBss) Locked & Loaded ★★★★
Ultra-classic line. Sit low on right by wrapping your hands around the huge lower flake horn on either side, power up, then cross over to the super incut jug on the main fin, and finesse a final move to top out.

VB Pistol ★
South aspect offers a basic run.

Winchester Boulder ⚠

The ultimate boulder hi-ball rock face at the Wild West knoll; a string of impressive powerful problems with enticing sequential madness.

V9 Mag Seven ★★★★
The ultimate power line at the knoll. Start at the crack, and power up left along the 25' long rising left leaning classic 20° overhanging prow. The ultra thin crux is at mid-point with a long reach

to latch a flat jug, then continue on positive holds up leftward till you top out on the block. **Magnum** is a variation right exit.

V0 (V6ss) Winchester ★★★★ ⚠ ☐
This is a 25' tall crack with slightly overhung standing start opening moves, then solid easy crack with jugs and steps on the upper half. The full Winchester sit starts under the 65° overhanging jam crack (V6), crank out with finger and foot jams, then up the entire route. FA onsite Mr O, full sit Mr A. The alternate Slayton variation is **V7** (**Pistol Whipped**); start on Mag7 and join higher in Winchester crack.

V5 Breach Loader ★★ ⚠ ☐
Just right of Winchester. Face crimp start then merges up left into Winchester.

V0 Gutter Ball ⚠ ☐
The deep chimney.

V4ss Born on the 5th of July ★★★★ ☐
A superb line that begins sit start under an arête, power up the arête to finish on easy terrain. Immediately right of the deep chimney.

V3 Girls with Guns ★★ ⚠ ☐
Slightly hung scoop with tricky hi-ball move to top out.

V5 Run For Cover ★★ ⚠☐
Thin techy face starts on steep nose just right of a scoop; finish on steep slab.

V4 Surrender ☐
Crimps on a seam on steep face.

VB ____ ☐
Low angle slab (the rightmost problem).

Cannonfire Boulder

V2ss Cannonfire ★ ☐
Large oblong boulder uphill from the Four Minor Fins in front of the Obelisk. Low angled traverse problem. A V4ss low direct exists.

The Obelisk

AKA THE SHOEBOX

At the rim-top overlooking the West Cluster is a stunning

Larch Mtn West Fin

Larch Mtn Winchester Stone

156 COLUMBIA GORGE

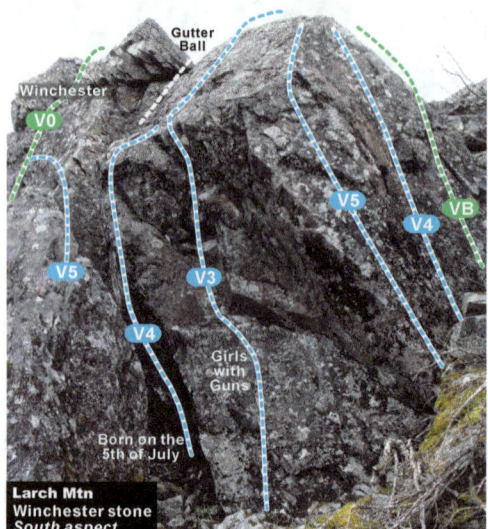

Larch Mtn Winchester stone South aspect

four-sided stelae-shaped block perched on the edge on a 15' vertical drop. It is a stunning powerful looking block with bouldering on the north aspect. Beta is left to right.

V0 Left Face
Minor face left of the crack.

V0 Pharoah ★
The short north side jam crack.

V_ (?) _____
North face thin crimps face potential.

V6 Fortes Fortuna Adjuvat ★★
The exposed vertical hi-ball northwest arête.

Directly below the Obelisk on the west side is a short 11' tall bluff with 4 minor problems (range VB-V0) and a short jam crack.

Rimtop Face

Immediately uphill (east) of Obelisk is a short 12' tall bluff. Beta from right to left as if departing from the Obelisk.

V2 _____ ★
The thin crimps face (rightmost).

V3 Right to Remain Silent

★★
The left thin crimp face.

V0 Crack ★
The basic corner crack.

V4ss Meatish Sweetballs
Prow immediately left of crack cleft.

Several more problems exist as the bluff trends downhill northward (ratings VB-V0).

EAST SIDE (WILD WEST BLUFF)

A group of boulders, outcrops, and fins located on the east side of the butte formation known as the Wild West knoll.

East Fin

This exhilerating fin has three cool problems on a well overhung 45° slice of rock.

V6ss East Fin ★★★
Sit start low on undercling, then mid-crimp, and long reach for lip.

V3 Straight Out Of Camas ★★
Start mid-face on face holds, then catch the lip out right.

V2 Mobile Chunks of Liquid Carbon ★★
The whole rail start-

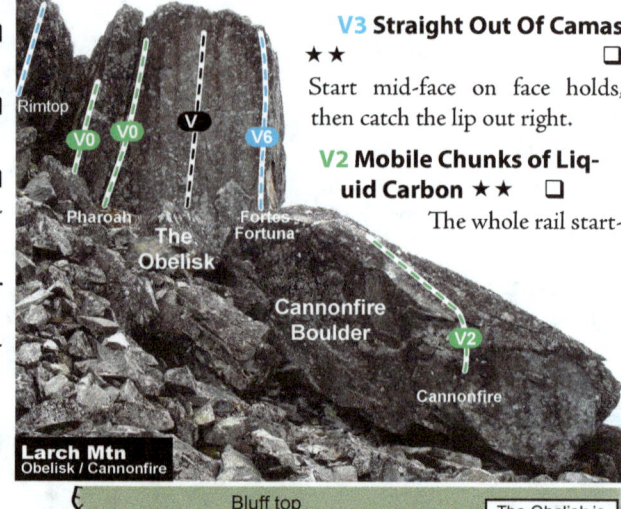

Larch Mtn Obelisk / Cannonfire

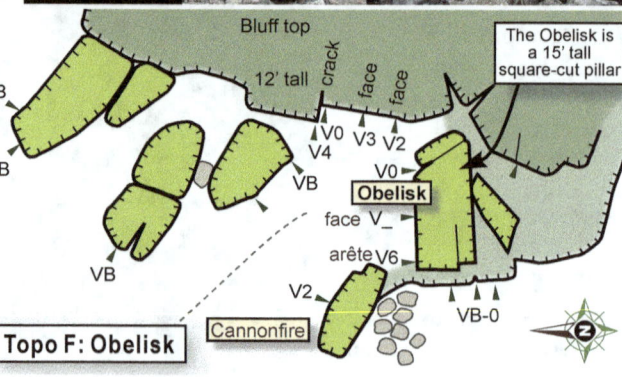

Topo F: Obelisk

Larch Mtn Boulders ✦ OR&B

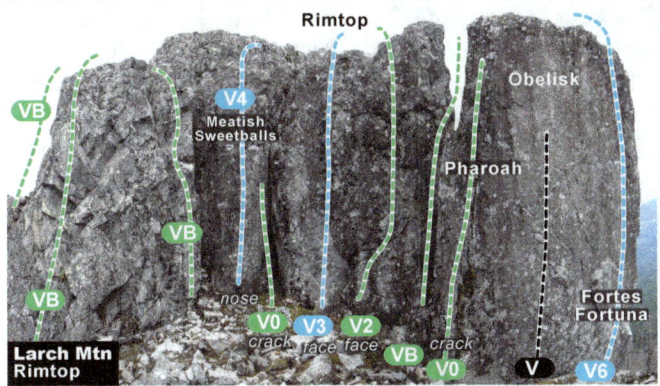

Eastwood Boulder

This is the reason to be at Larch Mountain boulders.

V7ss Eastwood Traverse ★★★★

A flat laying 25' long thin block of rock with a stellar hand-foot rail traverse. This is the premier attraction. The rail is an upside-down wrestling match, a horizontal traversing physical enduro power line 4' off the ground.

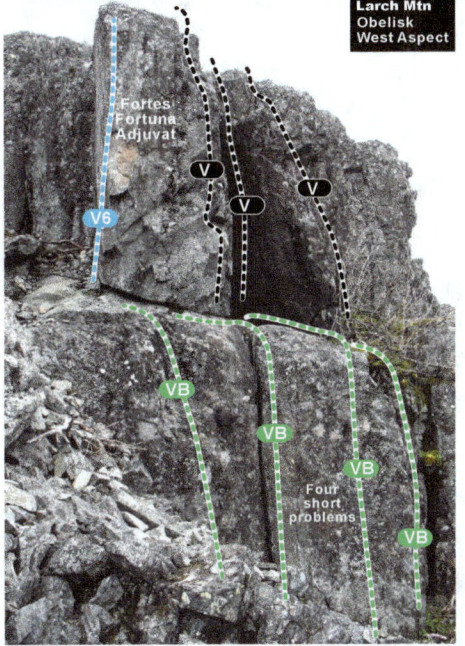

ing low on the right going up to far left.

Triple Threat Fin

Just to the right of East Fin is this overhanging tall fin with jugs on the entire upper part.

V1 (V3ss) Triple Threat ★★★

Standing start uses the uppermost undercling. The triple undercling sit start (V3ss) begins on a crack undercling on left outside and an inside right undercling, then go up to the second and third undercling onward to the top.

The rocky rimtop formation behind the two primary fins offer five VB faces, corners, or off-widths (all done). The main bluff reaches highball status (usually avoided) to the left of East Fin.

158 COLUMBIA GORGE

Larch Mtn Eastwood

V4ss Eastwood Direct ★
Starts on a hollow flake and goes out the center overhang as a mantle.

Bonanza Boulder
A few yards downhill from Eastwood Boulder is the Bonanza Boulder, a 17' hi-ball with 3 problems on a cool vertical rock face. Beta is described left to right:

V7 Shooting Gallery ★★★★
This route rides the left arête and crescent moon undercling as high as you can (a right hand-heel match will help), then small face crimps and foot smears.

V7+ (?) _____
A difficult center line (project).

V0 Jewel Heist
This is a long reach from a jug to a jug, mantle to a stance, then easy corner to top.

North Face Bluff ⚠
From the Wild West Bluff formation walk north to a rutted track and follow this west to its end. There is a north facing wall 15' tall by 45' long which may offer steep bouldering.

Roadside Boulder ⚠
This is one single large 17' tall roadside block just under the gravel access road near a parking spot on the south side of the Wild West knoll. Beta is left to right. Nothing special; just tall.

V0 _____
On the west part of the tall slab.

V1 _____
The center route on a tall slab.

V1 _____
The tall spooky slab (center right).

V1 Broken Arrow
The east face route.

V0 _____
The northeast face.

Larch Mtn Bonanza

ALPENGLOW BOULDERS

Certainly noted for being one of Portland's finest bouldering areas, Alpenglow holds a concentrated spectrum of VB-V10 problems situated on an open south-facing talus slope, surrounded by a fir forest with impeccable scenery, superb quality bouldering on stones ranging in size from 9'-18' tall, with the fattest stone measuring at nearly 35' in diameter. Alpenglow is a high-altitude locale overlooking the Columbia Gorge. The weather-scoured dacite rock is ideal for 'chalk-and-send' bouldering (about 50 problems and several traverses). The rock surface texture is composed of a slight fine grain quality (no moss), natural divots, edges and smears, rippled textured surficial features, steep vertical faces (both thin techy and jug lines), overhung aspects, dicey hi-ball lines, VB fun runs, and prows. All the quality you could ask for merged into a single core site offering a fine back-to-back list of classic boulder problems found in this region. This is a 1-2 crashpad recommended site.

History:

This site was specifically tapped by Mr Abbott and two close associates (Dave and Shane) starting way back in early 2002 (the team did 85% of all problems). As they returned late one October day from 3-Corner Rock bouldering they spied the Alpenglow cluster just above the tips of the trees. They parked along the roadside and walked up to the untapped site and were very impressed. But alas, the next day fall season rains began in earnest and neither were able to conquer the place until spring 2002. The site was aptly named Alpenglow Boulders by Abbott after seeing quality late in the day sunset hues. A few very stout problems were tagged in about 2014 by several locals and a few more in 2018 by Sam. Today, only a few random lines remain untapped on Shark and Hood Boulder.

Seasons:

Weather dependent conditional temperate variances exist at this site (it can get hot in July) based on the time of day, the season, if its a bright sunny windless day, or an overcast breezy afternoon. Until you experience the flavor of Alpenglow you have missed one of the finest this region has to offer.

Directions:

From State Route 14 at Beacon Rock, drive north on paved road Kueffler Road for 2 miles, then of NF1400 road for six miles till you reach the power lines. Park in a wide spot there, and walk 200' back down the main gravel road, then angle up slope (off-trail scramble) into the thick forest, aiming for a cluster of stones about 300' above the road.

Alternate: a very long alternate option exists by driving up the entire Washougal River road to the pass, then south on a rough gravel road that circumnavigates the west slope of 3-Corner Rock to reach Alpenglow Boulders from the north.

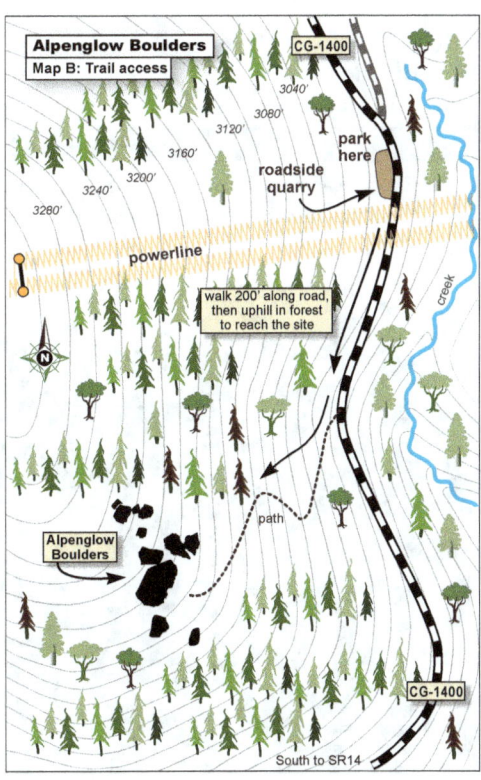

Alpenglow Boulder

This is the big long beast boulder with a string of high quality problems along its SE aspect. The hi-ball Alpenglow line beckons for those who relish savvy with spice. A great spot to warmup and catch a scenic view. Beta is listed from left to right:

V2 Mazama ★ ★

This is the leftmost problem tucked in the vertical scoop.

V1 Sunshine ★★
The next scoop to the right.

VB South Side ★★ ⚠
A series of small sloped steps and edges leading up into a prominent slot corner near the top.

V1 Alpenglow ★★★★ ⚠
Alpenglow tackles the tall section of the stone in the center of the face using a series of down sloping fat ramp rail edges, then delicately moves past the high rounded bulge onto the slab (hi-ball).

V5 The Spur ★★
Tackles a slight bulge using two tricky downward sloping fat rails (behind a small tree).

V4 Ice Feathers ★★★
This is a quality series of pockets and sidepulls on a slight hung double nose feature.

V4 Sunspot ★★★
This involves crimps to a slight notch at the lip, then follow the seam past the notch onto top slab (a V5 variation also merges into it).

V7ss Bring It On
A techy crimp line on the far right at slot.

THE TRAVERSE:

V5 Alpenglow Traverse ★
Entire base traverse (exclude the V7).

Cathedral Boulder
A long cigar-shaped block with a set of problems facing the sunshine. All short problems, but

Tymun on Shark Fin Arête

this boulder has some very cool problems, too.

V6 Cathedral ★★
This is a series of rounded slopers. Start at the far left at a nook where the boulders jam together (alternate ending V6 var).

V3ss Heather ★
A face with several tiny crimps.

VBss Bear Grass
A minor shorty groove.

V1ss Lip of Light ★
Start low just left of the next problem using several crimpy features on a short face.

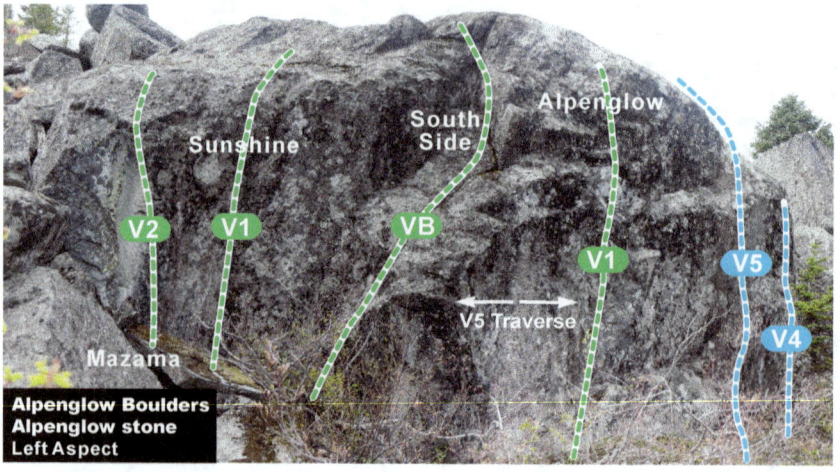

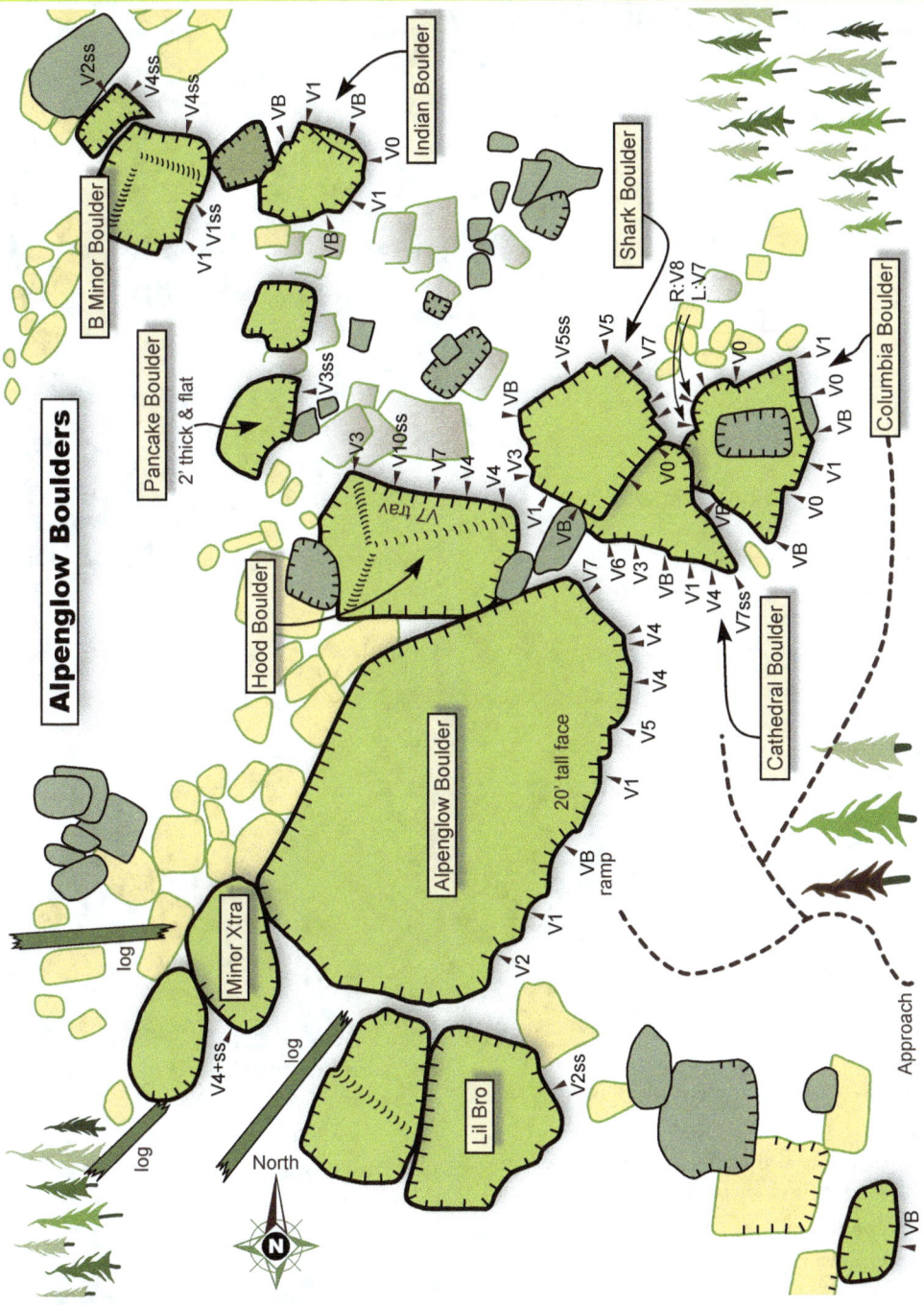

V4ss Cathedral Arête ★★★★
The lower prominent classic overhung nose. Sit start and punch directly over the entire thing.

THE TRAVERSE:

V7 Cathedral Traverse ★★★
Sit start on the Cathedral Arête, then traverse left uphill to the last problem and top out.

162 COLUMBIA GORGE Alpenglow Boulders

Columbia Boulder

This is a big square-*ish* boulder with a smaller squat block perched on top of it. The east face aspect is a tall hi-ball slab, while the shorter uphill section is tucked in a nook created by a group of blocks. Beta is left to right starting on the lower left end facing Mt Hood:

VB Modus Operandi ☐
March up steps, and minor groove on far left.

V0 (V1ss) Mea Culpa ★★ ☐
Use the giant gas pocket. Nice move, but can boost the power by doing a low sit start.

V1 (V3ss) Ex Nihilo Nihil Fit ★★ ☐
Start at overhang using a leftward slanting seam. Bump up the V by doing low sit start.

VB Cooper ★★★ ☐
Start on a small base stone, step onto an incut gas pocket, then cruise up the fun slab run on small pockets.

V0 Sandy ★★★ ☐
The right part of the same tall slab but starting at a slight notch, then cruise up left on the small pockets on the face.

V1 Wy'east Arête ★★★★ ☐
The classic sharp profiled arête which is always worth doing it. Start as previous but use the right hand arête.

V_ (?) _____ ☐
There may be a futuristic line on the face immediately right of the arête on its north side.

V0 The Groove ★ ☐
An obvious minor groove on the north side of the boulder.

V5ss Vanilla ★★ ☐
A short slightly overhung rounded face (using a minor round prow).

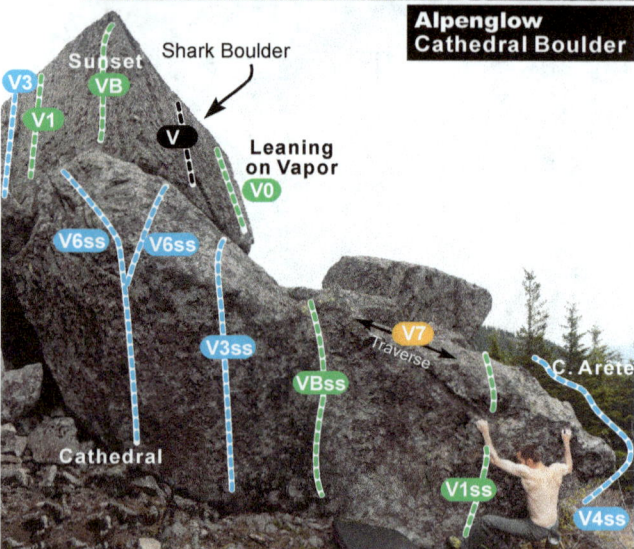

V8ss Don the Armoire ★★ ☐
An overhung face tucked in a small nook created by several nearby blocks.

V7ss Don't Sweat the Technique ★ ☐
Tucked deeper into the same deep overhung nook. With left hand on hung rail, power out an

overhung roof.

Shark Boulder

This is located just uphill from the Columbia Boulder. This high proudly perched boulder is stacked on part of the Cathedral Stone. The first problem listed below is the basic line on the southwest aspect. Beta is described clockwise from right to left:

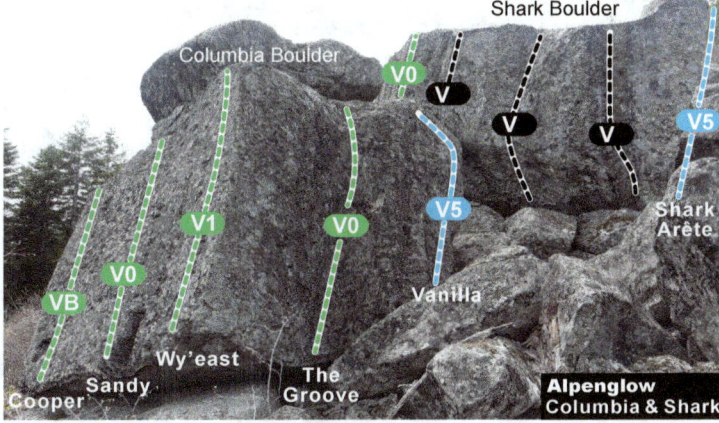

VB Sunset ★ ☐
Ascend it by standing on the Cathedral Boulder, make one move up, grab top, and mantle onto summit.

V1ss Northern Lights ★★★ ☐
A cool short crimp problem. Climb a slight vertical seam on a flat face.

V3ss Edge of Life ★★ ☐
Squeezed in there just left of the previous line. Use your right hand on a sharp lip.

VB Mantle ☐
Just a brief jug mantle.

VB Descent ☐
Well...the descent of course.

V5ss+ (?) _____ ☐
A possible corner-*ish* nuance that is tucked in further right of Shark Fin Arête [a block is in the way though].

V5ss Shark Fin Arête ★★★★ ☐
The super cool and classic problem that ascends the sharp arête. Sit start.

V7+ (?) _____ ☐
Start on the immediate left side of previous routes arête, go up left on crimps to the flat lip.

V7+ (?) _____ ☐
An unproven overhung groove on a vertical face.

V8+ (?) _____ ☐
Another unproven overhung groove.

V0 Leaning on Vapor ☐
Stand on the Columbia Boulder, and do a high step one-move onto this stone (with a partner as your backup).

V8-9ss+ (?) _____ ☐
Down in a pit, is this powerful seriously overhung crimp climb on the east aspect.

Hood Boulder

One of the other great spots to bring a crashing set of pads and work on some ultra power. The beta is left to right.

V4 (V6ss) Fait Accompli ★★ ☐
Start low on the far lower left and power up the overhung rib, then over lip.

V4ss The Native ★★★ ☐
Start low and make several crimps moves that end on a groove then the lip mantle.

V7ss Shattered ★★ ☐
Sit start low using a sidepull and reach tiny crimps, then catch lip and power over.

164 COLUMBIA GORGE — Alpenglow Boulders

V10+ss (?)
Very thin crimpy face on right half of boulder.

V3ss Columbine ★
Just a nice warmup on a rounded right nose.

THE TRAVERSE:

V7 Tilly Jane Traverse ★★★
Quality and very powerful slopers rail traverse. Begin on leftmost route down low and run rightward along the entire lip.

Pancake Boulder

Very flat boulder, easy to mistake as you wander past it. But yup thars something on it, too.

V3ss Pancake ★
A minor flat 2' thick block with a low traverse.

Indian Boulder

The next several boulders are fairly minor, but a few of the problems offer unique enough variety for the easier grades. Beta is left to right:

VB Teepee ★
Climb a scoop and keep right hand on a fin.

V1ss Indian Scout ★★
Use your left hand on a fin while going up face.

V0ss Peace Pipe ★
A minor rounded face.

VB Palamino
On the north aspect is a series of steps.

V0ss Bring Your Bow
A minor point and rightmost problem.

B Minor Boulder

Definitely a small boulder. Beta is listed from left to right:

V1ss Nolens Volens
Sit ultra low, catch lip and up. On SE aspect.

V1ss Hypnotic
Sit ultra low, face hold, grab lip, and up (all using low hung prow really). On the SE aspect.

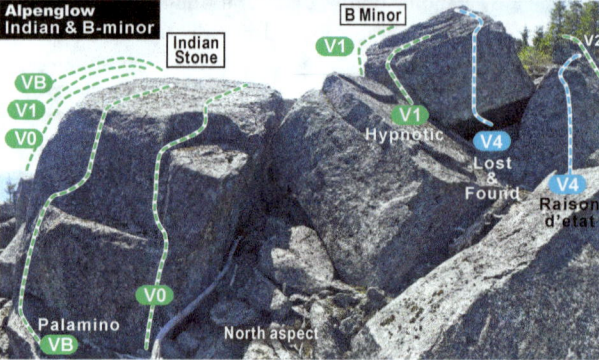

V4ss Lost & Found ★
Under the lowest part of stone on the north side. Sit start, using a short rail and get up.

C Minor Boulder

And right next to the previous stone is this minor stone. Beta is left to right.

V4ss Raison d'etat ★
On its outer steep aspect is this low crimpy sit start problem.

V2ss Hypnosis
A final minor sit problem on the uphill side.

Minor Xtra Boulder

And way over on the SW upper side of the Alpenglow Boulder is a brief block that got just big enough to yield a minor sit start problem.

V4ss Alpen Extra
Start low and crimp an overhang to the lip and over the top.

BRIDGE OF THE GODS BOULDERS

When it came time to explore beyond the confines of Carver way back in the day, the locals delved into the Gorge and tapped these boulders. The Bridge of the Gods Boulders (BOGB) is set in a extensive talus field as pocket clusters of quality andesite stones, ranging in height from 9' – 16' tall, and a few taller ones. The talus field originated from Table Mtn to the north, and sloughed off into the Columbia River long ago.

There are two popular areas – the Lower Powerline area, and the Upper Area (+ the Dome near the knoll) one mile up a rough gravel road. The common established areas are good destinations during the good weather months from May-Oct (and virtually year-round when its sunny). BOGB is a south-facing site in the rainiest part of the Gorge, but strong prevailing wind patterns can dry out the stones in 1-2 days in winter. One to two crashpads are the minimum recommendation. Considerable loose, rough talus limits future exploratory interest to the boulders nearest to the road. The area is infested with substantial poison oak growth, surrounded by forested sections and brushy ravines. Rock type nuances: the andesite stones yield powerful overhangs, techy crimper lines, traverse smear-fests, on a light grain crystalline phenocryst matrix that gives the problems a quality sticky appeal.

Directions:

Drive I-84 to Cascade Locks (or State Route 14), cross the bridge into Washington. Ashes Lake is just to the east of the bridge. Take the paved road that wraps around the northwest side of the lake, then drive up a steep gravel road en route to the quarry at Blue Lake, but when you reach the first set of power line towers, turn onto a minor dirt road, and park here (see map). A path wanders east 200' to the first primary cluster of blocks.

POWERLINE AREA

LOWER MAIN ZONE

Boulder A

As you walk the path east to reach the big cool popular boulder you pass this tiny creature off to your right a few yards.

V3ss _____ ★ ☐
Do just the left rib.

V4ss _____ ★ ☐
Angle right using center crimps.

VBss _____ ☐
Run the rib up leftward.

Boulder B

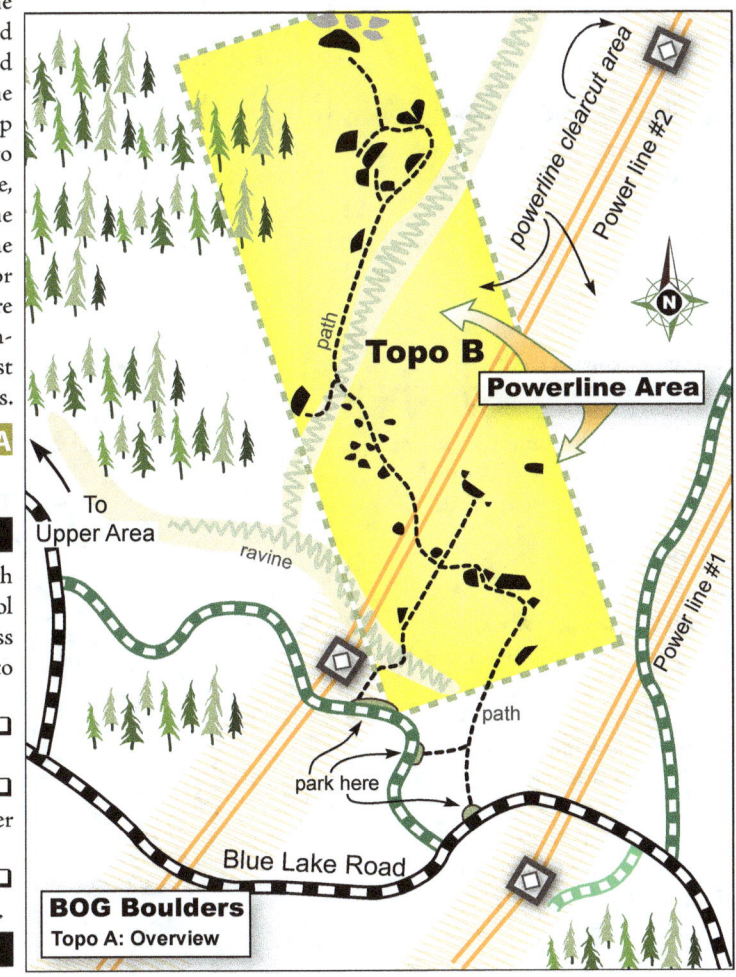

BOG Boulders
Topo A: Overview

166 COLUMBIA GORGE — BOG Boulders

BOG Boulders
Stone C

VBss ☐
Ultra low shorty.

V3ss ☐
Ultra low shorty.

Boulder C
A nice sized stone immediately south of the big mega boulder.

V4 ★ ☐
Tall nose.

V4 ★ ☐
Nose start, then up right on face.

V3 ☐
Just the slab on the right

Boulder D (Jury)
This is a very common spot to visit at BOGB because of convenience and quality lines. Beta starts on the SE side at the stout line.

V6 All Right Jury ★ ☐
Southeast prow and face.

V8 All White Jury ★★ ☐
Hung south face, crimps up right into previous line.

V5 El Percy ★★★ ☐
South nose starting on a big jug.

V6 Roller Skates ★ ☐
Thin face on the west aspect.

V3 Itchy & Scratchy ★ ☐
A thin seam on the west side.

V2 Land Down Under ★ ☐
A slabby face on the west side.

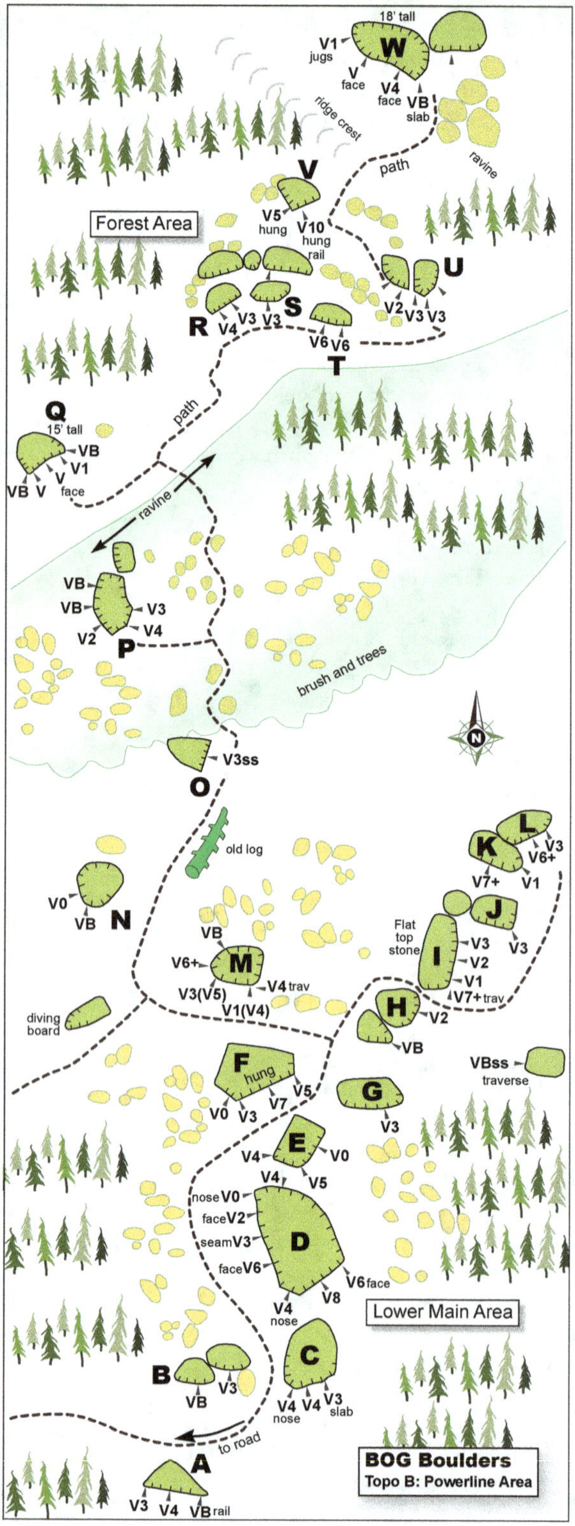

BOG Boulders
Topo B: Powerline Area

BOG Boulders ✦ OR&B 167

V0 ☐
The short north side nose.

V4 Tsunami ☐
The short north face.

Boulder E

V4ss ☐
Begin sit start low on west bulge.

V5ss ★ ☐
Sit start; hung crimps on south aspect.

V0 ☐
A minor located on the east side slab.

Boulder F

Prominent, enticing overhung flat south face.

V5 ★★ ☐
Climb hung crimps on far right up to the lip.

V7ss ★★★ ☐
On a hung face make a long reach up right to an edge, then reach again to the lip. Quality line.

V3ss ★★ ☐
Start on hung face but go up left onto easy slab.

V0ss ☐
A low start using the left edges on left side.

Boulder G

V3ss ☐
Low start and short.

Boulder H

V2ss ☐
Sit start shorty.

Boulder __

VBss ☐
On another small stone to the left of #H.

Boulder I

A long stone lacking height, but offering several low start problems.

V7+ Traverse ☐
Do the entire traverse along the lip.

V1ss ☐
On the left; get up over the lip.

V2ss _____
Mantle in middle & get over the lip.
V3ss _____
Rightmost problem; get over the lip.

Boulder J

V3ss _____
Sit in low spot, pull over lip and up rib.

Boulder K

V7+ _____
Climb up on the left side of the stone.
V1 _____
Climb the nose of this stone.

Boulder L

V6+ _____
Climb up on the left.
V3 _____
Climb up on the right.

Boulder M (Quality Time)

Quality time boulder and a favorite.
V4ss Traverse ★★
Traverse entire lip leftward & top out.
V1 (V4ss) _____ ★★
Positive holds bump up along incut rail and moving left to point and over lip.
V3 (V5ss) _____ ★
Low crimps on south aspect.
V6ss+ _____ ★
Sit start just the over hung west nose.
VB _____
Ascend slab on the NW face.

Boulder N

V0ss _____
Sit start minor (on the left).
VBss _____
Ultra low start minor (on the right).

Boulder O

Located on the path so it's a popular problem to experience. Quite short but quality.
V3ss _____ ★★
Sit low, power crimps on the hung east face.

Boulder P

Large stone just west of the path with fun tall lines. Beta is R to L.

V3ss ____ ❏
The east hung aspect near center.
V4ss ____ ❏
The east face using left point.

And the next are on the west side:
V2 ____ ❏
Crimps on short slab face.
VB ____ ❏
Fun run on center slab.
VB ____ ❏
Left section; west side slab.

Boulder Q

A large boulder with a hi-ball south aspect (and poison oak). Where the path splits, go left for 100' to reach this boulder.

VB ____ ❏
Do a brief face just left of nose.
V_ ____ ❏
Left nose, but with left hand on left rib.
V_ ____ ❏
The powerful center face exiting high right.
V0 ____ ❏
Right face using good small edges.
VB ____ ❏
Far right on brief round nose.

Boulder R

A triangular shaped stone on the path.

V4ss ____ ★ ❏
Climb up on hung left face using lip then move

BOG Boulders Stone N

BOG Boulders Stone O

BOG Boulders Stone P

BOG Boulders Stone P

170 COLUMBIA GORGE — BOG Boulders

left onto slab.

V3ss ☐

Climb hung smears, sloped crimps to start, and catch rib, exit right onto the slab.

Boulder S

V3 _____ *(minor problem)*

Boulder T

V6ss _____ ★

Smooth hung face with slight foot smears and dicey crimps (left hand on rib). Top slab is often mossy. Sit start.

V6ss _____

Hung crimps, then crimps on mossy slab, and tough to exit up onto the slab. Sit start.

Boulder U

A split block that is roughly shaped like a big heart. Beta is described right to left.

V_ _____

Just the far right face.

V3 _____ ★

The center flat nose using crimps.

V3 _____ ★

Climb crimps on the vertical face (where the two blocks split apart).

V2 _____ ★

The rib on the left block.

V_ (?) _____

Do just the left face of the left block.

Boulder V

Poison oak at base, but several powerful lines.

V8 (10ss) _____ ★★★

Right face starting low on powerful overhung slopers/crimps, move up to a sloper rail, then cruise left along rail to top point.

V5ss _____

Start low on left hung face using reachy crimps and jugs.

Boulder W ⚠

From the last boulder, walk north briefly into a ravine choked with mossy boulders to find this huge 18' tall beast. Beta is described from Right to Left.

VB _____ ★

Long cool southeast prow slab

V4 _____ ★

The vertical direct center face.

V_ (?) _____

Another powerful possible face.

V1 _____ ★

Steep jug run on the left.

BOG Boulders — Upper Area Trail Block

UPPER AREA

The Upper Area has perhaps the finest double set of leaning pillars in this region perfectly designed for ultra cool quality bouldering. These two stones are White and Lotus Boulders. A visit here is a must-do on everyone's hit list.

To reach the Upper Area drive up a rough gravel road (past the natural gas pipeline) one mile (toward Mosley Lakes), then turn right onto a cul-de-sac road and park at its end (see map). A rough path scrambles down slope (from the parking spot) and across a talus zone to the lower end of a minor wooded knoll.

Trail Boulder (#1)

BOG Boulders
Topo C: Upper Area

172 COLUMBIA GORGE — BOG Boulders

The first substantial boulder you see alongside the path. It's in a low trough and well worth doing all the fun lines. A unique fun boulder, about 11' tall, and loaded with five enjoyable warmup problems. Beta is listed right to left.

VB _____ ★ ☐
Juggy outside nose on far right.

V0 _____ ★ ☐
Hung crack on right (the sit start is harder).

V3 _____ ★★ ☐
Crimps on face over top lip.

V0 _____ ★★ ☐
The fat hung crack using all of the right side of the crack. Fun run.

V1 _____ ★ ☐
The far left rib going up right.

Boulder 2

V_ss _____ ☐
Sit start; power over a hung bulge.

Bouncer Boulder (3)

V11 Yojimbo ★★★ ☐
Start low in center, power up left over slightly hung sloped lip.

V5ss The Bouncer ★★★★ ☐
Start low on rail in center of face, move up right over bulge, commit to thin crimps.

White Boulder (4)

Walk right along a path around the corner about 30' to two parallel free-standing pillars. White Boulder is the tall left pillar.

V3 _____ ★ ☐
The west aspect of the pillar (V4 rules).

V7 (V11ss) Rodeo ★★★★ ☐
The classic hung leaning left arête.

V6 White Lines ★★★★ ☐
This is the impressive right arête of same block that angles up leftward.

V2 Grey Lines ★★★ ☐
The slabby face between the two pillars.

Lotus Throne Boulder (5)

This is the unique tilted tall right pillar.

V10 Lotus Throne
★★★★ ☐
The left arête. Toss to a side-pull, then series of left-handed slaps up the arête.

V8ss Upsetter
★★★★ ☐
This is the classic right arête. Start low on the arête and arc up leftward to top.

V2 Springtime ★ ☐
Smears on the long east slab.

V0 _____ ☐
Minor problem on the northwest outer corner.

BOULDER #6 & #7

This next set of stones are tucked behind (north of) the White / Lotus Boulders. To reach stone set #6 walk between White/Lotus. To reach stone set #7 walk around the left side of White to access it.

Boulders 6a & 6b

V2ss Ballrog ☐
Low start at lip with jug, move up onto face (on #6a stone).

V3ss Log Jam ☐
The taller unit on the right (#6b stone).

Boulders 7a & 7b

Two options: V2 to V4 (one can be done as a sit start or standing).

From the Lotus Boulder walk right a few yards to the next stone.

Boulder 8

Beta is left to right: V0 crack, VB face, VB crack, VB crack. Further north along the path is a minor rock finger (V3, V0, and V0).

Boulder 9

The next stone (#9) juts out over the path but has a poor landing.

Stretch Arm Boulder (10)

From the previous boulder, walk a short distance eastward to the final tall stone.

V5ss One Move Wonder ☐
Southwest face reaching up left to catch rib then cruise up rib to top.

V7 Stretch Murphy ★★★ ☐
South face crimps using the seam and face moving up leftward.

V5ss Four Star Arête ★★★★ ☐
Tackle vertical east arête straight on. Classic.

V2 _____ ★★ ☐
On the north aspect but using some of the same east nose (with left hand).

V5 (V7ss) Stretch Arm Strong ★★★ ☐
North aspect using an arête (with right hand).

V6/7ss Lightning ★ ☐
Same as previous but use only right back prow.

THE OUTCROP

About 40' north of Stretch Arm Boulder is a tiny but tall-*ish* rock bluff. It has several hi-ball x-rated problems (L to R): **V4** (**V5ss**) **High as a Kite** (tall arête), **V3ss Tornado** (on the backside of previous line). **V2ss Wave** is another nearby low block.

An isolated stone about 100' east of the of Stretch Arm Boulder has several short V0-V1 problems (beware of poison oak).

THE DOME

This is a compact boulder zone with a large hung rock bluff scarp, yet most problems are hiball status. Located uphill closer to the forested knoll. History goes back to the early days when Jered Bernert and friends discovered and tapped a few lines such as Vato Loco. Problems here tend to be hi-ball.

V7 Vato Loco ☐
Incut powerful line on the right portion of the bluff.

V7 _____ ☐
Dyno from last jug on Vato at 15' up.

V6 _____ ☐
The arête about 15' left of Vato.

V4/5ss _____ ☐
Sit low and climb overhung small roof (left of previous line). Alternate left holds make the climb easier.

V1 _____ ☐
Prominent section of rock next to previous line, has a hi-ball problem.

EMPIRE BOULDERS

The Empire Boulders is certainly the gem quality site Portlander's have been long awaiting to see. Packed into a remarkably compact zone of about 700' square with a wide variety of sizable boulders that are loaded with every rating possible from VB to V-insane (including hi-ball lines) the Empire is truly destined to become a locally popular, highly favored site.

For those folks who prefer nationally famous places like Buttermilk Boulders (or any global bouldering site) this little site is very good. For those who live in this micro-region this site is a cool gem that seemingly fits a miniaturized version of one of those ultra-stellar destination bouldering places. When compared to other bouldering sites in this region few compare with the sheer magnitude of the technical nature, quality, and difficulty found at this one bouldering site.

Empire's combined total number of problems on the boulders and on the bluff outcrop exceeds 325 problems (90%+ of it tapped by just two persons). The height of many boulders are in that spice and dice range where several crashpads stacked minimize the jump-off gambit.

The bouldering ratings are suitably broad for both entry level boulderers and skilled experts, with plenty of warm-up lines VB-V4, a lesser string of mid-level power lines V5-V8, followed with a select upper string of V9-V12+ futuristic lines. All the boulders tumbled long ago from a minor cliff band just above the dense stone cluster. The bluff offers a plethora of power problems (some substantially overhung) with beastly lines trending upward to 25' tall.

Empire Boulders is easily reached by a convenient paved road to a parking pullout spot (there are residential dwellings nearby so think low-key non-noise environment) and a short path.

Bring more than one crashpad, especially if you plan to do anything hi-ball. Bring a chalkbag for your waist especially if you are there on a warm summer day doing hi-ball lines. When the moss regrows you may need to apply a brush to some lines a bit though the many overhung lines will not see much regrowth. Fir needles become a slight nuisance in the spring season so consider bringing a small whisk broom to knock off the excess needles. Certain 18-27' hi-ball boulders and outcrops have a top anchor (or nearby tree) if you desire a top-rope.

History:

Empire is ultra secluded in a forest grotto. It's discovery would have been impossible except for the sleuthing skill of a local mushroom hunter. Therefore, considerable appreciation goes to our close friend Mr. B who stumbled upon this site long ago and kept it secret for many years. He eventually revealed it to Mr O, who, after an additional several years elapsed invited Mr A to the site so that he could get that renewed spark for bouldering. His comment pretty much sums it up, "...I've been waiting a life-time for a place like this near home base." So this exclusive team tapped into the site even more heavily in 2015-2018. These two folks are the highly valued primary site development stewards at this site (as well as many of this regions other sites). Yet there are a few remaining untapped breadcrumbs at EB (albeit some hi-ball and extreme power lines). The V9-V12+ lines, though stunning, tend to be few in totality (no more easy sugar cookies).

Stepping briefly back into a historical time frame, it can be noted that for many years Bridge of the Gods Boulders were thought to be charting the next golden age of Portland bouldering. Then, along came a string of gems such as Alpenglow and Three Corner Rock to shake up the scene (if you were part of that inner circle). Then along came Lost Lake Boulders which in its own way is an earth shaking site for this region. Yet all of these places missed just a few minor details; ultra compact site, hi-ball lines with natural soil landings, summer time bouldering in a forested scene (imagine boiling hot days at Hamilton Boulders), gargantuan stone beasts, easily accessible boulders from a paved county road, superb quality stone textural nuances, and virtual all-year bouldering. With a few days of dry weather in the winter this site may be viable even in the winter months. This lengthy combination of unique factors make Empire Boulders this micro-regions prime bouldering site.

In this northwest USA micro-region the boulder size does not necessarily equate to quality boulder problems, but this compact site offers a surprise, in that even the tall V0 sketch lines are crimp/smear adventure spicy problems that can satisfy even the most ardent chalk warrior. So just how big is the biggest stone here? The Roman Boulder is a triangular shaped beast that logs in at 36' x 34' x 28' girth, and 19' tall on its east aspect. OK...super wow! Surprisingly, this yields a rare single massive stone that is both easily accessible and of a quality composition ideal for bouldering (within a short drive of Portland). The tallest single stone is 27' tall (Inca Boulder). The tallest part of the cliff outcrop is over 25' tall.

Rock type and rock surface nuances:

The bluff formation and boulders are broadly classed as a pyroclastic or volcanoclastic rock deposit, and was likely laid down under rapid volcanic processes that enhanced the stratified layering effect with heat compaction under pressure. The strata is duo-tone gray welded lithic (e.g. solidified) ignimbrite-*like* ash bed. The strata contains vesicular pockets, small scooped out spheroidal surface weathered divots, distinct internal stratified banding, including considerable embedded fragments of basaltic rock chips of various small sizes, and limited quantities of various scattered minerals such as quartz.

The rock textural nuances are very amenable for bouldering, and offer a well textured friction-friendly surface, some large angular flat aspects, substantial overhung sections, considerable gas pockets of variable sizes (usually rounded but sometimes incut) from micro to 7", small embedded basaltic nubbin protrusions (up to 5") welded into a gray ground mass.

Pesks and other Nuisances:

Yes, there are some. Poison oak exists in very limited spotty places, varieties of flies, horseflies, mosquitoes, spiders, etc., pretty much all the typical things one might find in the forest except gorillas. The flying pests are active primarily in early summer but relatively inactive on cool cloudy or breezy days. Evenings will bring out the mosquitoes. Hornets are a difficult encounter (they give no advanced warning) and there are known to be nests in the general vicinity (use caution when marching off to go pooh). Moss and various dust lichens occur mainly on less traveled boulder problems.

And did we forget to mention the bears. If you are bouldering silently for considerable periods, bears may wander unexpectedly through the bouldering area (sing a little jingle if you are there alone).

Advantages:

The site is shaded all year by tall Douglas fir trees, so summer time is quite viable here, even in July so long as there is a breeze. It's a low elevation (1050') site so it seldom gets snowed in, but it can be damp in the winter months, therefore its seasonally viable 12-months of the year *when* its dry. On boiling hot summer days (90°F or higher) that lack a breeze the humidity factor tends to limit your ability to crank V-hard. Contrary to most bouldering sites in this region the Empire Boulders do offer parameters highly favorable to *family-friendly* bouldering outings (approach, some low angle boulders, non-rocky terrain). Cell phone reception is good. Additionally, the site is on US Forest Service managed land.

Site Variety:
A multi-use site offering fall season bouldering, mushrooming, and perhaps minor top-roping. Power is always needed for the crimpy stout lines, but a sustained level of endurance and steady focus is beneficial for the lower grade hi-ball lines. For the low-ball fanatic there are plenty of short lines and traverses to tweak your tips.

Grades:
The boulders yield a suitable range of difficulties conducive to most persons in this sport. The total problems here exceed the 300 goal post. The most common grade of course is V0-V3 (40%); the next most common is VB (30%) [anything 5.0-5.9]; a lesser group of V4-V8 (20%); and only a smattering of extreme V9-V14 problems (10%).

Naming convention of boulders:
The ideological naming conventions seen at the Empire Boulders are generally attained from obsolete empires, emperors, dynasties, or autocracies from the various imperialism's of centuries past. And due to a friendly local bear population we dedicated a few stones to the furry black creatures, too. Part of the outcrop bluff formation is broadly named the Great Wall of China with correlating dynasties (or prominent regional features) to pinpoint each specific smaller outcrops. All this and more at a curiously fascinating bouldering site spiked by a wealth of history.

Stewardship:
There are residential dwellings nearby along the primary paved road, so common etiquette is required for long-term viability of this site. Enjoy the quiet forested appeal of the site. Avoid using boombox stereos, keep pets in control (i.e. leashed), use the established path network, bury your pooh in a distant location, etc. You might consider not smoking here (a LNG natural gas pipeline is located nearby) for everyone's safety. The vine maples around the boulders keep the poison oak from growing too easily, so keeping as much undergrowth growing is vital. The site steward is Mr A; he frequently boulders here with friends, and he often emphasizes site values, promotes safety, user discretion, and courteous interaction. If you send a new line (a rare day here indeed) provide your latest project 'send' info to him, and be of valuable service to this site by assisting the 'caretakers' in various stewardship opportunities at this site.

Path Access:
A brief 500' long path gently ascends an open forested slope passing several smaller stones en route to the Roman Boulder. When you reach this big stone, the path splits. A prominent deer path ventures horizontally from the upper west cluster, eastward past the main central cluster (just above the Egyptian Boulder), continuing eastward just above the Babylon Boulder and over eastward to the lower east cluster. Various foot paths branch off from this deer path to reach other stones and outcrops. Some of the forest between the paved road and boulders is a tangle of low brushy growth, wind fall, random hornet nests, and poison oak, so its best to follow commonly used paths.

Site Orientation:

This site is encompassed by a long east-west randomly outcropping very short bluff. Below this bluff formation the entire group of boulders are found concentrated into generally four primary areas; the initial trail cluster (the Bear Cluster is located here), the central cluster (the Roman Boulder is located here), the upper west cluster (where the Greek Boulder is tucked in a low trough), and the lower east cluster (the massive Inca Boulder is located here). The site is nicely wrapped in a deep forest canopy of fir trees.

Camping arrangements:

Timberlake Campground and RV Park is located less than one mile down the road, and it offers quality seasonal camping arrangements for those travelers who are on a road bouldering tour of the US west coast region. Another quality seasonal campground is located at the Skamania county baseball park (east end of park). This county park and campground offers riverside access and free shower facilities. The county campground is open from May 1st – Oct 31st . With two very nearby quality camping facilities, do not camp at the bouldering site, nor at the end of the paved road at the parking spot.

Amenities:

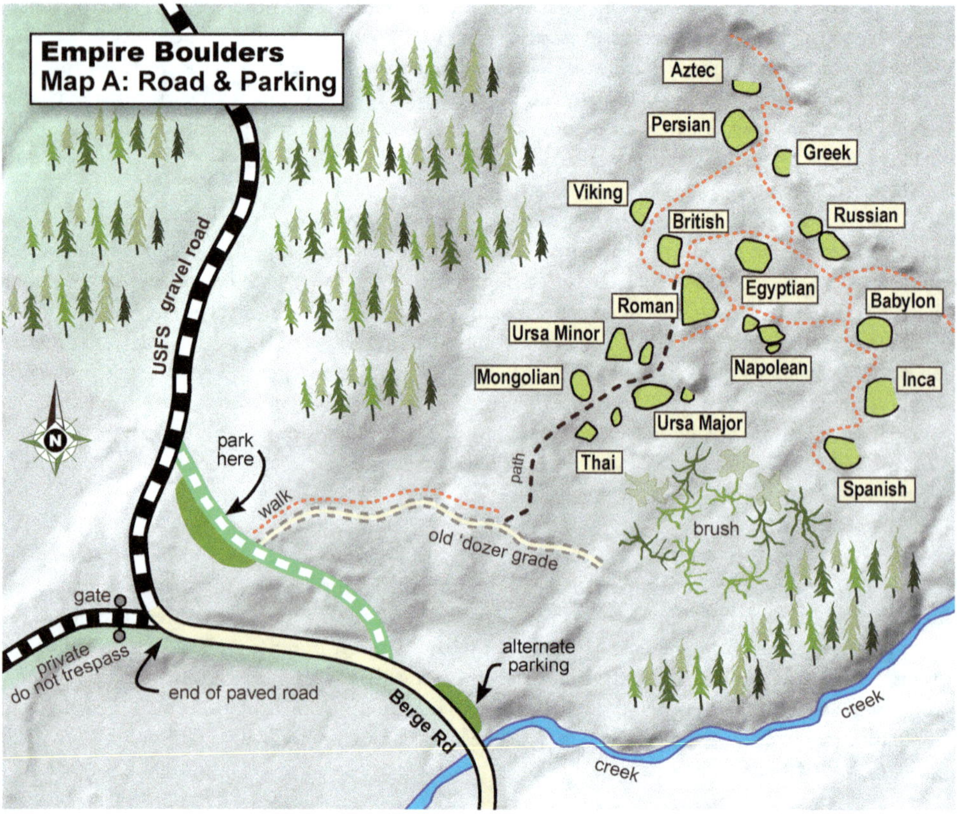

The nearest large grocery store is located in Stevenson, Washington, though a good tiny mart exists at Home Valley (⅛ mile east of Berge Road junction) for basic items. Stevenson also has a variety of shops and fast food arrangements, and is the county seat for administration and emergency services.

Directions:

Drive east from Portland, Oregon on I-84 freeway. At Cascade Locks cross the Bridge of the Gods bridge. From the north end of the bridge on State Route 14 continue east (passing Stevenson, WA) for 8.3 miles. When you enter the small community of Home Valley turn left (north) onto Berge Road and drive uphill for 3.6 miles to the end of the paved road and park alongside the paved road (do not block the private driveway, nor the USFS road), or park on a dirt side spur (*see map*). Walk uphill on a narrow path for about 500' to rach the first boulders. Anticipate about 1¼ hours drive time from Portland-Vancouver.

THE BEAR GROUP

The Bear Cluster is the first series of six boulders that range in height from disgustingly short to invitingly tall, yet each seems to have quantitative gems certain to wet your palette. So, let's begin this famous site tour with our first stone, the Pax Mongolia.

Mongolian Boulder

This is the initial minor low laying oval-shaped boulder with an obvious sloped lip wrapping around its south aspect. Its the first stone you encounter walking up the path en route to the main area. Beta is left to right:

VB Ultima Ratio Regum (aka War) ❑
Minor problem; easy get down method.

V0ss Mandate from Heaven ★ ❑
Brief set of small crimps over lip onto slab.

VB (V3ss) Khublai Khan ★★ ❑
Fat hold mantle. Sit start adds a long lunge.

V3ss Hwacha ★★★ ❑
Crimps at the lip, and a tough dead-point to reach crimps on the slab face above.

V6ss The Scourge ★ ❑
Start on two sloper edges, use lip moving right up over the very point of overhang.

V4ss Genghis Khan ★★ ❑
Start very low on left pocket and right side pull, then lunge for the jug, and power mantle over the lip yield a superb line.

Siam Boulder (aka Thai Boulder)

Technically, this is the first boulder on the hike uphill, though due to its low profile its easy to walk past it without realizing that a few lines exist on the east aspect. It's situated about 30' downhill from the Mongolian Boulder just east of the trail. Beta is listed left to right.

V1ss Siamese Twin ★ ❑
Low bulge left of the fir tree.

VB White Elephant ★ ❑
Brief flat face just right of a fir tree.

V0 Little Buddha ★ ❑
Also just right of tree (very close to left VB) but more on the subtle round point.

VB Red Curry ❑
A short vertical scoop.

VB King and I ❑
A short vertical face.

VB Angkor Wat ❑
Brief east point.

VB Sticky Rice ❑
Odd traverse along north slab.

VB Kneejerk ❑
Minor kick on the north point.

The south aspect has four very short family/kid friendly VB's (2 smears, 2 mantles).

Ursa Minor Boulder

The next substantial sized boulder on the hike uphill. Its a superb 13' tall trail-side stone that has a vertical south-facing aspect with a treasure

180 COLUMBIA GORGE ✦ Empire Boulders

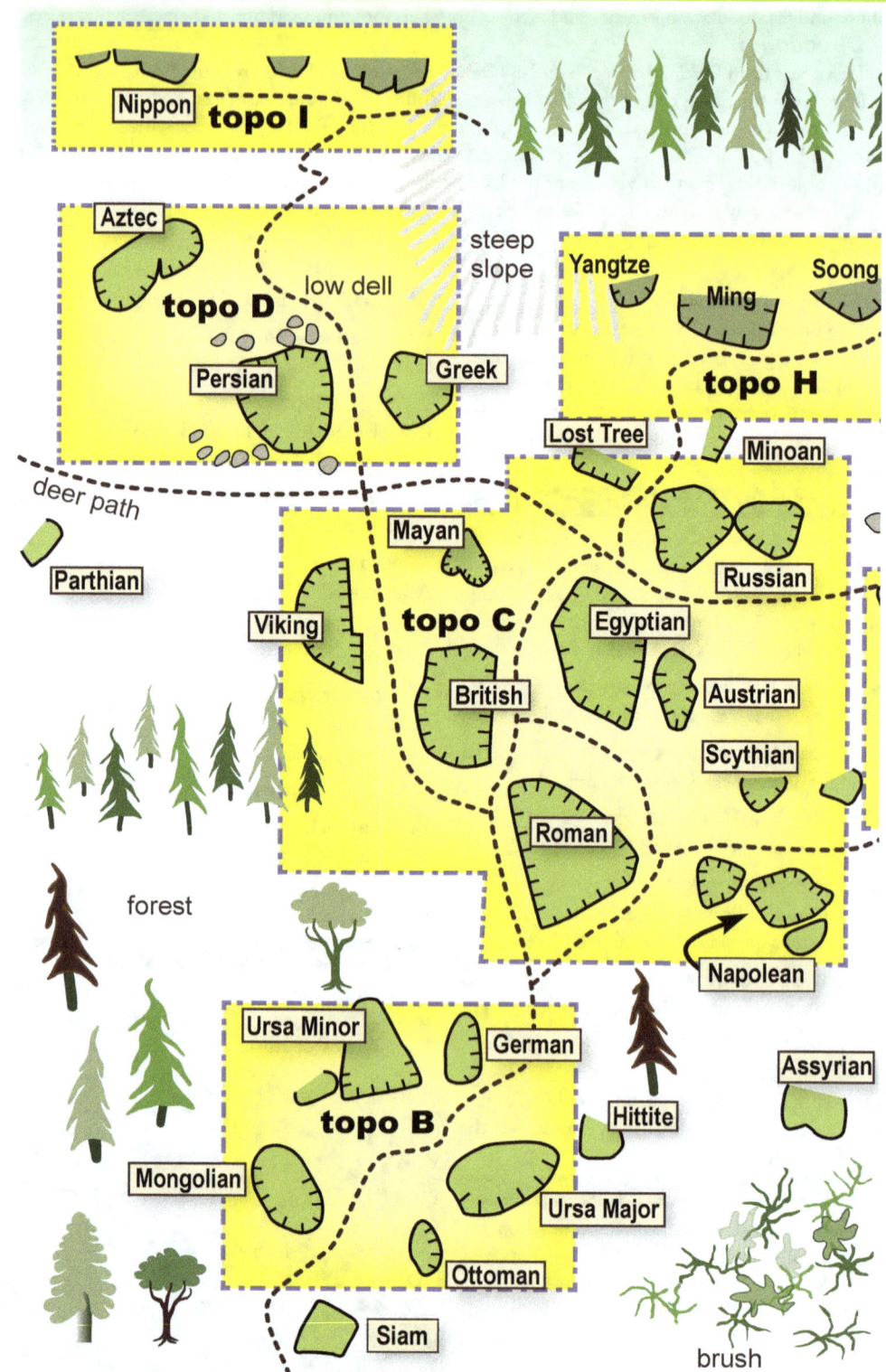

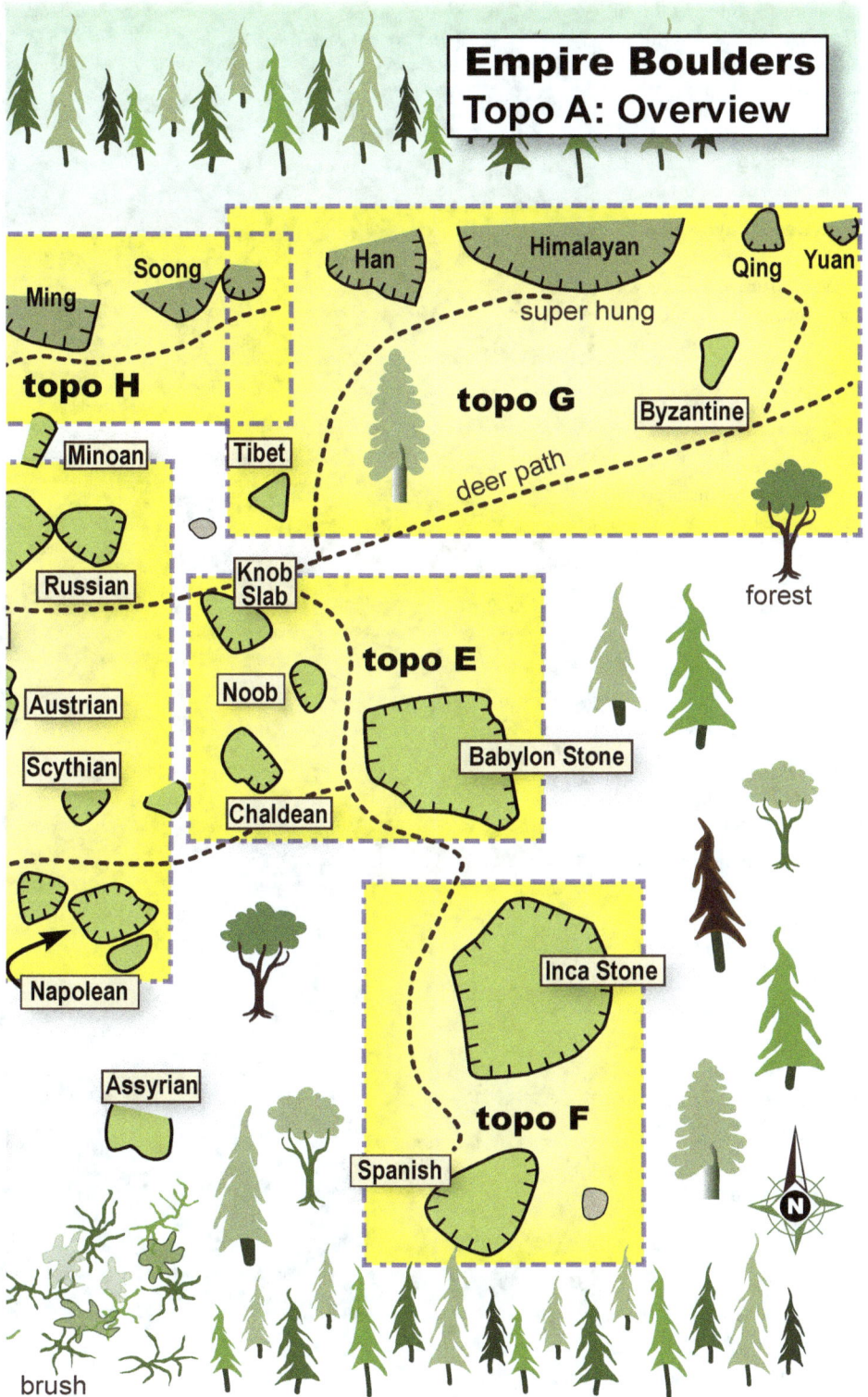

of serious problems on it. The first beta is for the independent round low blob on the far left. Beta is left to right.

VB Bear Rug
Minor variant on far left.

V4ss Bear Claw ★★★
Traverse from left all the way right into the V0 and then bump up and mantle over bulge.

V0 (V4ss) Chubby Huckster ★★★
Sit low on left dish & crimp, then bump to next crimp, then catch lip, then mantle. The standing start merely starts on both good crimps and bumps for the lip and mantles over.

...And on the vertical south face of the main big boulder (beta L to R):

VB Pocket Rocket
Use the obvious natural pocket on nose.

V5 Bear Minimum ★★
Left face using a sloped pocket and reaches for more sloped holds.

V6 Big For Your Boots ★★★★
Center power line – pinches, balance, dead-point reaches (exit right V6; direct to top V8).

V7 Three Bears
Power line in the center of tall face cruising a partial seam.

V3 Bearly There ★★★
Skinny face on the right with surprisingly subtle

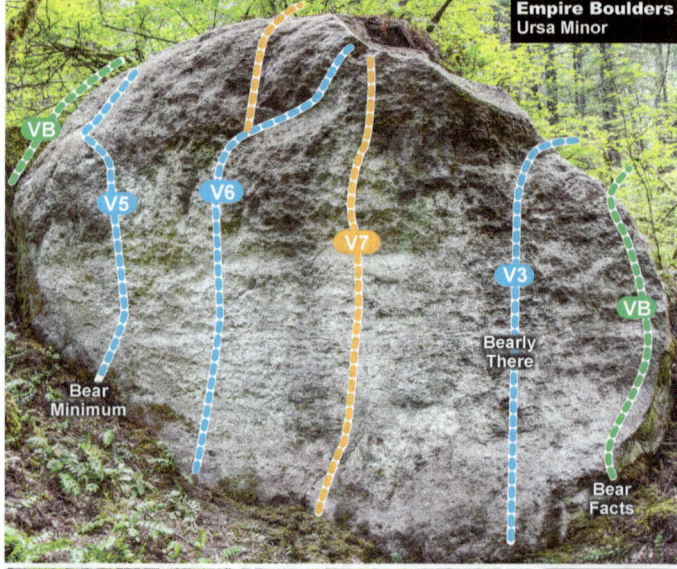

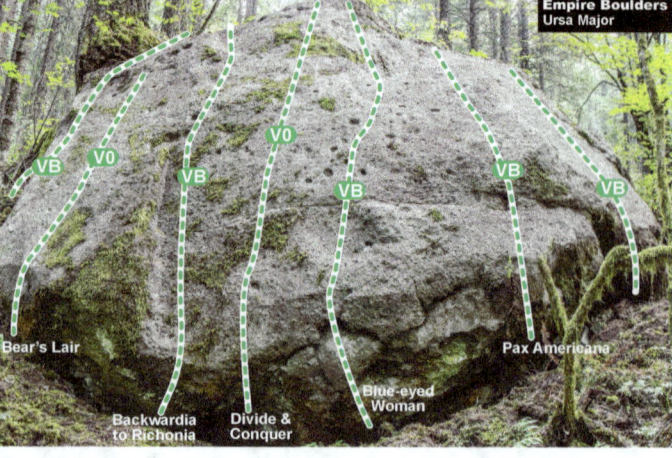

Empire Boulders ✦ OR&B 183

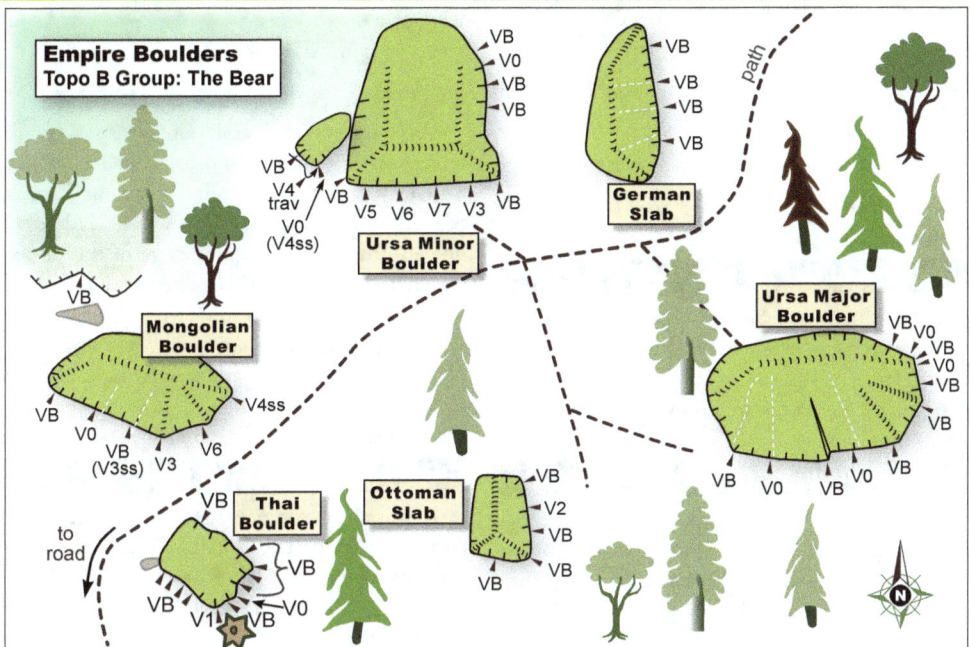

holds.

VB Bear Facts ★★ ☐
Right nose doing just one-two move.

...And on the east side of this same large stone is some family-friendly stuff.
VB a brief face left of crack.
VB Bear Bait is the crack on a slab.
V0 Bearvilla. A thin rounded face on a slab.
VB Grin & Bear It. Low angle ramp.

While standing on the path looking up at Ursa Minor Boulder, directly downhill you will find the two following boulders.

Ottoman Boulder

A small minor east-facing slab located about 25' below the path. Beta is L to R:
VB ___ short leftmost low angle steps.
VB Stairway. It's steps & jugs on a nose.
VB ___ short face.
V2 LP ★★★ ☐
This is a quality yet tricky pure smear slab line well worth doing (facing east).
VB short round right face.

Ursa Major Boulder

Large 24' tall stone with a substantial south-facing slab. Located 30' below path. Beta is left to right:

VB Lost Art ★ ☐
Nice brief line below the big fir tree on far left.

V0 Bear's Lair ★★ ⚠ ☐
A quality skinny opening crux section on a long smear slab.

VB Backwardia-to-Richonia ★★ ⚠ ☐
The prominent central sloped trough creates a popular hi-ball fun run.

V0 Divide & Conquer ★★ ⚠ ☐
Tackles the hi-ball face and has a skinny crux at mid-height. Cool fun run.

VB Left-handed Blue-eyed Woman ★★ ☐
Series of prominent pockets make for a fine fun run on long slab.

The following are on the eastern part of the Ursa Major boulder.

VB Pax Americana ★ ☐
This is a minor blunt rib on a slab.

VB Bondage ☐
This is a minor series of edges and steps on the far right. On east part of stone.

V0 Spoofed ★★ ☐
Quality very short east prow (rules by staying on

face) starts with left hand on sidepull.

VB Eulachon
East steps to smear slab (plus variation).

V0 Git Lost
One move face onto a north facing slab.

VB Pax Europa
Low angle slab on north side.

Hittite Boulder

A brief ultra low boulder a few yards east of previous (Ursa) boulder. Four lines (L to R). **VB Kitty** (face), **VB Cool Cat** (one-move crack), **VB Dog** (slab), **VB Pony** (one-move onto right slab). No photo.

German Boulder

This is the minor trail-side low angle eastern-facing slab stone. All four problems are VB (including a cross-all-routes variation). A quality family and kids friendly low angle slab. Beta is left to right:

VB Eagle Claw
This is a left slanted groove.

VB Gothic Art
This is the shorter central face.

VB Boar's Tusk
This is the taller central face.

VB Berlin
And doing just the right rib.

CENTRAL BOULDER CLUSTER

This concentrated and popular spot entails four massive boulders and four smaller stones, primarily wrapped around the famous Roman Stone. Its the area where you will likely hike to first in order to get a quick taste of the power, punch and quality this little site has to offer. The primary approach path splits from this cluster of stones, one path traveling northwest (to the upper west grotto), one path travels northeast (up to the deer path), and a brief path travels southeast to a small set of two minor stones.

Roman Boulder

This is the prominent really big boulder you encounter when the trail lands at a compact cluster of boulders. The Roman Boulder is the *tour-d-force* at EB with everything from mundane to absolutely extraordinaire. This large stone offers a host of quality 360° bouldering. The path directions to reach the remaining stones in the area are coordinated from this major stone. Beta starts at the north point and is described clockwise:

VB Empirical Dreams ★ ★
The north point fun run and often used as the down climb. This is the *first* line established on

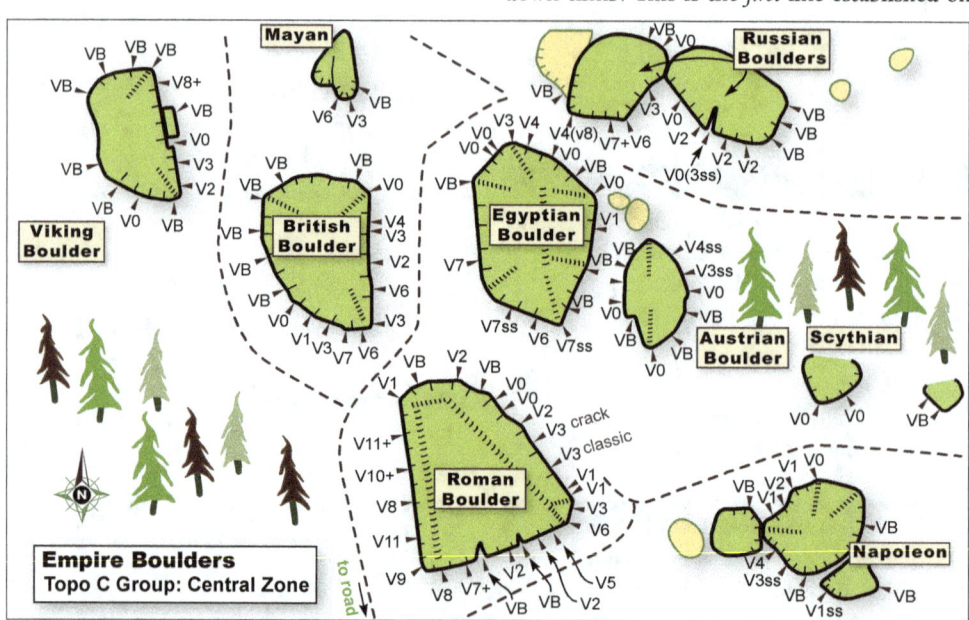

the Roman Stone and at the Empire.

V2 (V3ss) Etruscan ★★★ ☐
Several short enjoyable variants on a slight overhang (all end the same on next VB).

VB Via Appia ★★ ☐
Goes up easy steps; viable as a down climb.

The next six are 18' hi-ball problems.

V0 The Empire ★★★★ ⚠ ☐
Classic. First half of seam then right face. Start up the leftward angling seam till you reach mid-height, then aim up right on smears.

V0 Rome ★★★★ ⚠ ☐
Ultra classic full angled seam. Start at a large pocket on a slight bulge at seam, then go leftward up the seam to the top.

V2 Centurion ★★★ ⚠ ☐
This starts at the crack, pulls the initial bulge using a large pocket then angles up right crossing Rome and finish on The Empire (or finish on the Rome route).

V3 Gladiator ★★★ ⚠ ☐
The prominent center crack. Crimps till the crack widens at mid-height, then balanced movement to finish. Crack can be lead with small stoppers and cams.

V1 Gladiator (Var.) ⚠ ☐
Start same as Gladiator crack but bust up right as an ending variant.

V3 Aqueduct ★★★★ ⚠ ☐
Ultra classic at Empire. Tiny crimpy pocket moves to attain large mid-face pockets, then dicey moves to finish. Way to go Mr A!

V1 Colosseum ★★★ ⚠ ☐
Crux opener move to sloped stance, then calmly reach up left to jug, then jug again.

V1 Colosseum Direct ★★ ⚠ ☐
The same crux opener move to sloped stance, then reach up right to catch a sloped rail and a big flat jug. Pull past the jug to the top.

V3 Damascus Steel ★★★ ⚠ ☐
This is a superb tall 17' hi-ball line using an inner scoop of the overhung southeast prow utilizing good crimps and holds (if merged right near top into Colosseum it's V2).

V6/V7 Ritual Union ★★★★ ⚠ ☐
Tall overhung blunt prow with a series of unique holds and crimps that yield a classic bold hi-ball problem. Great send Sam!

The next set of problems are all on the south aspect of this boulder.

V5-7 Vesuvius ☐
Short vertical face with skinny skinny smears (project).

V5 Via Delarosa ☐
Start with two small pockets, one for each hand.

V2 Nero ★ ☐
Thin short face with a few pockets.

VB Preston's Nemesis ☐
Corner-*ish* nuance.

V2 Cobblestone ★★ ☐
Everything on short face with pockets.

VB The Scramble ☐
The walk up and walk down.

V8+ Prima Facie ☐
Thin crimps just left of the down scramble. Project.

V9 Architect ★★★ ☐
The right aspect of prominent overhung prow on tiny crimps & slopers. V8 if you got beta.

The next set of futuristic problems are all on the west aspect.

V9 Gladius ★★★★ ☐
Overhung technical round arête prow. Crimps to catch high sloper. This has an alternate 'sit start' on the right (V9-*ish*) with several power moves and then merges at the fat sloper.

V11 Caesar Salad ☐
Technical crimps face moves to a high sloper rail then into a slight groove at the top.

V7 (V8ss) B is for Brutus ★★ ☐
Overhung technical face. Standing start on high crimp and pop for sloped jug. The 'ss' uses a left low undercling.

V10+ ____ ☐
Tiny crimps and undercling pocket to knob on rail, and into groove at top.

V11+ ____ ☐
Overhung face with marginal crimp features.

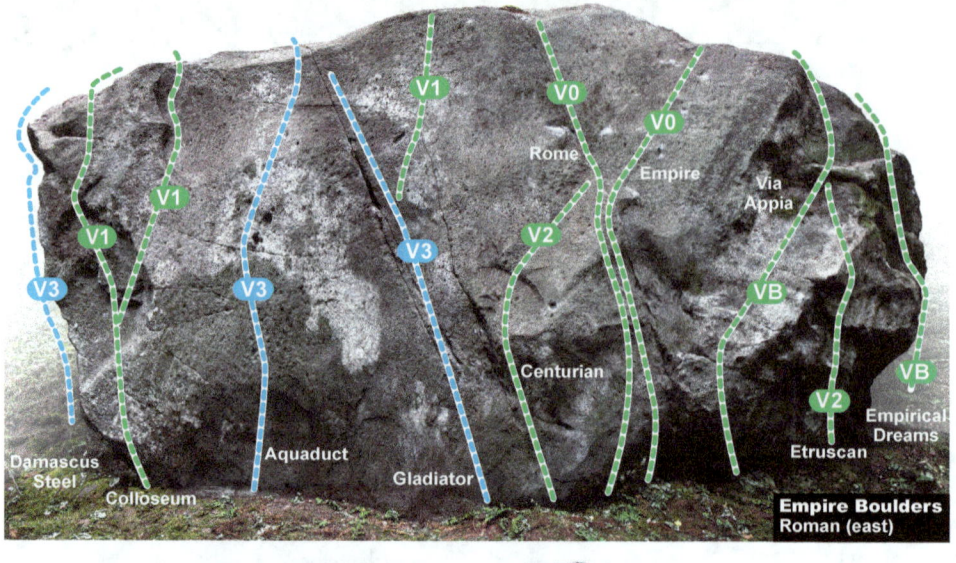

V1 Spartacus ★★

Minor shorty just right of the standard north point *Empirical Dreams* line. As rated V1 Sparticus Left (use left fingers in seam), and V2 Sparticus Right (is all crimps).

British Boulder

The Anglo-Saxon boulder has a broad rounded prow on the south end, and a slightly overhung flat face on the east side. Beta L to R starting on the far west face:

VB Left Coast

A brief move and mantle (+ minor var).

VB The Real & The Ideal ★

Go up a brief round rib (use or avoid pocket).

VB Boulderville

Basic slab run just right of rib.

VBss Cosmic Order

Low bulge mantle onto easy slab.

VBss England ★★★

Sit start low and reach over bulge high to grab giant gas pocket and pull up over.

V0 Balance of Power ★★★

Undercling pinch, high right smear, move up left to grab the giant 4" pocket.

V1 British Isles ★★

Start on same undercling pinch (as previous line), high right smear, then move up right directly over the bulge on just crimps.

V3 Mini Cooper ★★★

Overhung face using crimps directly up a seam. Start low on a good right hand crimp and a small left hand crimp.

V7 (V8ss) Notre Dame ★★★★

Start left hand side pull and right hand on good right side pull. Substantially overhung bulge with tenuous reach. Sit uses the undercling.

V6 (V7ss) Quasimodo ★★★★

Hung prow. Start under bulge, power to flat crimp.

...And on the east face of this same boulder:

V3 Bulldog ★★★★

The right side of an overhung prow starts by using underclings and a knob hold to reach better holds.

V6 Crusade ★★★

Powerful slightly hung thin face. Start with low right hand crimp pinch and dyno for the high sloper.

V2 King Arthur ★★★

Start at center of boulder below two under clings and climb straight up to the top.

V3 Excalibur ★★

Uses two small undercling sidepulls, but exit left using natural rail and committing top out.

V4 Excalibur (direct) ★★★

Start same as previous using the two small undercling sidepulls but continue directly up a blank section with a few reachy high pockets.

V0 Badge of Honor ★★

Minor seam going over a brief bulge.

VB Fabric of Deceit

Face going over bulge (rightmost line).

Viking Boulder

Immediately NW of Roman Stone is the Anglo-saxon Stone, and another 25' NW is the Viking Stone which has a sheer east face about 16' tall. Beta is left to right:

VB Raven's of Odin

West face angled slab.

VB False Peace ☐
Brief moves going up left onto slab.

V0 Force Majeure ★★ ☐
Smears on face with small sloper holds.

VB Tectonic Shift ☐
Obvious step prow next to tree.

V2 Greenland ★★★ ☐
Vertical face between two trees. Crimps to jug rail, then a side pull.

V3 Ulfberht ★★★ ☐
Tall prow with long committing reaches.

V0 Doublethink ★★ ☐
Vertical corner that steps up onto the stacked blocks, then several minor moves in the right facing corner to top out.

VB Uncaused Cause ☐
Get onto a stacked block, then mantle the short face above.

V8-9[?] ___ ☐
A skinny face with improbable holdless features maybe.

VB Noble Savage ★ ☐
The minor face at NE nose.

VB Cultural Suicide ☐
Minor short face merging left.

VB Standard Bearer ☐
Minor short rounded north face.

Mayan Stone

A minor short slanted hung prow-like stone a few yards uphill from Brit Stone with a few in-

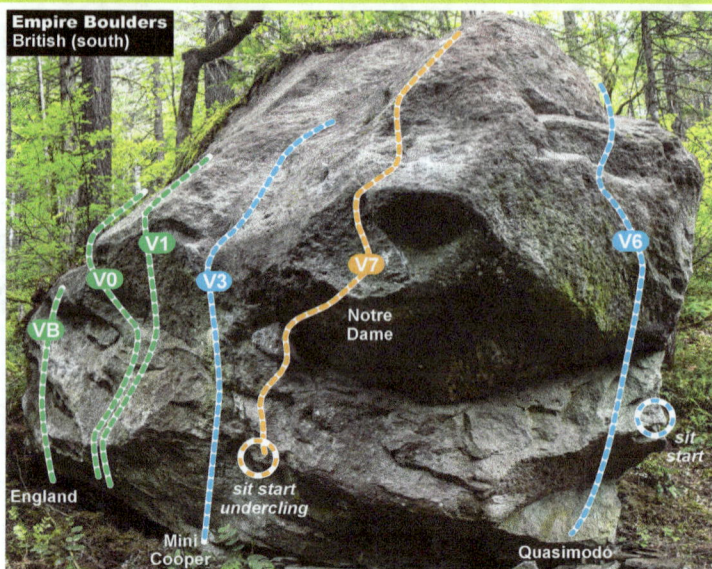

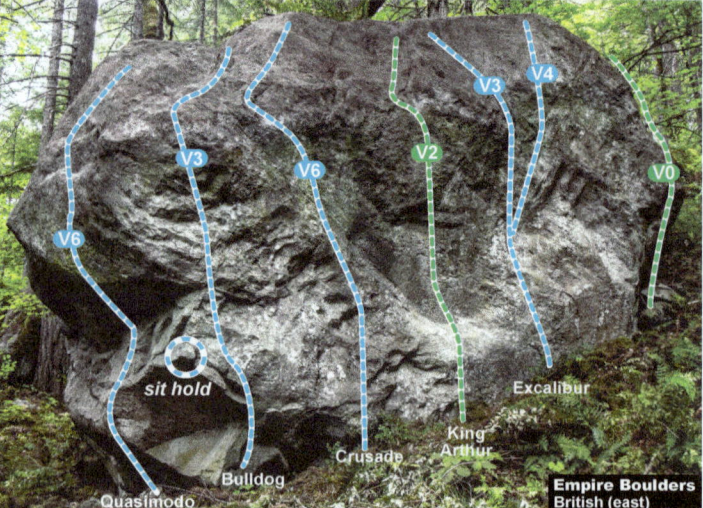

triguing lines on it. Beta is right to left.

VB Chai Frappuccino ☐
The east side shorty.

V3ss Sclerotic Stagnant Superstate ★ ☐
Crimp prow, move up right onto slab.

V6 Downtown Funky Stuff ★ ☐
Crimps & palm on left side of prow to lip and mantle exit.

Egyptian Boulder

About 30' northeast of the Roman Boulder is the Egyptian Boulder, a tall, yet roughly pyramidal shaped beast with a long slab on its west aspect with a slight overhang to start each problem. Beta runs clockwise starting with the easy lines on the east side:

VB Cheops ★★

The basic up/down line on the east side.

VB Hatshepsut ★

Another basic up/down line on east side.

V8ss Chi Jin Yu ★

Full under prow utilizing incut holds, power out and up. Ends at head height by merging into the previous VB. This is right of fir tree.

V6 Ancesters Protect Me ★★★

Left of fir tree. Start on smooth face, utilize a sidepull undercling to make a long reach.

V7ss Only God Forgives ★★★

Sit low on left in hung nook, cruise several incut holds rightward, then up using a slight crimp and a very long reach over a round bulge.

V7ss Magpie Moments

On round overhung nose is a crux sequence using a small knob.

VB Hieroglyph ★

Easy steps up onto the slab, then run the center of the easy slab.

V0 Sand of the Sahara ★★

Traverse lip leftward, then use the crack with your left hand to surmount the bulge.

V0 Sphinx ★

The jam crack straight on over lip.

V3 Valley of the Kings ★★★

Using the crack with your right hand, move left along the lip, around to north aspect, then surmount the north side of the hung prow.

V4 King Tut ★★★

Cool direct start with long reach on north aspect of hung prow.

V0 Pounding Sand ★★★

Climb up using the 7" diameter pocket.

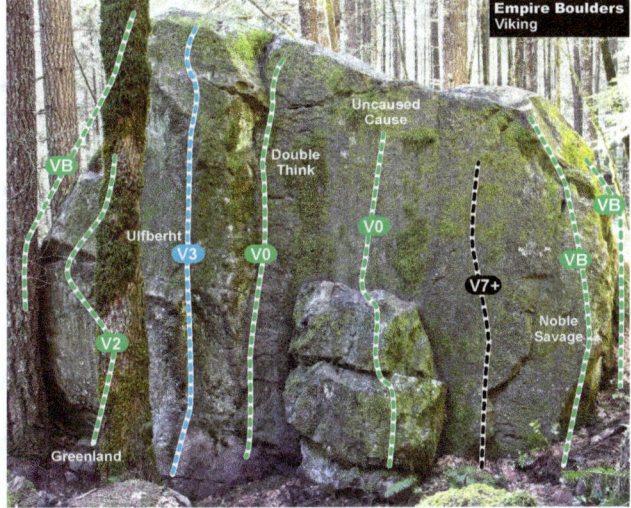

VB Giza

Face-crack next to a detached flake.

V0 State Of DeNile ★

East prow (and large crack of detached block).

V1 Pharaoh ★★★

Quality face with small crux crimps (rules avoid crack on right).

THE TRAVERSE:

V6 The Nile ★

The north side traverse (R to L) starting on the Sphinx problem.

Austrian Stone

A minor block on the immediate east side of the Egyptian Stone. Beta L to R:

VB Slab (short slab on westside)

VB Alps

Short face crack with incuts.

V0 All Things Nice

Brief vertical face on west side.

VB Symphony ★

Steep corner steps on the west side.

V0 Last Waltz

High step getting onto the south nose.

VB One Move

Short one-move onto slab face.

VB Globalize Me

Doing just the east ramp.

V0 (V2ss) Renaissance ★★
Brief vertical face on east side starting with hand in the pocket.

V3ss Tic Tac ★★
Good quality crimps problem utilizing a series of sloper crimps and a slap finish.

V4ss Little Red Monster ★
A series of punchy short right facing sidepulls on the east side.

Russian Boulders

Uphill NE of the Egyptian Boulder is this double set of impressive stones. Beta is left to right (starting on left big boulder):

VB Urals
A short move on far left side.

V4 (V7ss) Kremlin ★★★
Outer left overhung nose above block. Pinch start, power up to a good edge. FA sit: Sam A.

V7-8 Vodka
A hard send on the overhung face using an insipient seam (project).

V6 Natasha ★★★
The first V6 established at the site (way to go Mr A). Start on the boulders inner aspect on two small gaston's and move up a short crimpy face to small sloped holds. V7ss variation starts at the same spot then goes up right to finish.

V3 Czar ★★★
Scooped face using left undercling pinch and high reach to catch small crimps.

...And on the right boulder:

VB Volga
The deep wedge slot between both blocks.

V0 Mockba (aka Moscow) ★★★
Vertical short flat face on the right block.

V2 Ikon ★★★
Power up a jutting prow just left of a deep overhung OW crack.

V0 (V3ss) Gulag ★★
The offwidth crack itself is a viable challenge especially if you sit start it.

V2ss Caviar ★★★
Start about 4' right of crack very low, traverse left upward on positive lip holds (the original line is harder (V3) - missing foot flake). The quality and cool V2ss direct begins with left hand in

Empire Boulders Egyptian (west)

Empire Boulders Egyptian

offwidth and right on undercling, then punch up right merging into Caviar.

V2 Russian Bear ☐
Start same as previous line, but mantle right over onto slab.

VBss Dr Zhivago ☐
Kids stuff. Left edge of crack. Far east side.

VBss Politburo ☐
Kids stuff. The short crack. Far east side.

The following two problems are on the north side of the boulders.

V0 Siberia ☐
A nice short crimp smear line.

VB Russophobia ☐
Basic short slab move.

Minoan Boulder

A brief low boulder just uphill from the Russian Boulders.

VB King Crossis ☐
Basic low traverse.

History Boulder

VB Scrapheap of History ☐
A minor face with a big fir above it (about 15' NE of Minoan Stone).

Lost Tree Boulder

Brief boulder with short vertical face (about

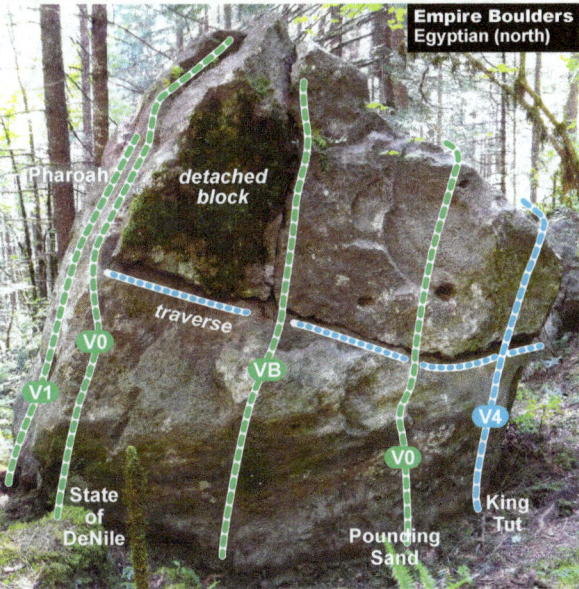

15' left of Russian Boulder). Beta is R to L:

V1ss Sleepy Salamander ★ ☐
Immediately right of the tree on rounded face.

V0 (V4ss) John Deere ★ ☐
Left of the tree. Starts on crimps with foot near a flake.

V2ss Minimum Bark ☐
Undercling right, reach high with left.

V2ss Flakey Flake ☐
Brief short crimps. The leftmost shorty.

Napoleon Boulders

Also known as the French Boulders. About 35' southeast of the Roman Boulder is this a triple set of short boulders nested low in a bowl. Beta is left to right starting on the north side:

VB Arch De Triumph ☐

Minor move left onto a fat stance, then up a short slab face on crimps.

V1 The 1812 Overture ★★★ ☐

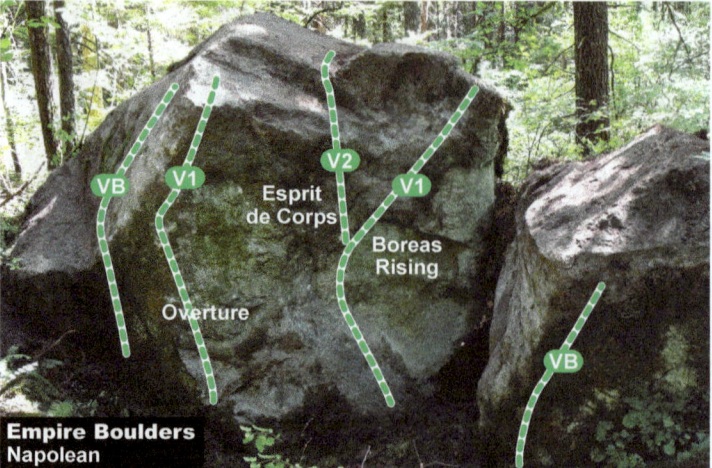

Empire Boulders — Napolean

Tackles a vertical round nose straight on, culminating with an interesting top out finagle.

V2 Esprit de Corps ★★ ☐

Start in the overhung scoop, move up to catch the obvious flat rail, then go straight up over.

V1 Boreas Rising ★★ ☐

Start in the overhung scoop, catch the obvious flat rail, then move right to exit up right.

VBss Last Waltz ☐

The low minor step on a short west stone.

On the south side of the same big boulder (beta left to right):

V3ss Revolution ★★ ☐

The direct start of the next problem.

V3ss Waterloo ★★★★ ☐

Start low on right, cruise leftward and up rounded prow, hand wrap and bounce up the rounded nose. The classic line on this boulder.

VB Trampling March of Power ☐

Minor move; it starts at the slot but use left face only.

And...on another small stone which is on the south side of the big boulder:

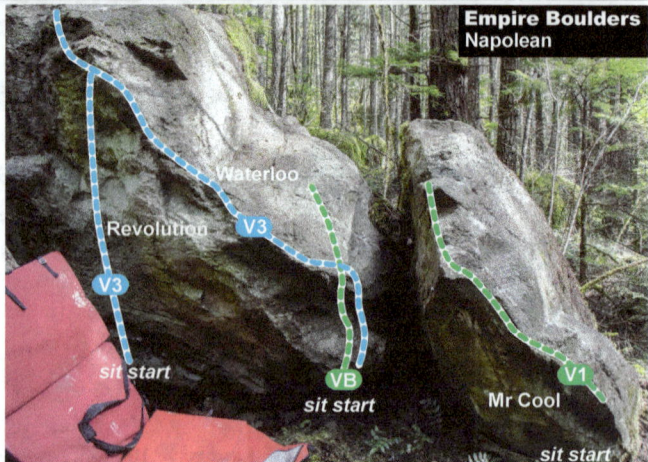

Empire Boulders — Napolean

V1ss Mr Cool ★★★★ ☐

Fun hung warmup arête. Sit start on ground grasping jugs up leftward onto the fun arête.

VB Paris ☐

Short slab on east face of main boulder.

Scythian Boulder

About 20' directly north uphill from the Napoleon Boulders is this small boulder.

V0ss Agnostic Babble ☐

The left mantle at the vertical nose.

V0ss Pagan Idol ☐

The right mantle just right of nose.

UPPER WEST CLUSTER

From the Rome Boulder a path extends uphill westward to a low dell or trough, where you will encounter three large boulders. The west cliff

Empire Boulders — OR&B 193

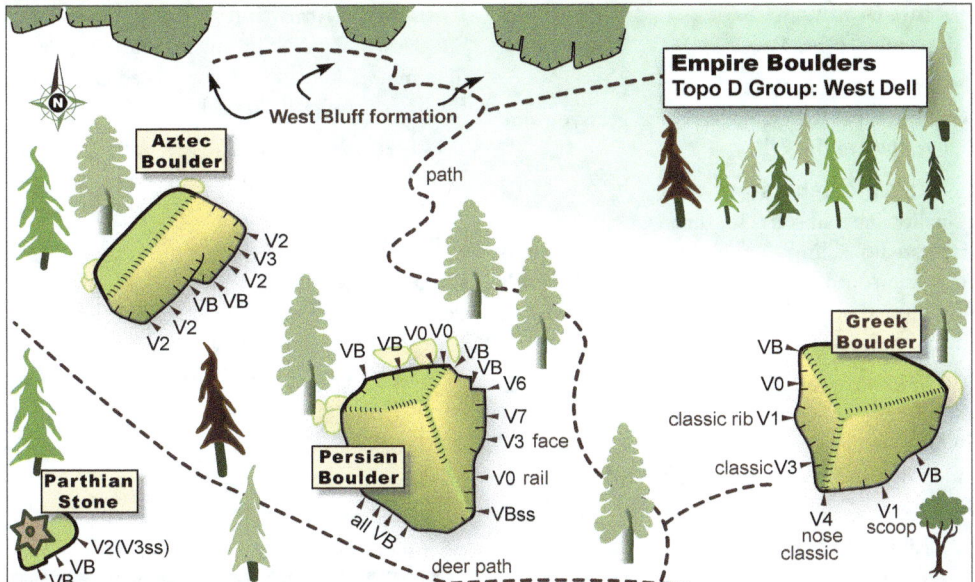

formation outcrops perch above this minor dell like little political sentinels glaring down at your slow progress. The narrower tall east-most proud stone is the Greek Stone.

Persian Boulder

This giant boulder has an excellent vertical east face with superb quality problems. The north aspect has some quality fun runs. Beta is left to right:

VB Boar's Head
A minor short crimps mantle on left.

V0 Silk Road ★★★★
A great quality fun run up a steep, slightly overhung left angling rail.

V3 Trojan Horse ★★★★
Excellent vertical crimp line on a slightly overhung portion of face.

V7 Meel Time ★★★
A tech climb which starts at a series of minute pockets in a seam, and utilizes the left trending seam for the left hand. Powerful and quality.

V6 Ante Bellum ★★★
The superb 16' tall prow with a tree close at your backside.

The following are on the north aspect of this large boulder:

VB Idle Dreams
The sloped corner steps.

VB Masters & Slaves
Off the top of the smaller block gets you one move up onto the slab.

V0 Rattling Sabers ★★★
Quality line that starts low in an trough between two stones. Climb a slightly hung scoop, and transition onto flat right face at mid-height, catch top lip, and mantle out. A minor variant runs left out of the scoop.

V0 Laka Educayshun ★★
Start same as previous line and transcends up right to a large pocket (crossing over next line) and continues on face up rightward to top of stone.

VB All Hat 'n No Cowboy
Step off the top of the large flat block into a large foot pocket, then pull onto the top lip.

VB Genie ★
A minor steep face with a variety of crimps and edges make a nice fun run. Last problem on the uttermost northwest side.

...and on the south aspect of Persian Boulder is some family friendly short slab stuff.

VB Diva
The left subtle nose onto a low angle slab.

VB Doubledip
Scoop then onto the low angle slab.

VB High Five
Seam smear then onto the low slab.

VB Deep-Six
Bulge smear landing on the low slab.

Greek Boulder

This is an excellent 15' tall stone in the upper west dell. It offers a solid string of high quality problems always worth doing.

VB Mossophobia
The down climb on the far left.

V0 Croton ★
Thin face crimps with a reachy move.

V1 Imperial Ambition ★★★★
Super classic line. Start low in center and cruise up a minor rib using various angled crimps and small edges (15' tall). Its tall.

V3 Alexander the Great ★★★★
Utilize three finger pockets to start up a vertical face. Ultra-classic line. Definitely tall but not hi-ball.

V4 Zeus ★★★★
Powerful line that starts on two pinches (left & right) and moves up into a scoop aiming for the obvious fin up high on the prow. A tech classic not to be missed.

V1 Gatekeepers ★★
Scoop-seam, mantle onto sloped slab to finish.

VB Drunk on War
Brief set of minor edges on far right.

Aztec Boulder

About 35' west of the Persian Boulder is this last sole remaining challenger, a squat unit with a

Empire Boulders — Greek stone

nice spat of brief lines on it.

V2 Aztec ★ ☐
Leftmost mantle problem onto a slab.

V2 Beast ★ ☐
Mantle a bulge onto a low angled slab.

VB Fault Line ☐
Grab rounded hung prominence and move up obvious crack rightward.

VB Sombrero ☐
Just right of the same crack, slither up onto slab (its just left of a tree).

V2 Total Depravity ★ ☐
Right side of tree at hollow flake. Punch over round bulge onto slab.

V3 Utopian Visionaire ★ ☐
Crimps on rounded bulge reaching for a pocket on a slab.

V2 Sanity Awakening ☐
Use crimps on rounded bulge on far right.

LOWER EAST CLUSTER

In the east cluster are three massive boulders with a broad variety of high quality lines. Many must-do lines exist on the Babylon, Inca and Spanish Boulder. A prominent trail goes directly east from Roman Boulder to Babylon Boulder.

Babylon Boulder

This is a very massive stone, and a fine spectrum of quality lines await for those who like lower spectrum grades. Beta is clockwise starting on the north side. The problems on the south aspect are definitely tall, nearly hi-ball.

VB Ur ★★★ ☐
A fun quality short string of pockets leading up to a slight round dish.

V0 Graveyard of Empires ★★★★ ☐
Obvious string of small pockets ending with sloper crimps. A minor variation exists between this and the previous.

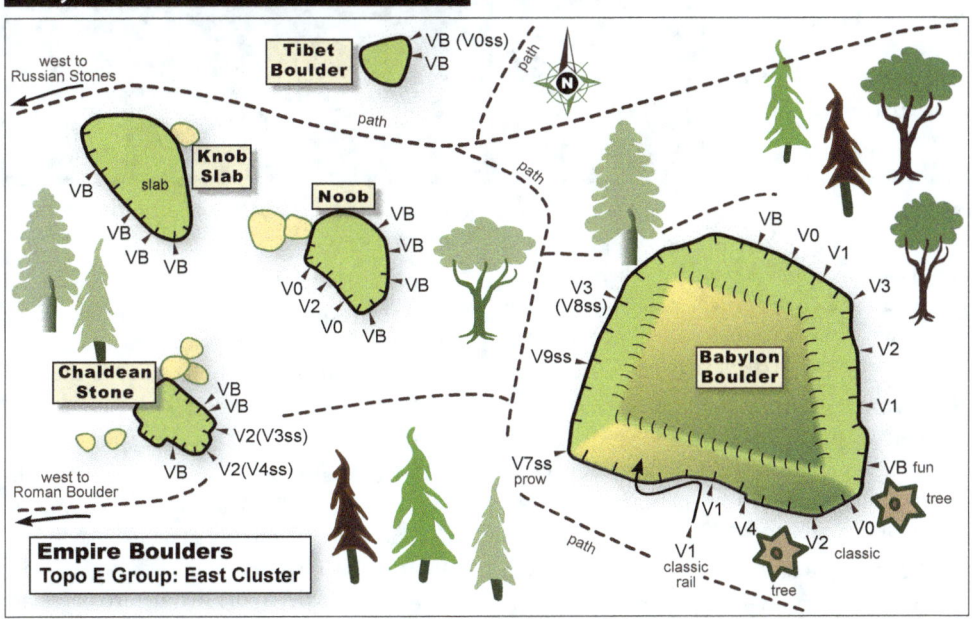

Empire Boulders
Topo E Group: East Cluster

V1 Enemy Within
★★★ ☐

Several nice jugs to start, then ends with a few skinny crimps. Cool spook.

V3 Nebuchadnezer
★★★★ ☐

Start up a seam, smearing and crimps will get you a fair high hold, then a series of tricky thin crimps (crux) at the top give you a quality tall finale.

V2 Darius ★★★ ☐

Initial starter move, and crux cross-over gets you into the slight groove to several nice pockets, then ends with a flat topped finale.

V1 Xerxes ★ ☐

Initial step move, then steepens to vertical dicey thin face crux at the top.

VB Imperial Dreams
★★★★ ☐

Start on the immediate right side of the large fir tree, grab a large obvious pocket, and dash up the easy terrain to a brief vertical crux move. Fun tall climb.

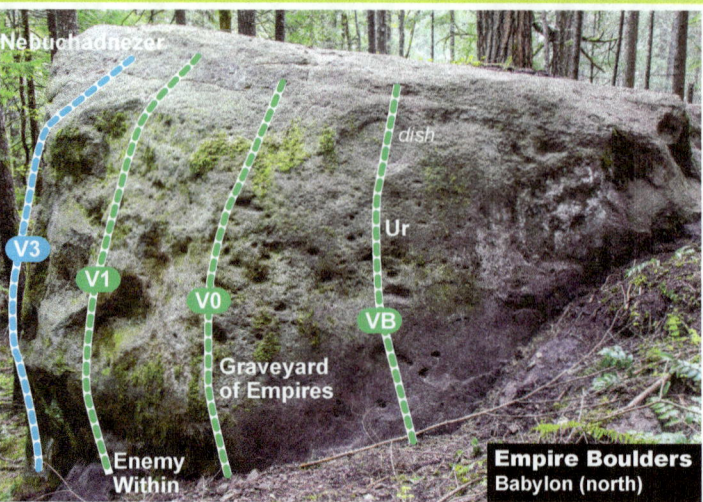

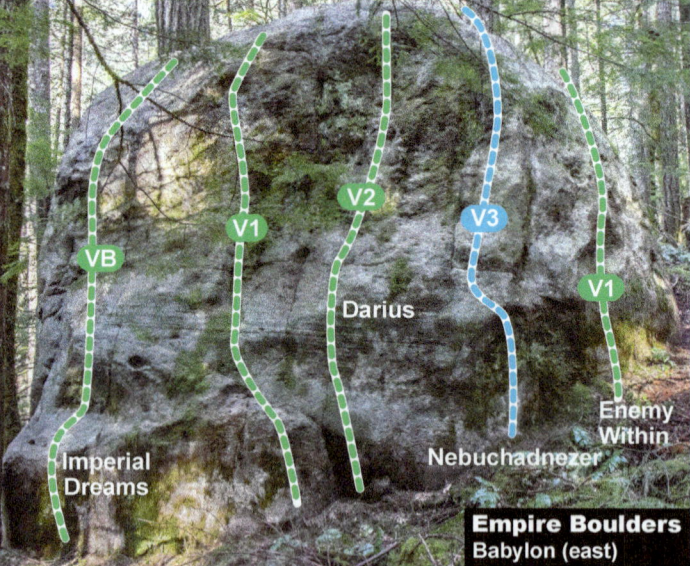

V0 Tower of Babel
★★★ ☐

Start on the immediate left side of a large tree, and dance up numerous holds. Where it steepens, a series of large pockets await with a minor crux move. Fun tall problem. Located between the two fir trees. Excellent problem.

V2 Seventh Wonder ★★★★

A superb very tall problem on a vertical face with several big pockets on its upper portion. Located between the two trees. This is the left of two cool side by side routes. Classic!

V4 Fiery Furnace ★ ☐

A right angling corner-ish seam, that gets vertical and very dicey at the last portion of the problem. Crux is the very last move.

V1 Spice & Dice ★ ☐

Start low in center of face (same as for next line), move up left a few moves along the rail system, then punch straight up using a series of small crimps on a vertical face. Better holds save you at the exit.

V1 The Emperor ★★★ ☐

A quality line at EB. Start low in the center of south face aspect. Run the rail monkey style leftward, then as a high bulge of rock begins to jut out, crimp directly up the slightly overhung face

Empire Boulders — OR&B

Empire Boulders
Babylon (south)

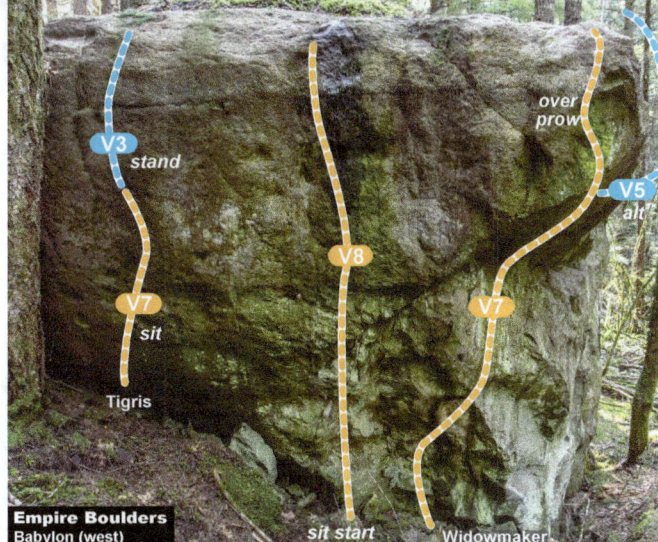

Empire Boulders
Babylon (west)

on crux small holds.

V7ss Widowmaker ★★★ ☐

The powerful techy super overhung west prow. An alternate (V5) popular top out is done slightly to the right of the small high pocket.

V8ss Enemy ☐
Thin rounded pockets and scoops on short overhung face.

V3 (V7ss) Tigris ★★ ☐
Next to the tree trunk is a brief power set of moves with a sloped top out.

Inca Boulder

This is the tallest tumbled boulder at Empire, logging in at a wildly majestic 27' tall on its west aspect. The beta begins on its north side (Left to Right), ending on its south side:

VB Stone Stairs ☐
Basic steps on far left (north side).

V1 Native Soul ★★★
Quality enjoyable short sequence of moves using two small crimp slopers.

V0 At The Table Or On The Menu ★★

A tall rounded face with series of angled seam-edges for crimps and smears (very close to a fir tree). Fine quality line.

V6 Pyramid ★★★ ⚠
Tall techy face with pockets and knobs ending on an arête on upper portion.

V6 High Priestess ★ ⚠
Tall face that goes up through a slightly hung scoop to a high crux, then exit left at a pocket to

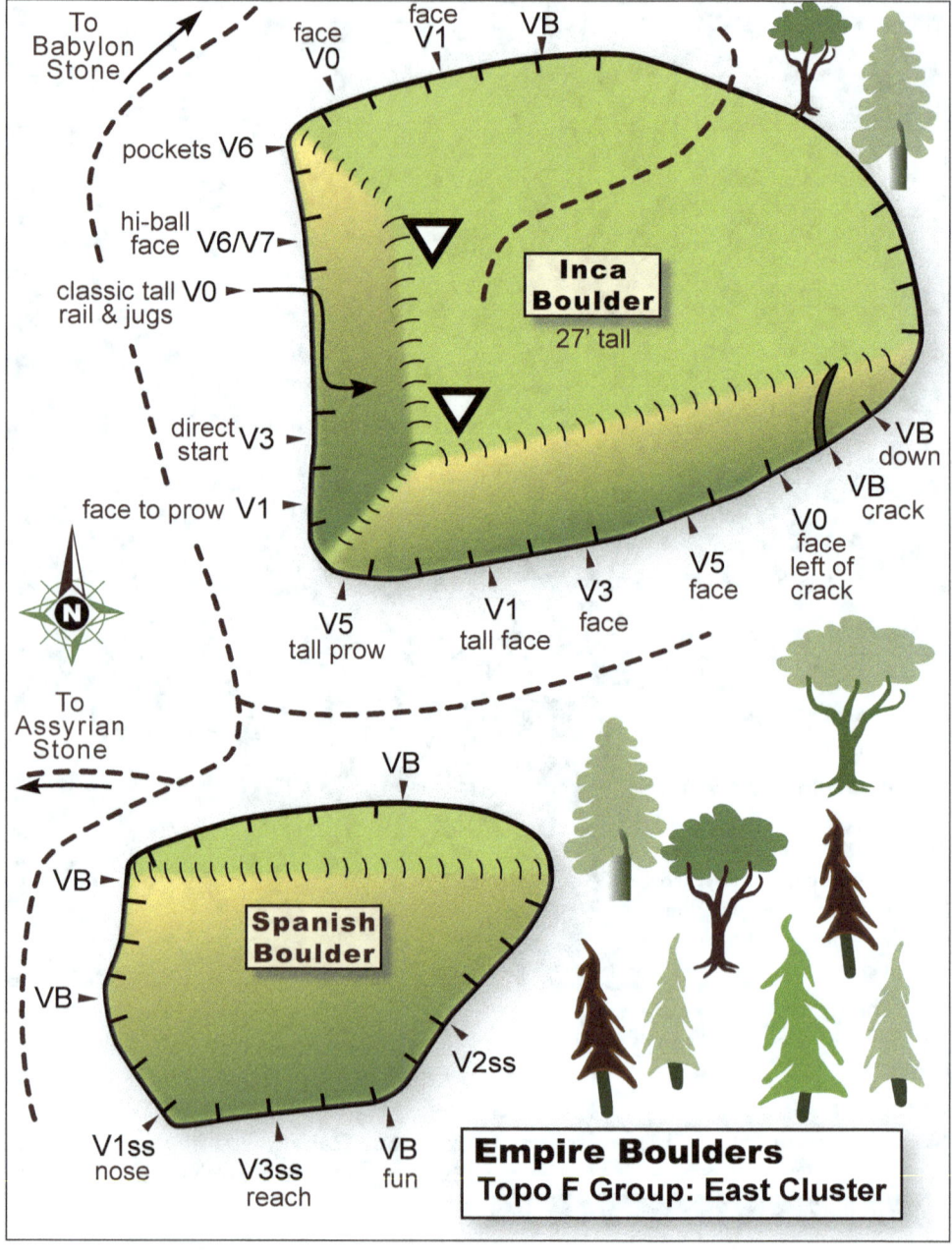

Empire Boulders
Topo F Group: East Cluster

the prow. The alternate stout direct finish top out is done at V7.

V0 Machu Pichu ★★★★ ⚠

The premier central route on the tall west face. Crux opening move to jugs, and crux exit move. Great hi-ball problem.

V3 Directissimo ⚠

Vertical direct that merges into the previous route.

V1 Imperial Hubris ★★ ⚠

Vertical face with nice pockets; merges onto arête at mid-height to finish.

V5 Blood Sacrifice ★★★ ⚠

Long arête with low crimps crux, then from mid stance upward are easier rounded reachy holds.

V1 Pulmonary Edema ★★★★ ⚠

Superb classic route on the tall south face. Go up arched seam, then up steep slab on better holds.

V3 Manco Capac ★★★ ⚠

Crux opening move is a single small inclusion, then continue on small holds on a tall face. Excellent route.

V5 Bleeding Edge ★★★

Superb techy line. Thin opening moves to a slight hung rounded lip. Dicey crux slopers above lip.

V0 Nowhere Fast ★★★

Start of small holds on left side of crack system (rules left of crack for all holds). At stance make a crux move to small pocket up right.

VB Ibex

The fat curved OW crack system.

VB Fen Fu

Far right down step.

Spanish Boulder

Empire Boulders Inca stone

Just a few yards to the south of the Inca Boulder is the Spanish Boulder. Though squat-like with a broad slab top-out, the south aspect does offer several nice lines. Beta is left to right:

VB Hobgoblin ☐
Minor slab seam on the north side.

VB Spaniard ☐
Round slabby west ramp.

VB Galleon ☐
Minor scoop and slab on west side.

V1 Columbus ★ ☐
The bulge at a round nose (onto slab).

V3ss Doobloon ★★ ☐
A bulge with a scoop that refutes the less than diligent. On south aspect of stone.

VB Realm of Uncertainty ★★ ☐
Vertical fun run using positive holds on center of the south aspect of stone.

V2 Mandolin ★ ☐
A nice string of moves that makes a high step onto the slab finish.

Assyrian Boulder

About 50' directly west of the Spanish Boulder is this extremely low obscure flat stone. Beta is listed left to right.

V2ss Blackball ★★ ☐
Left low bulge (rules: avoid seam).

V0ss Unthinkable Thinkster ★★ ☐
Up just the seam (rules: seam only). Low start.

VB Imperial Umpires ☐
Mere high step one move.

V0ss Fastball ☐
Low start using several incut small pockets (rules: just the pockets).

The next three minor boulders (Knob, Noob, Chaldean) are located in a cluster just west of

the Babylon Boulder about 35' distance.

Knob Slab

A fun low angle 12' slab with a liberal dose of knobs, located next to the main east-west deer path. No photo, but very kids quality.

VB Pork Bellies ★★
All four problems on Knob Slab (5.0-5.3).

Noob Boulder

An inconsequential argumentative uncooperative tiny stone. No photo.

V0 Noob. Squnched tightly left of the next unit.
V2 Motherland pockets (left-right), high step right, top slopers.
V0 Fatherland the high step south side.
VB All Noob. South and east side ramps, and two short kids east side lines.

Chaldean Boulder

Directly west of Babylon Stone about 30' is this stone with a brief sit start overhang. Beta is described right to left:

VBss Noob
Squnchable kids line on right.

VB (V1ss) Just Do It
Short crimps line.

V2 (V3ss) Whiskey & Whine ★
Start on right side, latch rounded nose, get up.

V2 (V4ss) Crocodile Tears ★
Start low on two finger slopers, left foot way out left, launch to fix on bulge jug, get up over.

Hittite Boulder

Minor stone between Chaldean and Scythian stones. Both problems are very short.

VB Schmoo

VB Whangdoodle

Tibet Boulder

A very minor small round-ish stone just northeast of Knob Slab on the path en route to the Han Face (on the bluff outcrop).

VB (V0ss) Broken Spear
Standing jug mantle, or sit start on crimps below the jug.

VB War 'n Peace
A one move smear left of the previ-

ous line.

Byzantine Boulder

Just north of the Babylon Boulder, walk the deer path for 80' to this minor 10' tall stone. The south side is flat faced and offers four brief odd

Empire Boulders Byzantine & Qing

lines.

VB Iconoclast
The left nose for a few moves.

VB Byzantine ★
Run the lip uphill from Left to Right ending high on rightmost VB.

VB Tetragram
Midway one move step-in.

VB Constantinople
Direct dance on the taller portion (rules out any big foot hold).

GREAT WALL OF CHINA

This refers to the bluff outcrops that protrude from a steep hillside. The Great Wall offers an exhilarating and extensive selection of serious hi-ball lines, some classic lines, and possibly even the stoutest mega overhung face at the Empire Boulders. Various outcrops are given a Chinese dynastic reference name to parallel the major dynasties. The outcrops are described from right to left (far east end to west end).

Yuan Dynasty Boulder

At the utter east end of the outcrops (beyond even the Qing) is a tipsy little speck of stone. This

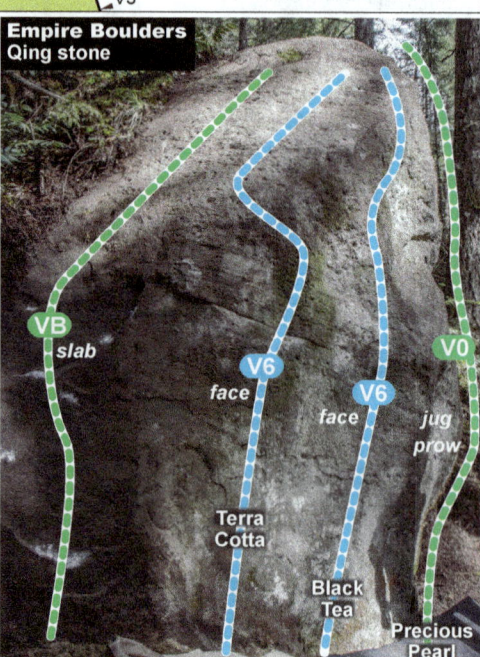

is the Yuan Stone with a very minor set of lines.

VBss Bondage
Left side low sit, then mantle over.

VBss Between Good & Evil
Start at pockets on center point, mantle over.

V3ss Enemy of Your Enemy ★★★
Just right of previous, run right horizontally

Empire Boulders
Himalaya (left)

around the hung prow, and mantle over far right side. Quality problem.

V0ss Gutless Wonder ☐
Mantle the far east side.

And another 150' further to the east is a VB minor on an isolated tiny munch block.

Qing Dynasty Boulder

Qing-Manchu is the second small outcrop along the cliffband. Beta is right to left:

V0 Precious Pearl ★★★★ ☐
Quality vertical layback rib with opening crux move (rules avoid big flat stance part way up on right).

V6 Black Tea ★★★ ☐
Powerful and thin. Right sidepull crimp, send middle part of face via left sloped crest.

V5 Terra Cotta ★★ ☐
Start on obvious fat flat hold on left, go up to small divots high on left face.

Empire Boulders
Himalaya

VB Polished Jade ★
Easy slab on the left side of stone.

⚠ Himalaya Face
Incredible super overhung face about 25' tall at its center. It offers about 5 futuristic hi-ball potential problems, some pushing the edge (V10-12+). Beta is right to left (east to west).

VB Lucky You ★
Basic rightmost low-angle ramp.

V5 Flying Pigs ★
Brief bulge mantle onto slab.

V4 (V7ss+) Divine Fury
Crimps at a seam. Powerful sit under entire.

V_ (?) ⚠
The super hung face.

V_ (?) ⚠
The super hung face.

V_ (?) ⚠
The super hung face.

V_ (?)
The super hung face.

V_ (?) ⚠
The super hung face.

Empire Boulders — OR&B 205

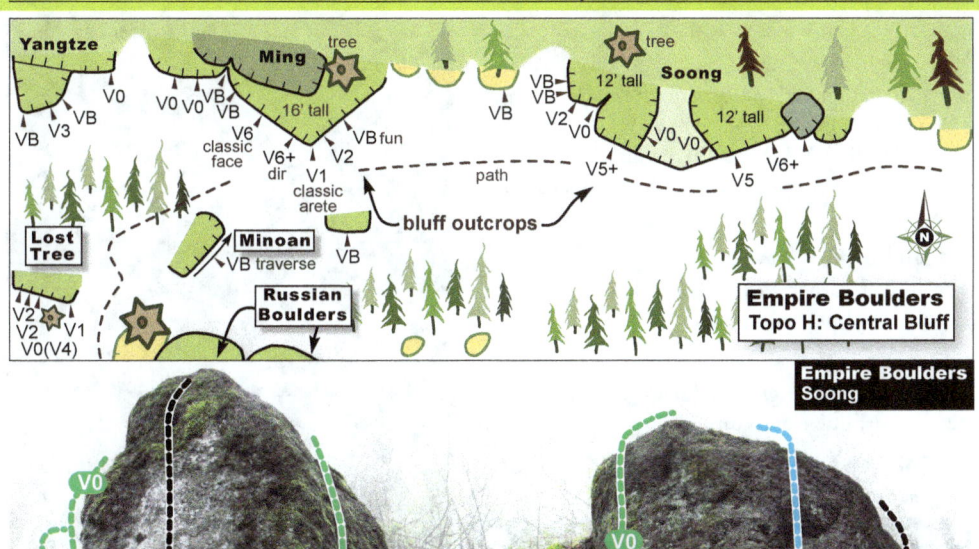

V4 The Sword ★ ⚠
Tall cool thin finger crack (p).

V4 Unreal Unperson ★★
Direct using smears and long reach to two pockets, then finish on seam.

V0 Logic ★★
Brief smear and crimps on rightward angling seam.

V0ss Szechuan ★★★
Crimp reach, pull to a crimp, attain top lip, mantle, done.

VB Manchu ★
Leftmost fun basic nose.

Han Dynasty Boulder ⚠
Prominent bluff with two main aspects with impressive 25' sharp arête. Beta is right to left:

VB Yes No Maybe ★
Basic groove next to a tree (on east side).

V9+ (?) ⚠
Vertical powerful thin crimps on east face.

V7 Red Dragon ★★★★ ⚠
The ultra classic arête and one of the great reasons to be here. Begin directly below arête on right side, then transition up onto its left side, while using right hand on arête to top.

V7 Automation ★★★ ⚠
Delicate face crimps to mid-stance, then techy moves up vertical face. Excellent line.

V7 The Empress ★★★ ⚠
Thin crimps, crux onto sloped stance, then crux exit at top lip. Stellar line.

VB (V0ss) Jade ★★★★ ⚠

Right angled tiny ramp [landing #3] to a block pinch, then high step up left into the crack corner system (the next VB). The V0 variant starts on second landing. V3 is the direct finish. A variant exists starting on the lowest landing crossing up into this line.

VB Shanghai ★★★ ⚠

Fun hi-ball corner with large pockets, crack-*ish* nuance, and bulge at the top.

V1 Loaded Dice ★

Up easy steps to a right hand pocket, then power over a short bulge onto top.

VB Cobwebs

Very short round groove corner.

Soong Boulder

A unique double-set of overhung outcrops with a flat ledge squnched between each outcrop. Several quality lines exist on both. Beta is right to left (starting at the east outcrop):

V6-9 (?)

The super hung crimps east face (project).

V5 Mass Production ★★★

Great opening jugs to start and powerful crimps to finish.

V0 Rampart Right

Short face starting off a high landing.

...and on the west part of this outcrop:

V0 Rampart Left

The other short face off a high flat landing.

V5+ (?) Mirabile Visu

Powerful hung techy crimp-*fest* (project).

V0 White Tiger ★★

Quality short hung crack.

V2 Jade Gate ★★★

Quality crimps. Start at the V0 crack, go up the left face to the next VB.

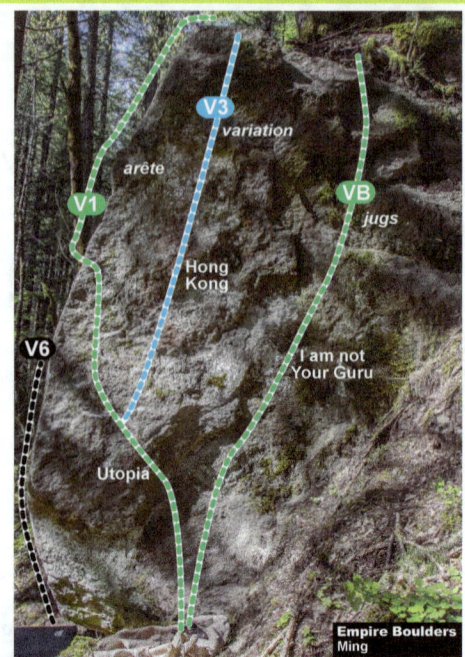

Empire Boulders Ming

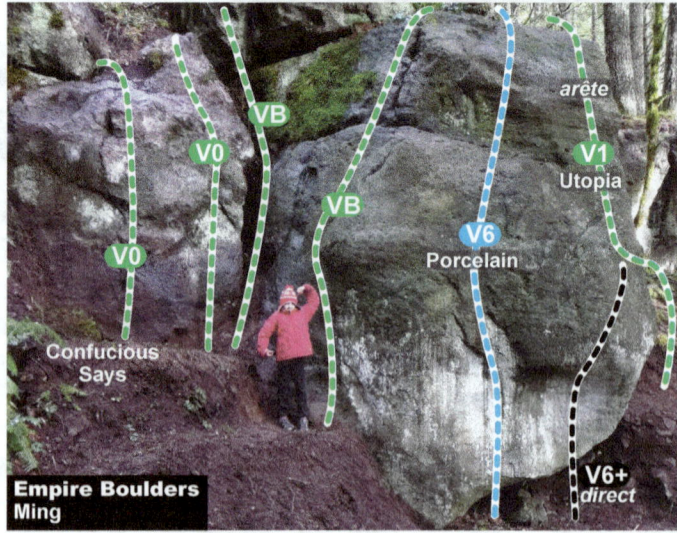

Empire Boulders Ming

VB & VB One Move

Two very short one-move boulder problems.

And on a minor stone to the left:

VB Rounder

A round very short bulge stone.

Ming Boulder

Just uphill northward about 30' from the Russian Boulders is this tall 17' high outcrop with

Empire Boulders ✦ OR&B 207

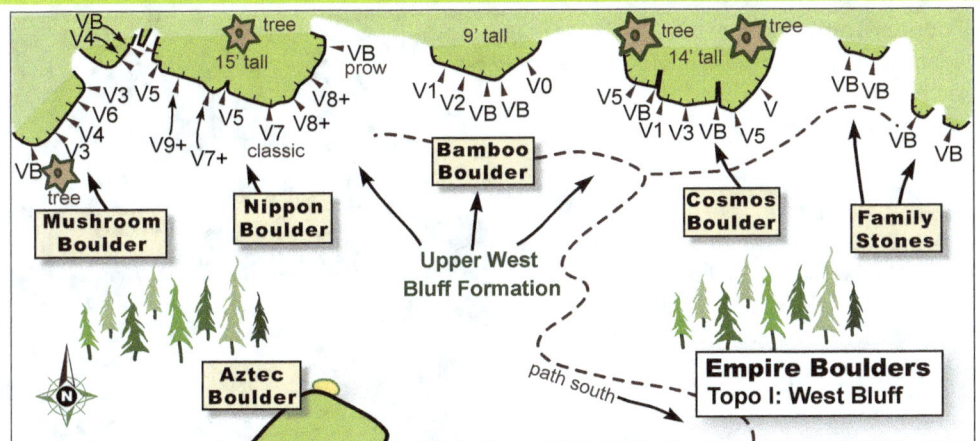

numerous stellar lines. Beta is from right to left:

VB I Am Not Your Guru ★★★★ ☐
Cruise up incut sidepulls and slopers on vertical face (right side of outcrop). The *first* boulder problem established on the bluff outcrops.

V2 Hong Kong ★ ☐
Stay on the right side of arête all the way (left hand on arête).

V1 Utopia ★★★★ ⚠ ☐
Classic arête. Cruise up east side, transfer to the arêtes left side at tiny mid-height stance, then dicey crux move to top. Exit left before crux is V0.

V6-7 (?) Mittimus ★ ⚠ ☐
Hung scoop face that merges into the upper arête of previous line (p).

V6 Porcelain ★★★★ ⚠ ☐
Ultra classic face and serious hi-ball. Begin in a slight overhung scoop and utilize tiny pockets, small knobs and slopers. Way to go Mr A!

VB Royal Blood ★★★ ☐
On left side of stone. Basic curved seams and edges (good fun run).

VB Huckypuk ☐
The fat dirty offwidth crack.

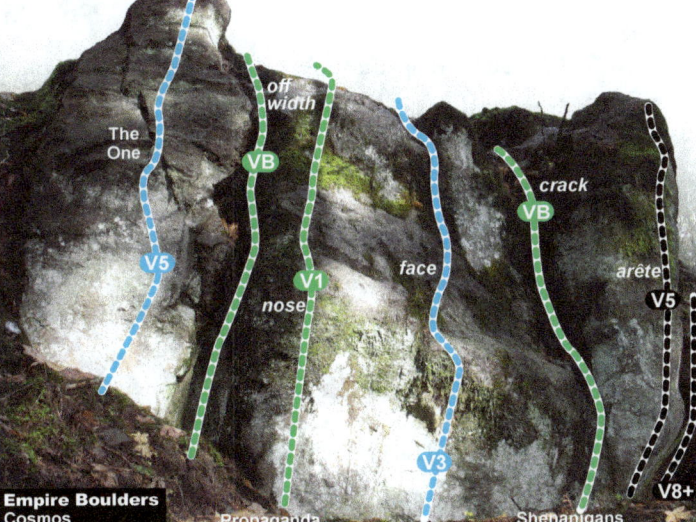

V0 Fuzzy Thinking ★★ ☐
Crimpy cool face immediately left of the off-width crack.

V0 Confucious Says ★★ ☐
A short crimp seam on a short face.

Yangtze Slab

A low angle slab with a midway landing, then a brief vertical second tier (kind of like a multi-pitch climb). Just uphill from Lone Tree Boulder. Beta is from left to right:

VB WhoWhatWhy ☐
A basic initial crux smear move, then a slab run. Step right at dirt landing to tackle a V0 finalé on the next shorty tier.

V3 Dirt Bag ☐
Start low on right at odd crimp maneuver.

VB Boorish Crack ☐
No cookies; send the crack up onto a slab.

UPPER WEST BLUFF

In the upper west dell (about 40' above the Greek, Persian and Aztec Boulders) is a series of bluff outcrops. These outcrops yield a variety of fun runs, packed with plenty of ultra powerful lines that are the real deal.

Family Boulders

Three very tiny slow angle tones with a few basic brief **VB**'s for kids to dash up all located to

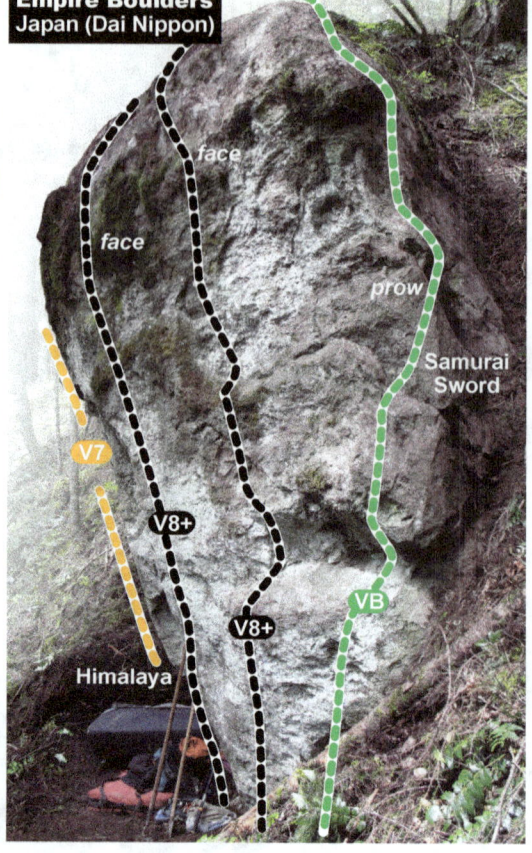

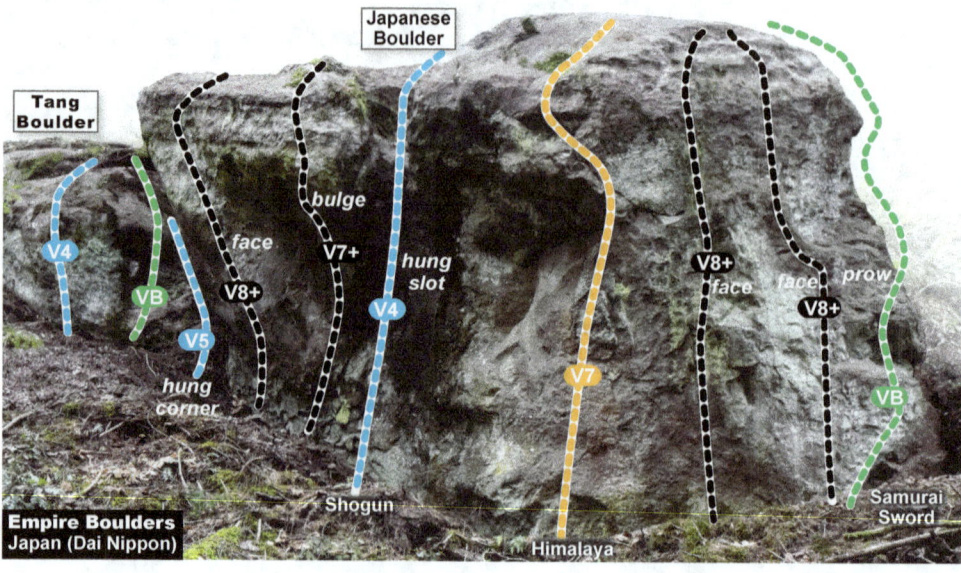

the east of the next boulder.

Cosmos Boulder

A fairly tall (14' high) outcrop with a vertical east prow. Beta is listed right to left:

V8+ (?) ___ ☐
Futuristic right face on thin crimps.

V6 Globalism ★★ ☐
Powerful crimps on tall jutting overhung arête (p).

VB Shenanigans ☐
Wide corner crack system on the right.

V3ss Copore Sano ★★ ☐
Sit start begins below jug, power over bulge, chill at stance, then finesse over the top lip.

V1ss Propaganda ★★★ ☐
Sit start low. Nice hung minor arête (the right side of offwidth) with crimps to a stance, then pull over the top lip on small crimps.

VB Cosmos ★ ☐
The left big fat OW crack.

V5ss The One ★★★★ ☐
Tricky initial setup and powerful crimps on this fine quality face line.

Bamboo Boulder

Midway between the two major stones is this minor shorty stone. Beta is right to left.

V0ss Far East ☐
Low minor one-move-two.

VB Nine Yak Tails ☐
Outer crack one move wonder.

VB Bamboo ☐
Left start on face ending in crack.

V2ss Kim Chi ★ ☐
Sit start low on crimpy short face.

V1ss Serpent ★ ☐
Sit start low on short crimpy face.

Japanese Boulder ⚠

Dai Nippon (the Japanese Boulder). Impres-

Empire Boulders Japan (left aspect)

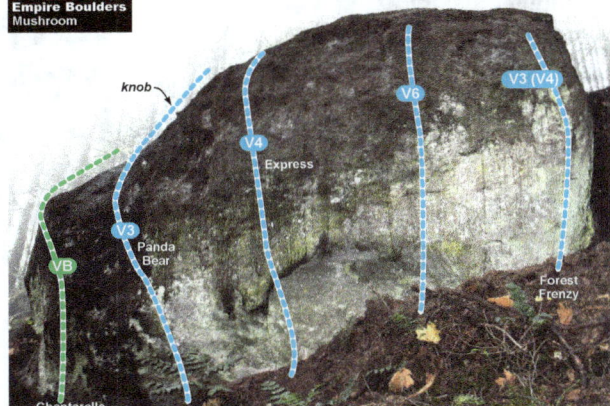

Empire Boulders Mushroom

sive tall outcrop with a serious overhang, and a fine string of ultra-wild lines. The beta is listed right to left:

VB Samurai Sword ★★★★ ⚠ ☐
Stellar warmup route using crimps on the hi-ball east prow. Always worth doing. Crux is the last move.

V8+ Yamamoto ⚠
Flat crimps face on right aspect (starts powerful, then gets more so). Project.

V8+ Fuji ⚠
Start on jugs, quickly morph to extreme sloper crimps (project).

V7 Himalaya ★★★ ⚠
Classic powerful hung prow just right of fat slot. Power flat crimps to hung lip, trend up left then over top bulge.

V5 Shogun ★ ⚠
Overhung fat slot full on.

V7+ Rising Sun ⚠
The jutting overhung bulge just left of the fat slot (project).

V8+ss Real Mojo ⚠
Technical hung crimps face (left hand uses edge of dihedral) (project).

V5 Velocity ★★★★
Far west overhung short dihedral corner involving unique crimps and moves. Classic, deceptive, powerful. Superb problem.

Tang Boulder

VB Intellectual Idiots
A minor short seam (the rightmost line).

V4 Emperor's Clothes
Crimps over a brief bulge.

Mushroom Boulder

The final westmost bluff outcrop at Empire. A shorty 9' tall stone, with a few punchy odd minor problems. Cheers to the mushroom man! Beta is listed right to left.

V2 (V3ss) Forest Frenzy
Minor round short face on the right.

V6 Spore ★
Power crimps on short face ending on slab.

V4 Express ★
Flat short crimps face ending on slab.

V3 Panda Bear ★★★
Make a move, catch the nob, reposition balance, mantle slowly. Phew!

VBss Chantrelle ★
Ultra shorty on far left.

Parthian Boulder

A tiny tiny isolated stone located about 100' southwest of the Persian/Aztec boulders. Beta is listed right to left.

V2 (V3ss) Square Peg Round Hole
Crimp the short rounded nose.

VBss Red Herring
The center shorty problem.

VBss Zero
The leftmost shorty problem.

And at that final tiny boulder we wrap up the entire discussion about the Empire Boulders. So how's that for a power packed group of boulder problems (VB to V-incredible), all of it stacked majestically into one single impressive bouldering zone this close to Portland, Oregon?

Totally cool....

Index

A

Abby Normal 128
Abducted 62
Achilles 132
Acoustic Kitty 44
Airtime 73
Alice 50
Alien Autopsy 60
Alien Invasion 62
Alien Lunacy 56
Alien Observer 61
Alpenglow Boulders 159
Alpha 18
Altered State 98
American Eagle 94
Archdeacon 130
Area 51 53
Atomic Dust Buster 50
Autumn Gold 97
Autumn Joy 97
Awesome Possum 49
Axe with a Passion 128

B

Balloon Knot 20
Barking Spider 50
Barramundi in a Billabong 98
Bat Stupor 107
Bearhug 70
Beginner's Route 96
Big Al 53
Birds on a Shelf 138
Black Market 52
Black Ops 60
Black Raven 93
Black Ribbon 74
Blind Ambition 101
Blind Deaf Old Goat 84
Blue Highway 73
Bookmark 99
Bottlecap 37
Bottle Rocket 70
Boxcar 68
Boxtop 68
Bridge of the Gods Boulders 165
Broken Hand 93
Bronze Whale 93
Brown Rice 134
BSD 16
Bucket o' Ribs 137
Buckwheat 101
Buffalo Hunter 98
Bullah Bullah 96
Bulo Dancer 49
Bulo Point 46
Bungee's Crack 74
Burning Zone 23
Burrito 65
Butterfinger 72
Butt Shiner 106

C

Calf's Gash 25
Calm Before The Storm 23
Camel Back 135
Captain Jim 60
Carl's Route 106
Cathedral 132
Cattle Guard 49
Cattle Mutilation 56
Cattle Trough 49
Cave Man 135
Chicken Burrito 65
China Man 17
Climbing Theme 134
Climbs with a Fist 49
Close Encounters 60
Columbina 107
Committed Convenience 74
Conquistador 66
Conscious Haze 94
Conspiracy Lake 63
Conspiracy Theory 63
Contrail Conspiracy 90
Cosmic Debris 58
Cosmic Journey 90
Count of Monte Cristo 84
Covert Research 63
Crankenstein 18
Crash Landing 55
Critical Conundrum 126
Crooked Finger 93
Crop Circles 57
Crowds of Solitude 100
Crows Feet 96
Cryan's Shame 44

D

DaKind 53
Dark Side of the Moon 64
Death Star 60
Desert Dreaming 105
Dilithium Crystals 61
Dirt In Your Eye 41
Dirty Deeds 18
Dismantled Fears 29
Djali 132
Doctors Patient 38
Do It Again 19
Don't Call Me Ishmael 52
Don't Tread On Me 94
Dorkboat 65
Dreamland 55
Dunce 41
Dunlap 45

E

Earth First 56
Electric Blue 72
Emerald City 18
EMF left 31
EMF middle 31
Empire Boulders 175
Enchilada ala Carte 68
End of the Line 107
Enigma 89
Enola 21
Erased Memory 56
Escalade 42
Esmeralda 129
ET 57
Eternity 88
Even 37

Even Horizon 61
Eye Of The Needle 42

F
Fat Crack 26
Fat Rabbit 51
Fifty-seven 24
First Contact 58
Forbidden Zone 22
Forest Circus Fiasco 107
Forest Fright 98
For Pete's Sake 36
Fortune Cookie 26
Freak Show 67
French's Dome 13
Friend or Alien 57
Fully Horizontal 69

G
Get It 106
Getting Rich Watching Porn 68
Giant's Direct 20
Giant's Staircase 19
Global Warming 92
Glue Me Up Scotty 62
Golden Shower 21
Granny's Got A Gun 23
Great White Book 98
Griddle Cakes 90
Grits & Gravy 27
Groom Lake 63
Guillotine 36
Gypsy Dance 130

H
Hammerhead Shark 92
Hamunaptra 44
Hangin' with the Hunch' 130
Hanz Crack 138
Held Down 66
High Voltage 15
Hillbilly Hot Tub 24
Ho' Lotta Shakin' 132
Horizontal Delight 68
Horsethief Butte 107
Hostile Old Hikers 101
Hugo 132
Hunchback Wall 124
Hunch Sack 133

I
Iceberg in a Sauna 86
Indian Summer 90
Inner Sanctum 70
Inukshuk 92
Inversion Excursion 49
Itchy & Scratchy 106
It Taint Human 59

J
Jackie Chan 16
Jethro 26
Jet Stream 51
Jet Stream Variation 52
Jet Wind 52
Jon Pussman 134
Journey To The Sun 59
JRat Crack 50
Jugalicious 25
Just a Freakin' Rock Climber 101

K
K-9 Shanghai 45
King of the Moes 29
Kings of Rat 68

L
Larch Mtn Boulders 143
Latent Genes 138
Laverne 133
Leavenworth Boulder 145
Lies and Deception 61
Lights Over Phoenix 63
Line Dancer 49
Little Crow 96
Little Gray Men 57
Live Free or Die 96
Live Long and Prosper 60
Log Flume 138
Lonely Climax 100
Lord Frollo 128
Low Voltage 20
Luna 56

M
Magic 128
Magician 128
Major Tom 58
Manic Madness 97
Mars 57
MC Direct 86
Measure of Pleasure 136
Meatloaf 24
Meister Brau 126
Mellow Drama 133
Men in Black 55
Metamorphosis 126
Mighty Mite 73
Mighty Mouse 37
Mirage 127
Mists of Time 71
Molly's Route 106
Monte Cristo Slab 75
Moonshiners Arête 28
Mosquito Butte Crag 121
Mothership 60
Mothership Supercell 126
Motional Turmoil 71
Mouse in a Microwave 138
Mr Hair of the Chode 25
Murky Water 130
My DNA 84

N
Naked 72
Niceline 73
Nook and Cranny 51
Northern Pearl 69
Norwegian Queen 100
Not For Teacher 40
Notre Dame 132
Nuggets 136
Nuked 49

O
Oasis 128
OCD 105
OH8 101
Opal's Arête 27
Open Space Plan 106
Open the Pod Bay Door

HAL 60
Outback BBQ 84
Outer Limits 45
Out Of This World 58
Oz 18

P

Park Her Here 20
Paul's Route 106
PB Direct 30
Pearl's Jam 69
Pedestal 37
Peloton 128
Penstemon 106
Pernicious Picklefest 99
Persistence Is Futile 131
Pete's Pile 31
Philanthropy 17
Phoebus 132
Phone Home 57
Pig's Knuckles 22
Pigs Nipples 22
Pissfire 65
Plaid's Pantry 131
Plaidtastic 73
Play Palace 90
Plumberette 31
Plumbers Crack 51
Plum Butt 31
Pop Quiz 40
Power & Politics 49
Probe 61
Progressive Climax 74
Prohibition 26
Psoriasis 20
Psycho Billy Cadillac 27
Ptero 138
Pumpin' For The Man 43
Pumporama 18

Q

Quasar 96
Quasimodo 129

R

Raging Sea 92
Raiders of the Lost Rock 50
Ramble On 42

Rat Cave 65
Rattler 136
Rattlesnake 101
Raven's of Odin 94
Raven's Revolt 96
Reckless Abandon 42
Redneck Knuckle Draggers 96
Reed's Route 106
Resistance Is Futile 63
Retro Cognition 89
Return of Yoda 51
Rhoid Rage 15
Risky Sex 106
Road Face 15
Road Head 21
Road Kill 16
Road Rage 16
Rock Climbing 13
Rock Creek Crag 69
Rocketman 58
Rock Thugs 53
Ron Love Verly 101
Roswell 59

S

Sacagawea's Route 106
Salmon 135
Salmon River Slab 134
Samurai 23
Sands of Time 72
Sasquatch 101
Scene of the Crime 53
Schoolroom 40
Scorpio 74
Scorpion BBQ 24
Sea Hag Roof 27
Seasonal Anxiety 97
Separated at Birth 50
September Morn 94
Serpentine Arête 24
Seven Eleven 136
Seven Pearls 99
Shape Shifter 56
Shine 28
Shorty 106
Silence of the Cams 49

Silence the Serenity 86
Silk Road 97
Silver Streak 18
Single Wide 28
Sky's the Limit 90
Slanted and Enchanted 129
Slice of Pie 50
Slim Pickins 100
Slow Dance 69
Sluice Box 137
Smokin' 40
Solar Flair 59
Sombrero 65
Spring Breezes 107
Squatch's Travesty 98
Squirrel's Stew 106
S.T.A.R.D. 37
Stargate 61
Static Cling 20
S#@t Fire 68
Stinger 37
Straw Man 18
Streamlined 52
Sunday's Best 86
Sunspot 59
Super Burrito 66
Superchron 89
Swine of the Times 26

T

Tailgater 28
Take Me To Your Leader 56
Taken 62
Temptation 36
The Borg 62
The Chain Gang 106
The Cover Up 58
The Dark Side 17
The Eagle Has Landed 56
The Easy Way 25
The Fang 28
The Gap 107
The Maverick 68
The Plum Arête 31
The Shuttler 107
The Siege 17
The Stiffler 66

The Swine 21
The Tallest Pygmy 128
The Truth Is Out There 60
The Watchman 71
The Wormhole 61
Thin Edge of Reality 138
Thin & Lovely 31
This ain't yo momma's five-nine 31
Three Martini Lunch 132
Tibbet's Crack 23
Tidewater 101
Tilting at Windmills 126
Times Tardy 40
Tin Man 18
Tin Tangle 18
Tipsy McStagger 26
To Boldly Bolt 60
Too Cool 27
Tor the Hairy One 84
Tour de France 93
Toveline's Travesty 100
Tres Hombres 30
Tribes 37
Trouble With Tribbles 57
Tuffnerd 67
Twenty Year Hangover 27

U
UFO 58
Uluru 86
Uncle Rick 20
Uranus Has Rings 59

V
Victor 132
Vulcan Mind Meld 60

W
Walk on the Wild Side 88
Wankers Columns 135
Warmnerd 67
Warm Up 65
War of the Worlds 55
We Are Not Alone 62
Welcome to the Swine 30
Wendell's Big Mistake 136
White Lightning 28

Who's the Choss? 53
Wind Dummy 101
Wobbegong 89
Wyde Syde 72

Y
Yellow Brick Road 20
Young Jedi 55

Z
Zeno's Paradox 131

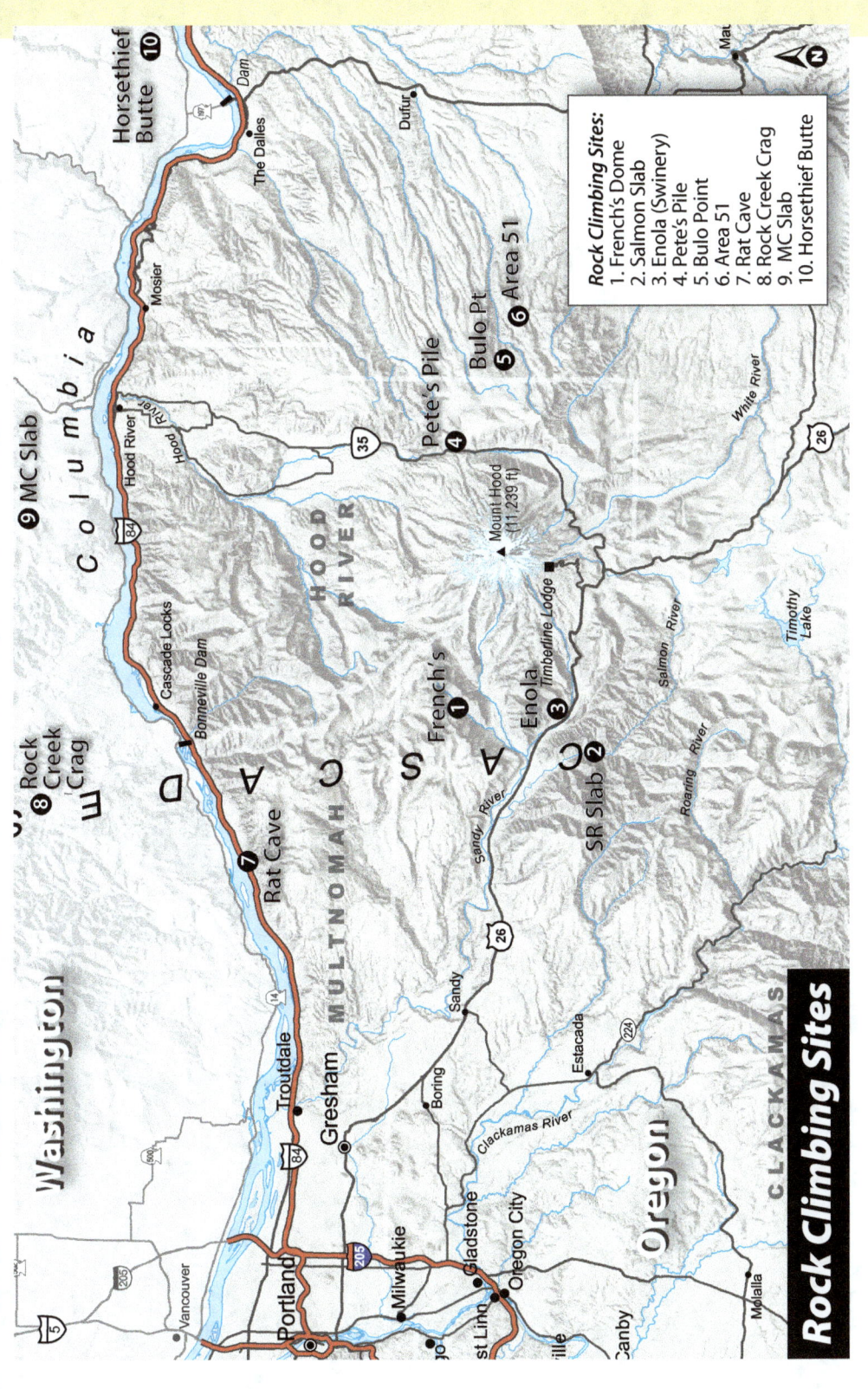

www.ingramcontent.com/pod-product-compliance
Lightning Source LLC
Chambersburg PA
CBHW070733020526
44118CB00035B/1248